HERE FIRST

SAMOSET AND THE WAWENOCK OF PEMAQUID, MAINE

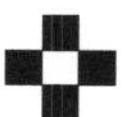

JODY BACHELDER

To Marcia Sewall,
for Samoset and The Wawenock—
Jody Bachelder

Down East Books

Down East Books

Published by Down East Books
An imprint of Globe Pequot
Trade division of The Rowman & Littlefield
Publishing Group, Inc.
4501 Forbes Blvd., Ste. 200
Lanham, MD 20706
www.rowman.com
www.downeastbooks.com

Distributed by NATIONAL BOOK NETWORK

Book design by Lynda Chilton, Chilton Creative

ISBN 978-1-68475-006-1 (paperback)
ISBN 978-1-68475-007-8 (e-book)

∞™ The paper used in this publication meets the minimum requirements of American National Standard for Information Sciences—Permanence of Paper for Printed Library Materials, ANSI/NISO Z39.48-1992.

CONTENTS

AUTHOR'S NOTE

My connection to Samoset is geographic. I grew up in New Harbor, Maine on the Pemaquid peninsula where he and his people lived 400 years ago, and for thousands of years before that. Between my house and the neighbor's there was a path which, legend has it, was part of an ancient trail used by the Wawenock. I used to take that path to get to my grandparents' house, lured by the prospect of warm doughnuts in my grandmother's kitchen. Their house sat on Indian Trail, where the Wawenock carried their canoes across the peninsula to avoid paddling around treacherous Pemaquid Point. None of that made an impression on me when I was young. I rarely stopped to think about the Native people who lived there, because they weren't there to remind me.

As a descendant of European colonists who displaced Indigenous people from their homelands, I recognize that I may not be the best person to tell Samoset's story. I grew up with privileges that were denied to Native people. But 400 years after his famous walk into Plymouth Plantation his story has never been fully explored, and the Wawenock are not here to write it. So, I have approached this project with great humility and not a little trepidation and have finally come to accept that, though I may not get everything right, that doesn't mean I shouldn't try.

Throughout this process — and it is a process, one that will continue well after this book is published — I have learned a great deal, but mostly I have been amazed at all the things I didn't know. I don't think I'm unique in that regard. U.S. history tends to gloss over the less glamorous parts of our past, the parts where we don't come off looking like heroes. But I think we're ready to know more of the story, and it is much more interesting than the white-washed version many of us learned growing up.

In the book I've used the names of specific Indigenous communities when

I am relatively certain of the reference (i.e. Wawenock, Wampanoag, Penobscot, etc.). Even so, these labels might not be accurate. The boundaries between villages and groups of people were fluid. Indigenous people moved around a lot, married into other communities, socialized, traded, and allied with one another. The Europeans who were recording encounters and events in the early 17th century were probably meeting people who came together from many communities — Wawenock, Kennebec, Penobscot and many others.

Notwithstanding that Wabanaki is a term that came into existence after Samoset's death, I use it here because it is recognized and used today. It refers to people who lived in the region from Vermont to the Maritime Provinces in Canada and included the Abenaki, Penobscot, Maliseet, Passamaquoddy, and Mi'kmaq. (Abenaki is a collective term for all the small communities south and west of Penobscot territory, so Samoset and the Wawenock were Abenaki.) The Wabanaki came together in a confederacy to fend off Mohawk aggression in the late 17th century.

Though a great deal of historical and personal flavor has been lost in the translation, I've decided to modernize the spelling in quotes I've used in the book. The first English dictionary wasn't published until 1604 and it was not widely available to the common man, so spelling was a wonderfully inventive exercise and punctuation and capitalization were left to the discretion of the writer. The Davies journal of 1607 is my favorite, written by a sailor rather than a scholar, with passages like this:

Frydaye beinge the xjth in the mornynge early we Cam into the ryver of Pemaquyd thear to Call nahanada & skidwarres as we had promyste them but beinge thear aryved we found no Lyvinge Creatuer they all wear gon from thence the which we perseavinge presently departed towardes the ryver of Penobskott Saillinge all this daye & the xijth & xiijth the Lyke yett by no means Could we fynd ytt" or translated as

Friday being the 11th in the morning early we came into the river of Pemaquid, there to call Nahanada & Skidwarres as we had promised them. But being there arrived we found no living creature; they all were gone from thence. The which we perceiving presently departed towards the river of Penobscot, sailing all this day and the 12th & 13th the like, yet by no means could we find it."

I have many, many people to thank for helping to bring this book to completion. Chris Newell and James Francis, Sr. read the manuscript and offered honest and insightful feedback. I consulted with several historians and scholars who were generous with their time and knowledge. I credit my fellow librarians for their help procuring books and documents for my research. Family and friends read the manuscript (some more than once) and gave me encouragement for many years, even when they wondered if I was ever going to finish writing it.

Most importantly, I want to dedicate this book to my husband, Todd, who supported me throughout this odyssey from the very beginning in every possible way.

This book began with the question "Why was Samoset in Plymouth?" and the journey I have taken to find the answer has surprised and enlightened me more than I could have imagined. I hope you will find something that surprises and enlightens you too. I am not a scholar or a historian, just someone who wanted to know more about Samoset and the Wawenock people from Pemaquid and what they may have experienced when Europeans landed on their shores. Any mistakes that I have made, in fact or in interpretation, are mine alone.

Note: Photos without attribution were taken by the author.

INDIGENOUS PEOPLE AND PLACE NAMES

Abenaki	Wabanaki people living south and west of Penobscot territory, including the Wawenock
Acadia	French colony in parts of eastern Maine and the Maritime provinces of Canada
Agamenticus, or Aquamenticus	Present-day York, Maine
Algonquian	The family of languages spoken in a vast area of the northeast
Amenquin	Wawenock who visited the Popham Colony in 1607
Amóret	Wawenock who was kidnapped in 1605 and taken to England; possibly died in England
Apponick	Presumably present-day Damariscotta, Maine
Armouchiquois	People living in southern Maine, New Hampshire, and Massachusetts,as told to early French explorers
Bashabes	Penobscot sachem who was the head of the Mawooshen alliance; killed in the Mi'kmaq War
Black Will	Man unjustly executed on Richmond Island, Maine for the murder of Walter Bagnall
Capemanwagan	Present-day Cape Newagen in Southport, Maine
Capowack	Present-day Martha's Vineyard, Massachusetts
Cogawesco	Sagamore in the Portland, Maine area who invited Christopher Levett to settle there
Conway	Sagamore who, along with Samoset, was attacked by a rogue English trader in Casco Bay, Maine
Damariscove	Island off the coast of Southport, Maine
Dick Swalks	Sagamore who signed the Samoset deed of 1641
Easey Gale	Sagamore who signed the Samoset deed of 1641
Epenow	Wampanoag from Martha's Vineyard, Massachusetts, who was kidnapped and taken to England in 1611; killed Captain Thomas Dermer
Gluskabe	A deity who is a cultural hero of the Wabanaki
Haudenosaunee	People living in present-day New York called Iroquois by the French
Heggomeito	Land that Samoset sold in the June 1653 deed
Kennebec	People living along the river of the same name; fought the Wawenock during the Mi'kmaq War, but were close neighbors and more often allies
Lenni Lenape	People living in the present-day Manhattan, New York area who sold the island to the Dutch in 1626
Mahican	People living in the Upper Hudson Valley in present-day New York
Maliseet	People living in part of eastern Maine, New Brunswick and Quebec, Canada, especially along the St. John River
Maneddo	Wawenock who was kidnapped in 1605 and taken to England; may have been starved to death by the Spanish
Massachusett	People living north of the Wampanoag in Massachusetts
Mawooshen	An alliance of people from Saco to Penobscot Bay in Maine
Membertou	Mi'kmaq sagamore who led the Mi'kmaq into battle at Saco in 1607
Menawormet	Sagamore who met Christopher Levett in 1623-1624

Mi'kmaq (singular Mi'kmaw)	People living in part of New Brunswick, Nova Scotia, Prince Edward Island, Newfoundland, and Quebec, Canada
Miantonomo	Narragansett sagamore who observed the changes brought by Europeans
Mohawk	One of the Haudenosaunee peoples who fought the Wabanaki over beaver
Monhegan	Island off the coast of Pemaquid, Maine
Montagnais	First Nations people living in the St. Lawrence River Valley of Canada
Muscongus	A bay in Wawenock country east of the Pemaquid peninsula
Namasket	Wampanoag people living in the village of the same name west of Patuxet, Massachusetts
Nanrantsouak	Present-day Norridgewock, Maine and the people who lived there
Narragansett	People living along the bay of the same name in present-day Rhode Island; enemy of the Wampanoag
Nauset	Wampanoag people living on present-day Cape Cod, Massachusetts in a village of the same name; had the First Encounter with the settlers of Plymouth
Nequasset	Present-day Woolwich, Maine
Norumbega	A mythical city in the northeast believed to be full of riches
Opparunwit	Sagamore who met Christopher Levett in 1624
Ousamequin (Massasoit)	Great sachem of the Wampanoag
Pashipskoke	Presumably the Sheepscot River in Maine
Passamaquoddy	People living in part of eastern Maine and New Brunswick, Canada
Patuxet	Wampanoag people living in what would become Plymouth, Massachusetts; also the name of their village
Pejepscot	Present-day Brunswick, Maine
Pemaquid	Peninsula on the Maine coast that was Samoset's home; also the name of his village and the river on which it was located
Penobscot	People living along the river and bay of the same name, as well as north of Wawenock territory; close neighbors and allies of the Wawenock
Pentagoet	Present-day Castine, Maine
Piscataqua	Present-day Portsmouth, New Hampshire area and the river of the same name
Pocahontas	Powhatan daughter of Wahunsenacawh
Pometacom (or Metacom, Metacomet)	The son of Ousamequin known by the English as King Philip, for whom King Philip's War is named
Powhatan (Wahunsenacawh)	People living in the tidewater region of present-day Virginia; their leader was called the same name by the English, though his real name was Wahunsenacawh
Quadequina	Wampanoag sagamore and brother of Ousamequin
Remoboose (or Remobcose)	Land sold in the Samoset deed of 1641 which may be Round Pond, Maine
Roanoke	People living in present-day North Carolina in a place of the same name, where the first English colony was attempted
Sadamoyt	Great sagamore of the "east country" who met Christopher Levett in 1624; possibly the head of the Mawooshen Alliance
Sagadahoc	The mouth of the Kennebec River in Maine

Samoset	Sagamore of Pemaquid, Maine
Sasanoa	Kennebec sagamore who fought the Wawenock and died in the Mi'kmaq War
Sassacomoit	Wawenock who was kidnapped in 1605 and taken to England
Sawahquatooke	Present-day Saco, Maine
Skedraguscett (or Squidrayset)	Sagamore who met Christopher Levett in 1624 and killed English trader Walter Bagnall on Richmond Island, Maine in 1631
Skicowáros	Wawenock who was kidnapped in 1605 and taken to England; returned to Pemaquid
Soggohannago	Land that Samoset sold in the July 1653 deed
Sowams (Pokanoket)	People living in part of present-day Massachusetts and Rhode Island; home of Wampanoag sachem Ousamequin
Squanto	Wabanaki deity who brought good fortune
Tahánedo	Sagamore of Pemaquid before Samoset; kidnapped in 1605 and taken to England; returned to Pemaquid
Tanto	Wabanaki deity who brought misfortune and carried those who died to his wigwam
Tarrantine	English name for the Mi'kmaq
Tisquantum (Squanto)	Patuxet who was kidnapped and taken to England in 1614; became a translator for the settlers in Plymouth
Tokamahamon	Wampanoag interpreter to the Plymouth settlers who may have taken the place of Samoset
Unnongoit	Sagamore who signed the Samoset deed of 1625
Wabanaki	Abenaki, Penobscot, Maliseet, Passamaquoddy and Mi'kmaq people who formed an alliance in the 17th century to fend off Mohawk aggression
Wampanoag	People living in part of Massachusetts and Rhode Island, including the islands of Martha's Vineyard and Nantucket
Wawenock	People living on the coast of Maine, roughly between the Kennebec River and the St. George River; also spelled Wawenoc, Weweenock, Wewoonock, Wewonock; one historian gives the proper name as Wali•na´kiak
Wôlinak	Reserve in the province of Quebec, Canada where many Wawenock migrated

INTRODUCTION

Plymouth, Massachusetts March 16, 1621

Samoset prepared himself to die that morning. He took in his surroundings —the birds chatting to each other, the earthy smell of rotting leaves around him, the sun shifting through the branches overhead. It was warm for March, but the trees had not leafed out yet. Normally that would make it more difficult to conceal himself, but he was not concerned. These strangers often missed what was right in front of them.

He had been watching them for some time. When he heard some English words, he felt relieved; his English was passable. He was fascinated by the houses laid out in rows on either side of a wide path, with smoke rising from shafts built on top. He knew about English houses, but it was still a wonder to see them for himself. Despite the danger, he felt himself growing excited to see more.

The Englishmen gathered with their guns at one end of the encampment. Samoset knew how unpredictable the English could be, and he was about to surprise them. He took a deep breath to calm himself. The risk to his life did not change the fact that he was on a mission and honor-bound to carry it out. Resolved, he stood up tall and proud, wearing only his loincloth and moccasins, his long black hair flowing down his back. He thought of all his loved ones who had recently died and knew he might soon join them. If so, he was ready. Picking up his bow and two arrows, he left the cover of the woods and bravely walked into Plymouth Plantation, straight for the crowd of men.

The Plymouth settlers were suspicious and on edge. There had been several sightings in recent weeks of "savages" in the woods around them. Surrounded and outnumbered, they knew that if they were going to survive in this inhospitable environment they had to be stronger than their enemy. They had recently installed cannons on the hill overlooking the bay, and that morning the men mustered to go over military orders. There were so few of them left. The Atlantic crossing had been difficult, and half of the colonists had fallen ill and died during the winter, either from illness, exposure, or starvation. Afraid the Natives would see just how vulnerable they were, they had buried their dead in unmarked graves in the middle of the night.[1]

When they saw Samoset walk boldly into their village, heading directly toward them with a weapon in his hand, they could easily have panicked. It would have been instinctive to shoot him on sight. But he was smiling, and he saluted them.

"Welcome!"

The settlers were shocked to hear their own language coming from a Native person. It may have been what saved him. They quickly learned that he was no stranger to Europeans. This "tall straight man" was friendly and talkative; he even knew some of their own countrymen by name.[2] For hours he answered their questions freely and told them valuable information about the local people. After a while they began to relax. He asked for beer, ate their food with enthusiasm, and even insisted on spending the night. He seemed right at home.

Their first meeting with a Native was a success. The settlers began to hope that their fortunes were improving.

On that day, March 16, 1621, Samoset cemented his place in history. He was the first Indigenous person to make contact with the colonists at Plymouth Plantation, who have come to be known as the Pilgrims. The extraordinary thing about Samoset's story is that he was not from Plymouth. He was not even Wampanoag, or more specifically Patuxet, the people who lived in the area. Samoset's home was more than 200 miles away on the coast of present-day Maine. So why was he there? And why was he the man chosen to make contact with the English settlers?

It turns out that in addition to making first contact with the settlers at Plymouth, Samoset witnessed many extraordinary moments in history. His life coincided with the period of early contact with Europeans, and his home village of Pemaquid lay at the center of Indigenous-European interactions at the beginning of the 17th century. In fact, Europeans were exploring and fishing in the Pemaquid region many years before the Mayflower landed at Plymouth. Samoset and his people, the Wawenock, were well placed to have contact with non-Natives. As a result, they not only witnessed history but made it as well.

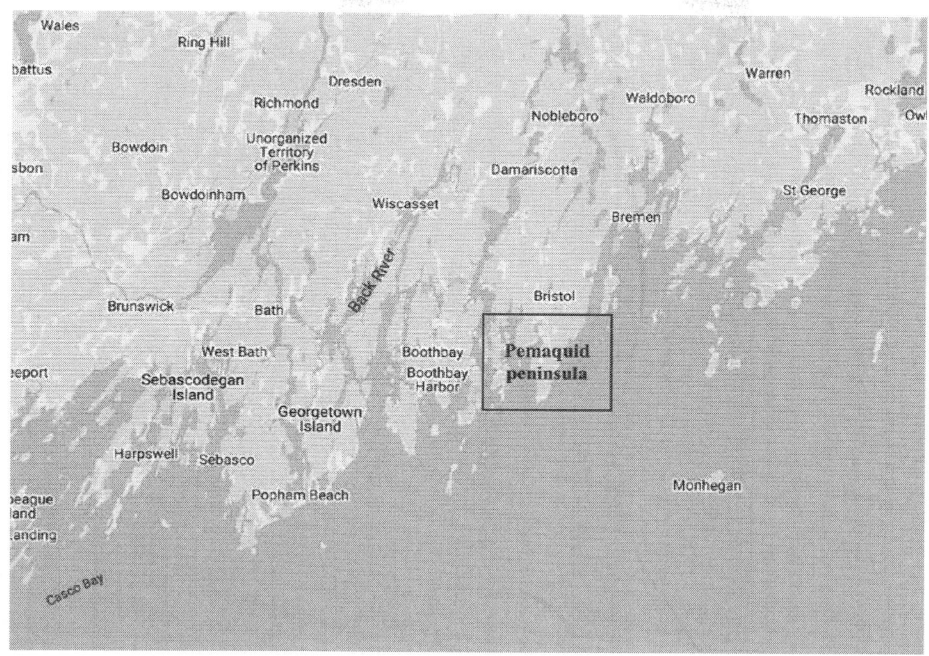

The word Pemaquid translates as "long point, or a point of land running into the sea"—in other words a peninsula. The word Wawenock, or Wali•na´kiak, is also descriptive of the place where they lived; it means "people of the bay country."[3] COPYRIGHT © 2021 GOOGLE

It was a period of incredible transformation. The Wawenock lived within a larger region known today as Wabanaki territory, which includes parts of Vermont, New Hampshire, Maine, The Province Quebec, and the Maritime Provinces of Canada. The Wabanaki, or "People of the Dawnland," were Algonquian language speakers who shared not only their language but also similar culture. When Samoset was born around 1590, there may have been more than 20,000 Wabanaki in present-day

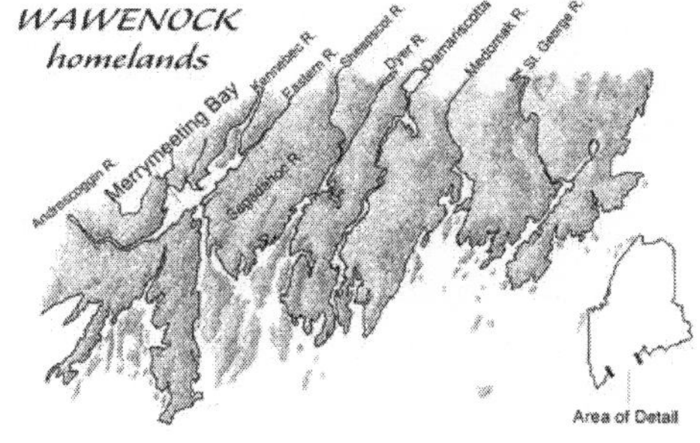

Wawenock territory spanned the area roughly from the Kennebec River to the St. George River. REPRINTED WITH PERMISSION FROM KERRY HARDY.[4]

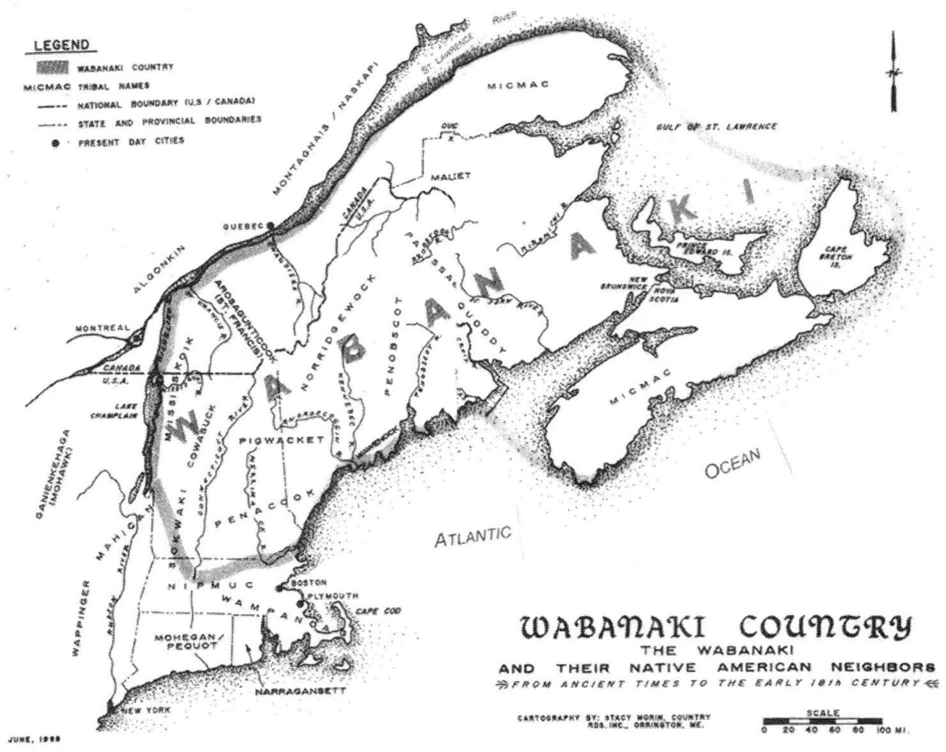

Map of Wabanaki country in the early 18th century. "It should be understood that there were many more villages and peoples found in the region anciently. This map just shows the major surviving groups now known to non-Indian governments and historians." - John Moody
REPRINTED WITH PERMISSION FROM H. STACY LABARE; MAP COMPILED BY JOHN MOODY[5]

Maine. By his death around 1653, that number had dropped to approximately 3,000, with some communities losing more than 75 percent of their people.[6] During his lifetime the Wawenock became increasingly dependent on European goods that replaced their own, and many lost the right to live on their own land. It was a time when people of different cultures met, often violently but sometimes in peace and friendship, and the impact they had on one another was profound.

The Wawenock survived many catastrophic events during this period including kidnappings, wars, epidemics, and a deadly hurricane. Perhaps less well known is the part they played in the failure of the Popham Colony, one of the earliest English settlements, and how closely their lives were tied to events happening in England. Samoset personally survived trauma and the threat of death again and again in addition to the famous walk into Plymouth Plantation. Though we will never know his thoughts, by looking closely we can see the traces of his footsteps through this moment in history. Native people left few records of their early encounters with Europeans and the oral history is scant, in large part because so few of them survived the contact period. Only books, journals, reports, and letters written by Europeans tell the story, and those were influenced by the culture, personal biases, and motivations of the writers.

One thing we do know is that Samoset was respected by his own people and non-Natives alike. As we will see, this clever, brave man with a passionate nature, who was quick to anger but also to love, has been remembered in history as a "man of most noble character" and a "prince of his race."[7] One Englishman described him as "very faithful to the English, and had saved the lives of many of our nation, some from starving, others from killing."[8] As a sagamore, or leader of his people, he maintained peaceful relations with Europeans during his lifetime and was allegedly the first Indigenous person to "sell" land in North America. These dual allegiances, to his own people and to the Europeans, leave his legacy open to interpretation. Was he being disloyal to his people for cooperating with the foreigners, or was he doing what was necessary to help them survive?

Ultimately this story is bigger than one man's life history. Through Samoset a greater narrative unfolds of the Wabanaki experience during the early days of contact with Europeans. We will see how a way of living that had endured for centuries changed dramatically over the period of one lifetime and how the Wabanaki were able to adapt to monumental changes in their world. But the Wawenock no longer live in Pemaquid. *What happened to them?*

PART I

Samoset's Early Life and Precolonial Times, approximately 1590–1605

1
BACKGROUND

Spring comes gradually to the northeast as snowstorms turn into rain showers that wash away the gray remnants of winter. After a few warm sunny days, green appears in dozens of different shades on grasses, shrubs, and trees. Violets, columbine, and dogwood burst into bloom, and birds that spent the winter in warmer places return. The miracle of earth's renewal is never taken for granted in a place that waits for it so hungrily.

The first humans in the Dawnland would have felt seasonal changes intimately. Based on archaeological evidence non-Native scientists say that they arrived in the northeast around 12,000 years ago, but according to Wabanaki creation stories they have always been here. When a massive sheet of ice covered the northern part of North America around 18,000 years ago, Passamaquoddy oral history recounts that their people moved onto the continental shelf (the coastline normally under water that became exposed when the sea was locked up in glaciers) until warming temperatures gradually melted the ice.[1] When conditions once again became favorable for plants to grow on the land, herds of caribou and large game, including now-extinct woolly mammoths and mastodons, migrated into the area from the south, and the Wabanaki followed the animals. As weather patterns and temperatures changed, people and animals adapted; those that could not died off.

The Wabanaki were hardy and resourceful by necessity. They lived in family units and larger communities, close enough to their neighbors so interactions were possible, but far enough apart so their hunting territories did not overlap, an essential condition for hunter-gatherer people.

By the 16th century temperatures were high enough to sustain crops like maize (flint corn), squash, beans, and tobacco. Being able to grow surplus food and store it over the winter meant more food security, and the Wabanaki became more settled, at least in some areas. Pemaquid may have been close to the outer limit where crops could grow; north and east of there, the growing season was very short. According to Helen Camp, a self-taught archaeologist who spent 14 years excavating the forts and early buildings at Pemaquid, "[The Wawenock] depended not only on game and fish for their food, but also to a large extent on corn. This they grew in summer, using fish for fertilizer, and it served as their most staple food in the winter."[2] Charred corn remains found at Pemaquid have been carbon dated to around 1445 A.D., and one of the artifacts found at Pemaquid is a pestle, used to grind corn.[4] Even so agriculture was unreliable and hunting and fishing remained critical to their survival, and they were impressively skilled at both.

Pestle excavated at Pemaquid. Courtesy of Maine Bureau of Parks and Lands —Colonial Pemaquid[3]

By this time Europeans had long been living in agrarian societies, giving up the hunter-gatherer lifestyle to become settled farmers. Theirs was a market economy with specialized professions. Things evolved differently in North America. To be clear, Indigenous people in the 16th century were not primitive, or simple, or lacking in ingenuity. They were highly intelligent and creative people with complex spiritual beliefs, a strong sense of social justice, and a deep understanding of the natural world. Many of their practices are considered more enlightened and progressive than those of Europe at the time. But when Europeans saw that they made their tools and weapons out of stone, wood, shell, or bone and their clothing out of animal skins and furs, that they had no written language and did not use the wheel as a tool, they quickly labeled them "uncivilized." What the Europeans did not know was that they had different resources and challenges as well as a different world view.

To begin with, Indigenous people in various regions throughout the Americas were mining copper, tin, gold, and silver before the Europeans arrived, so they knew about extracting and smelting metal. However, these soft metals are more appropriate for decorative items, not tools or weapons like shovels, hatchets, and swords. Copper was prevalent in North America, but only small deposits of it existed in the northeast. Iron deposits were sprinkled throughout the continents, and it is a mystery why Native people never took advantage of those—perhaps they had simply not discovered them.[5] Iron is the key ingredient in steel, which is what most European weapons and tools were made of. This technology imbalance would eventually prove deadly to Native people.

As for written language, the first known writing using symbols to represent sounds can be dated to around 5,000 years ago in ancient Sumer, an area in the Middle East that now roughly corresponds to part of Iraq and Kuwait. Writing also was developed in Egypt, China, and Mesoamerica, and though the invention spread throughout much of the world it had not yet come to North America.[6] Even after centuries of living with the written word, less than half of English men in the 16th century could read (for women the rate was probably less than 10 percent), and spelling was still a highly creative endeavor.[7] Indigenous people instead became prodigious storytellers who passed down their history orally.

Then there is the question of the wheel. What seems like the most basic tool was not actually invented until 3500 BCE in Mesopotamia (now the Middle East), and then it was first used as a potter's wheel.[8] In the Dawnland the wheel would have had limited use for two reasons: geography and a lack of farm animals. Maine in particular is covered with beautiful lakes and rivers, thanks to glaciers that dug holes and channels in the land which then filled with water. Maine is also known as the Pine Tree State because it is covered with dense forests. The terrain has changed some since 1590, but those two characteristics—waterways and forests—made it more practical to travel or move goods by boat or foot than by any wheeled vehicle. Wabanaki people had simplified travel on water by using canoes that were easy to carry around obstacles. Taking down large trees to build roads was difficult, so they created a network of footpaths around the trees. In the winter, they used sleds to transport their goods.[9]

Furthermore, a wheeled vehicle works best when pulled by a large animal like a horse or an ox. Many animals that were integral to the lives of Europeans simply did not exist in the Americas: horses, oxen, cows, pigs, sheep, and goats. With the exception of horses which died off in this hemisphere, these animals evolved in Europe, Asia, or Africa.[10] The only animals in the northeast large enough to pull a wagon were caribou and moose, and they do not have the temperament to be domesticated. Without large domesticated animals, the wheel had minimal value.

Given the tools and resources the Wabanaki had, they spent a good deal of time securing and preparing food, clothing, and shelter. This was not some unsophisticated, haphazard process. "It wasn't like we were bumping through the woods going, 'Oh, a berry bush—we eat today,'" points out James Francis, Sr., Penobscot Tribal Historian. "We knew where those berry bushes were, we knew when they would be ripe, and we knew the best way to get there."[11] The Penobscot were close neighbors of the Wawenock, with similar culture.

What the Wabanaki valued was different too. Given that they moved frequently, they were not interested in accumulating more material goods than they could easily carry. Wealth meant having plenty of food to eat and share with others, not more tools or goods than they could use. Contrary to European thinking, Wabanaki people were not unhappy or unprosperous before Europeans came to their shores. Even after contact most preferred their own way of life, which was rich with the closeness of their families and friends and a symbiotic relationship with the land.[12] They were not looking for change—it came to them, unbidden.

The coastline on the Pemaquid Peninsula.

Their life had a structured rhythm that revolved around the seasons. Every spring the Wawenock returned to the coast to plant crops and gather fish and shellfish after a long, cold winter in the woods. They looked forward to the bounty of the sea.

2
SPRING

Samoset would have entered the world with very little fuss. Not long after his birth, his mother was already back at her chores.[1] She laid her new baby boy in a bed of "cattail or milkweed fluff, duck feathers, or sphagnum moss," absorbent materials that were soft against his delicate skin and acted like a diaper.[2] His father built a wooden cradleboard, the Wabanaki equivalent of a backpack, and Samoset was trussed up like a tiny mummy and strapped into it. His cradleboard was packed with soft materials to protect him, and his mother carried him on her back this way; at times she might prop him up against a rock or a log or sling him over a tree branch while she ground corn or worked in the field. It is not hard to imagine a tree on the edge of a field decorated with black-haired babies sleeping in their cradleboards, like ornaments, while their mothers worked and sang nearby.

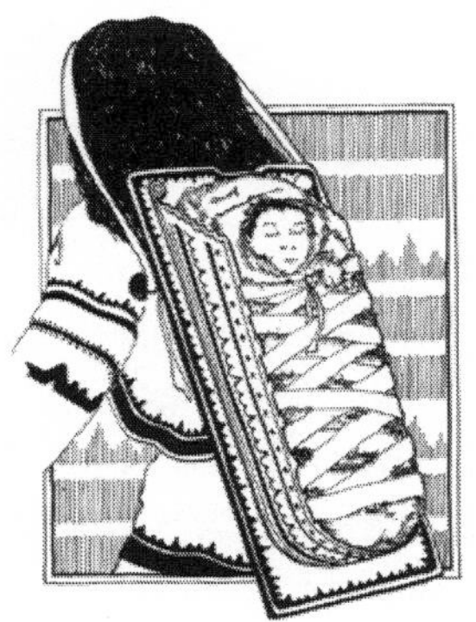

Illustration of a Wabinaki mother and baby in a cradleboard. ©Kathy Kaulbach, used with permission from Nimbus Publishing[3]

Once he was mobile Samoset roamed freely with little discipline. The English often found Native parents too indulgent for their puritanical tastes. They were also scandalized by their lack of clothing. In warm months the men simply wore loin cloths and moccasins, and Samoset and the other children ran naked—it was simpler than trying to diaper them. Black flies and mosquitoes were a problem, but they had natural deterrents for them. "They anointed their bodies with fish oil, eagle fat, coon grease, and similar emollients against sun, weather and insects."[4] Bear grease applied to the skin helped keep them warm when the weather turned cooler.

Spring was a busy season for the Wawenock. After a winter away, their camp needed attention. It was a time to repair the wigwam frames they had left behind or to build new ones. In the midcoast region where Samoset lived, wigwams were most likely constructed using bent saplings that came together at the top to form a cone shape. The saplings were tied together with supple tree branches or strips of cedar bark, leaving an opening at the top for smoke to escape from the fire built in the center of the structure. Then the saplings were covered with tree bark or mats woven from cattail reeds.[5]

Wigwam in the Wawenock style. ©KATHY KAULBACH, USED WITH PERMISSION FROM NIMBUS PUBLISHING[6]

After that it was time to turn their attention to food production. They had to clear the previous year's fields of weeds and prepare new fields for planting. Trees were taken down by chopping, burning, or girdling, where the bark is removed so the tree dies naturally. They carefully burned fields and brush, then turned over the soil with hoes and shovels made from the shoulder bone of a deer or moose, or a large, sharp shell tied to a stick. Women took full responsibility for the gardens, working together in community plots. They planted corn and probably beans and squash—known as the Three Sisters—but "only when the budding leaves of the white oak reached the size of a mouse's ear or a red squirrel's foot;" in other words, when all danger of frost had passed.[7] They paid close attention to the moon to determine the best time for planting, perhaps recognizing that the phases of the moon affected the moisture in the soil.

Samoset's mother had little time for rest. In addition to preparing fields, planting crops, and maintaining gardens, she took on the tasks of cooking for the family and caring for the home and the children. "[W]omen took this role both for cultural reasons, as well as to hold onto power. Women are seen as life givers [in Wabanaki culture] and take part in creation activities (having children, farming). Men are life takers and take part in activities which take life (hunting, fishing). Both are necessary in balance for the village to survive," explains Chris Newell, Co-founder and Director of Education of The Akomawt Educational Initiative and a Passamaquoddy citizen.[8]

The Three Sisters (corn, beans, and squash), grown throughout Indigenous communities, were planted together in a mound as a natural complement to one another. The corn stalk made a structure for the bean to climb, the bean provided much needed nitrogen to the soil, and the large leaves of the squash created shade to discourage weeds and retain moisture in the ground. Together they produced protein, vitamins, and minerals for a nutritious diet.[9] Some things were not on the Wawenock's menu, however. They never ate butter or drank animal milk because they had no cows, sheep, or goats, and they did not add salt to their food, choosing to season it with herbs and roots instead.

So, from the moment she woke there was work to be done. She might pin up her long dark hair with porcupine quills or tie it in a knot, then she would fan the embers from the previous night's fire and start a pot of soup using whatever was on hand: corn, squash, beans, herbs, animal fat, fish, shellfish, or meat. She even made the pot. It could be a large piece of birch bark that she steamed over a fire and molded into the shape of a bowl, or a clay pot with a cone-shaped bottom that fit snugly into the embers of the fire. She could also boil water by hollowing out a log, filling it with water, and dropping in rocks that had been heated in the fire. She roasted or boiled the game her husband caught, and covered clams and oysters with seaweed and roasted them over hot rocks. Nothing was wasted. Leftover water from boiled vegetables and meat was either drunk as a broth or used as a base in the next soup. Fish heads and animal bones were added to soups to improve the flavor, and only then discarded or made into tools. Their diet was varied, balanced, and nutritious, which led to healthy bodies that made Europeans—who suffered the scourges of rickets, malnutrition, dysentery, and other illnesses—envious.[10]

Indigenous people ate flint corn, which is not like the sweet corn we eat today. Women prepared it in a variety of ways. They roasted or boiled it so it could be eaten like we eat corn on the cob; they dried it, then ground it into meal and made it into porridge by adding water or animal fat; they also baked the meal into a type of bread called "pone."[11]

When Samoset's mother was not growing or preparing food, she was gathering edible roots, berries, nuts, and greens to feed to her family, as well as plants that could be used for medicinal purposes. She used a wide assortment of natural curatives, including balsam fir gum for wounds, beaver castor to stimulate menstrual flow, eelskins for "cramps, rheumatism and headaches," turtlehead to prevent pregnancy, lady's slipper for nervousness and convulsions, wild mint for croup and upset stomach, cedar for cuts and burns, and sweet flag for almost any ailment.[12] Her knowledge was gained from her ancestors' trials and errors over hundreds of years. Some of her tasks were endless, like fetching water from a spring or a stream or gathering firewood, so she must have been glad for the day when her children were old enough to help with those chores.

In addition to her other work she made clothing for the family out of animal skins and furs, which she might decorate with porcupine quill designs or natural plant dyes, feathers and shells. She was probably the basket maker too, using ash wood for the splints and maple for the handle. Many of these skills have been passed down for hundreds of years to Wabanaki descendants.

Work was divided along gender lines, and Samoset's father had plenty of responsibilities of his own. As the head of the family it fell to him to keep everyone safe and supplied with the game, fish, furs, and skins that were essential to their survival. His face was bare—Wabanaki men did not have much facial hair—and like his wife he wore his hair long, but either cut short in the front or tied up in a knot so it would not get caught in his bow. He crafted his bow out of a hardwood like beech, witch hazel, or maple, then strung it with animal sinew. For his arrow shafts he used wood from ash trees and tipped them with arrowheads made from sharpened rock or sometimes an eagle claw.[13] Turkey, hawk, or crow feathers lashed on the tail end kept them flying straight. Some arrows had no arrowhead; a blunt-ended arrow worked well enough to kill small game, without wasting an arrowhead if the arrow was lost.

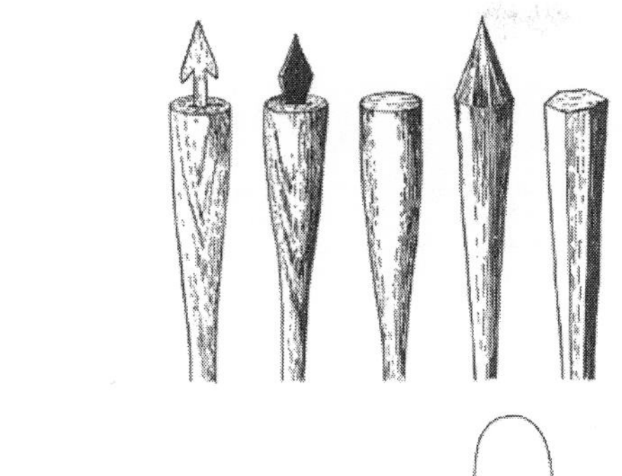

Illustration of early Wabanaki bow and arrow heads[14]

The men of the village worked together to clear fields for farming and also for hunting. Deer and bears are attracted to grasses and berries that grow in open, sunlit fields, so the effort to clear trees to attract prey was worthwhile. Samoset's father also set traps for beavers, rabbits, woodchucks, porcupines, and other animals. When he killed a turkey, he might pluck one of its feathers and stick it in the top knot of his hair, keep some feathers for his arrows, and give the rest of the bird to his wife. She used the remaining feathers to make clothing or bedding and then cooked the carcass.

Spring was a good time to check his canoe to see if it needed repairs, or to make a new one. A canoe was the principal method of transportation since waterways were plentiful. There were two types, the dugout and the birchbark. A dugout canoe was made by hollowing out a large tree with careful burning, then scraping away the charred part, leaving the bottom of the vessel intact. This also hardened the wood and made it smooth, so there would be no splinters to bother the occupant.[15]

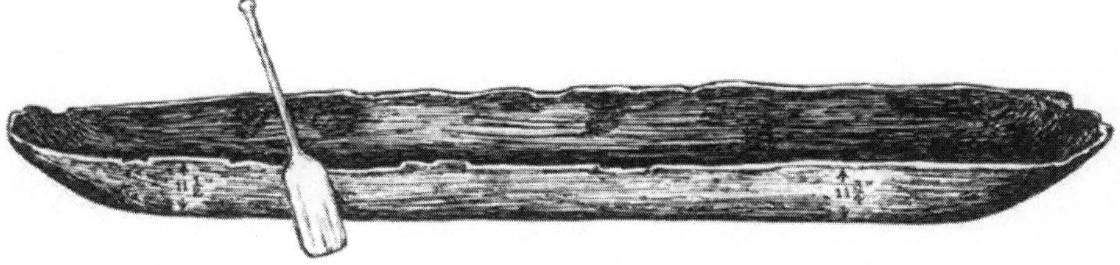

Drawing of a dugout canoe discovered near Weymouth, Massachusetts. The canoe dates to around the year 1500 and measures approximately 3 ft. wide by 11 ft. long.

Reprinted with permission from Globe Pequot[16]

In the northeast where Samoset lived, birch trees grew large enough so that they could be stripped of their bark to make birchbark canoes. This technique was more sophisticated and involved removing the bark in one large piece, laying it on the ground and weighting the central part with stones, then bending up the sides and attaching them to gunwales (the side rails). Samoset's father cut the bow and stern into shape and installed cross pieces, then sewed everything together using spruce root that he kept wet for pliability. He covered the bottom with thin cedar strips, and over those he installed cedar ribs which he bent to fit the bottom of the boat. The final step was to seal the seams with fir or spruce pitch.[17] Birchbark canoes were light and flexible, making them easier to navigate in the water. They were also easier to portage around waterfalls, rapids, or shallow water. In the spring, when snowmelt and rain fill the rivers with torrents of water, canoeing is especially difficult. Then the water can move at 4–8 miles per hour, or 6–10 feet per second.[18] That may not sound significant but putting a canoe into that kind of current feels a little like being shot out of a cannon. The Wabanaki also took to the ocean in their canoes, where sudden storms could cause dangerously heavy seas.

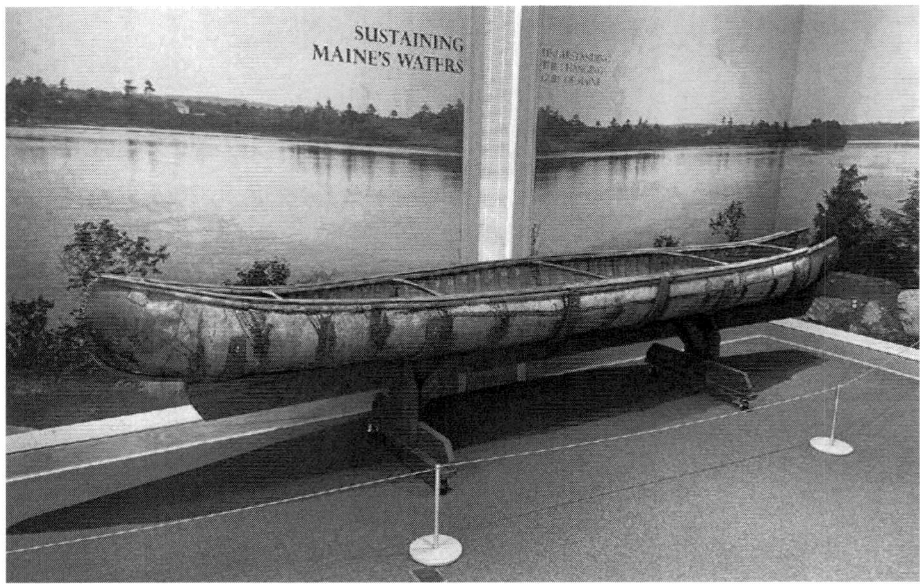

The Barnes Wabanaki canoe, possibly the oldest existing birchbark canoe in the world. Courtesy of the Pejepscot History Center. Photographed while on loan at the Maine Marine Museum.

Samoset's parents did not have the luxury of lingering over their tasks, because they had to be ready for one of the most important events of spring: the running of the alewives. Each spring these herring fish—and salmon as well—swam upriver in large schools to return to their spawning grounds, and for the Wabanaki it was a bonanza. They filled basket after basket with fish that they then smoked and preserved, or used as fertilizer for their crops. Another boon of the season was that bears came to feed

Portage technique using a modern canoe built in the style of ancient birchbark canoes.

Modern fishweirs on the Pemaquid River.

on the fish, making them an easy target for the hunter.

Samoset's family set up camp at a waterfall or a narrow bend of the river where the fish congregated. There they built a fishweir, a stone or stick structure that funneled the fish into an enclosed area, making it easier to scoop the fish out of the river or catch them in a net. According to a Jesuit missionary, the number of migrating fish in precolonial times was staggering. "[D]uring one month the fish ascend the river in so great numbers that a man could fill fifty thousand barrels with them in a day, if he could be equal to that work."[19]

Alewife and salmon populations have greatly declined in the Dawnland due to pollution, overfishing, and dams that inhibit their ability to return to their spawning grounds. According to *The Times Record of Brunswick*, "In 2017, 1,041 adult Atlantic salmon returned to Maine to spawn" compared to "100,000 that returned to the Penobscot River alone in the 19th century." Wild Atlantic salmon are an endangered species, but a program called Fish Friends out of Ellsworth is aiming to change that by providing salmon eggs to elementary school classrooms. Students nurture the eggs until they grow into fish, then release them into the wild.[20]

The alewives were such a plentiful resource and important part of the Wabanaki diet that people from villages near and far headed to the rivers during spawning season. Coming together for the alewife run was an opportunity to visit family members who had moved to distant villages, and for unattached men and women to seek out potential mates. No doubt they were all thankful to see new faces after a long winter apart. It was a joyous occasion and the Wawenock from Pemaquid and surrounding villages celebrated with enthusiasm. Their exuberance for life was innate; French explorer Samuel de Champlain marveled that the Wabanaki he met would often break into spontaneous dancing when they were pleased, as if their joy simply burst forth.[21] They sang and danced, feasted and told stories, and played sports and games when they came together in the spring.

Competition was fierce but good-natured. Men were anxious to test their

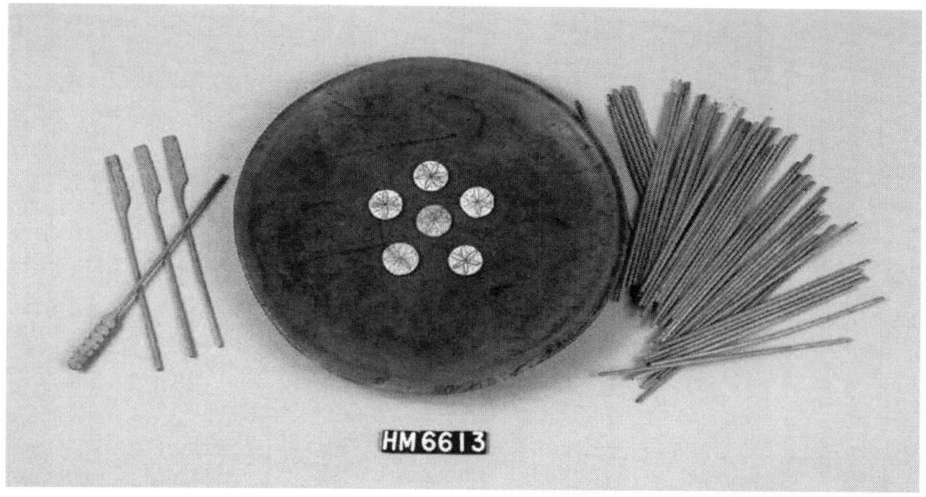

19th century Mi'kmaq version of waltes, also known as dice-game. HM6613 Mi'kmaq Waltes, c. 1850–1900. Hudson Museum, University of Maine[22]

skills, perhaps none more than the young men who were hoping to establish their reputations and impress the young women. There were footraces, wrestling matches, swimming races, archery contests, stone-slinging competitions, games of shinny (similar to hockey), football (like our soccer), and tossed ball. Tossed ball was played by inflating an animal bladder and tossing it back and forth, not allowing it to touch the ground. Game winners took home trophies of animal skins, clothing, or household goods. Not to mention bragging rights until the next year!

One of their most popular games, called waltes or dice-game, was played with "dice" made from moose or caribou bone, antlers, or beaver teeth. The dice were colored, painted, or carved on one side. Players used sticks to keep score, and a wooden platter or bowl to toss the dice. The general idea was to place the dice on the platter, then bring the platter down hard on the ground, which mixed up the dice in patterns that could be scored. The players would sometimes shout "Hub! Hub! Hub!" to distract their opponents, which Europeans heard as hubbub, but it was all done "in good spirit."[23]

Another favorite game was toss-pin and bundle. The game piece consisted of a stick or bone about eight inches long with a sharp point on one end; this was tied to a bundle of cedar boughs or moose hair. The object of the game was to hold the bone like a spear, toss the bundle into the air, and try to spear it. The player got points if the spear stuck in the bundle. The game was also used as a way for a man to court a woman. If the woman was successful at spearing the bundle but stopped playing, it meant that she had no interest in her suitor. Apparently this was a gentler way to let him down than telling him outright.[24]

On the other hand, according to Penobscot legend, a successful match was made when a suitor tossed an item—maybe a wood chip or a stone—at the feet of his beloved, and she picked it up. His marriage proposal having been accepted, the union would be celebrated with a wedding dance. Traditionally the couple would then live with the bride's family.[25]

While Samoset's parents were busy competing in games with the adults, Samoset and the other children had many games and toys of their own. Girls played with dolls made of "grass, or wood, or buckskin, or corn-cobs" and boys had miniature tools and weapons like "bows, slings, spears, and fishing equipment."[26] Girls were encouraged to learn skills for the home and boys were encouraged to hunt. Toys reinforced gender roles; they were meant to prepare children for their future lives.

Many of their games are recognizable in the games children play today. They played tag, calling the chaser "old woman" rather than "it." They played little sticks, what we call today jackstraws or pick-up-sticks. They played with tops made of wood, bone or stone; marbles made of little balls of hardened resin; and cat's cradle made from strips of rawhide. Naturally, they mimicked the adults too; footraces, swimming contests, shinny, tossed ball, and football were all popular.[27]

After having their fill of fishing and gaming it was time to go back to their summer camp by the sea. With their canoes filled with alewives, salmon, and bear meat if they had been lucky, Samoset and his family returned to Pemaquid.

3
SUMMER

Summer in the north is glorious and treasured because it is so short. After long, frigid winters and unpredictable spring weather, summer at last arrives sometime in June and by September is only a memory. The days are long, the sun is bright and hot, and the air is alive with birds, bees, and dragonflies. Salty air mixed with the smell of sweet grass is like a tonic. On the coast there is often a cooling breeze, but there can just as easily be thick fog that masks the ocean just a few steps away.

For the Wawenock it was a time for working in the garden, picking berries, gathering plants for food and medicine, and for fishing. Fishing was mostly men's work, and from a young age Samoset would have joined the men and older boys in the effort. The ocean and rivers were brimming with lobsters, crabs, clams, oysters, salmon, alewives, sturgeon, swordfish, cod, bass, mackerel, and eels. They fished with a hook made out of sharpened bone or by casting a hemp net weighted with stones. For larger fish a spear would do, though this took more practice. The men took to their canoes to hunt seals, dolphins, porpoises and—incredibly—whales.

The coasts of the northeast were prime whale territory. Hunting a whale from a canoe is nearly beyond imagining, but luckily we do not have to. James Rosier, an Englishman who sailed to the Dawnland in 1605, wrote a description of a whale hunt in his journal. (The "he" and "him" refer to the whale.)

> "[T]hey go in company of their King [sagamore] with a multitude of their boats, and strike him with a bone made in fashion of a harping iron fastened to a rope, which they make great and strong of the bark

> of trees, which they veer out after him; then all their boats come about him, and as he riseth above water, with their arrows they shoot him to death; when they have killed him & dragged him to shore, they call all their chief lords together, & sing a song of joy; and those chief lords, whom they call Sagamos, divide the spoil, and give to every man a share."[1]

Hunting an animal that was bigger than a school bus, armed with only spears and bows and arrows, was a brave endeavor. The Wawenock were probably hunting North Atlantic right whales, so-called because they were the "right" ones to hunt. They stay close to shore, swim very slowly, do not shy away from boats, provide an enormous amount of oil, and float when dead, making them easier to bring to shore. In Samoset's day, whales were common; today, it is much more rare to see a whale off the coast of Pemaquid.

North Atlantic right whales were especially vulnerable to hunters because they were relatively easy to kill and such a valuable prize. They may have numbered around 21,000 before contact with Europeans, then they were hunted nearly to extinction. Today the population is less than 400, and their biggest threats come from getting entangled in fishing gear, being hit by boats, and decreasing food supply due to warming ocean temperatures.[2]

The Wawenock would have celebrated a successful hunt with a ceremony to thank the spirits for bringing them good fortune. Ceremonies were used to ask for favors, like a good harvest, victory in battle, rain for their crops, or a cure for an illness. They also marked important occasions, such as marriages and births, a young man's first game kill, or the death of a member of the community.[3]

In James Rosier's journal there is a description of such an event witnessed by one of the young men on the voyage, Owen Griffin. Griffin spent a night on shore with the local people in Muscongus Bay, which was Wawenock territory northeast of Pemaquid. According to Griffin, a man rose up, the eldest in the group he guessed, and cried out a signal. When the women heard this they all fell down upon the ground, then the men went round and round the fire, stamping their feet as hard as they could. At times they took sticks tipped with fire and thrust them into the earth, or beat them on rocks, all the while crying out, sometimes changing the tone of their voices. After a couple of hours the men who had wives retired with them into the woods for the night—the implication not too subtle. The remaining revelers slept by the fire.[4] Griffin may not have known the reason for the ritual, but he was certainly impressed by it.

When Wabanaki people came together, it was a good time to do something else that they loved: smoke tobacco. Smoking tobacco has a very long history in the western hemisphere. "No tribal religious ceremony or intertribal conference began without the pipe and the smoke of tobacco. A pipe was the first courtesy offered guest or stranger."[5] Pipes were made from stone, clay, wood, or—along the coast—a lobster claw. Samoset's father probably carried his pipe and tobacco in a pouch made of animal skin or birch bark hung from his girdle, a leather strap around his waist. Men usually took on the task of growing tobacco and generally young men abstained from using it, because smoking impaired their stamina to fight an enemy in battle or chase down animals in a hunt, "a feat that might take more than a single day."[6]

Smoking was also an integral part of Wabanaki governance. Political decisions happened at council meetings where male leaders and other men of standing got together to make decisions for the community. Every family was represented in council and every council member got to speak his mind. Their goal was to come to unanimous agreement, and generally they would not end the session until they got there, even if it took days. Meetings would begin with the men lighting their pipes (or claws), and once everyone was relaxed, they began their discussion. Samoset's mother and the other women of the village were probably not invited into the council, though there is evidence that women exercised some influence with their men; in 1607 a Wawenock sagamore's wife was included in an important diplomatic visit with English settlers.

Wabanaki culture operated by strict rules of etiquette. Any visitor to the village was treated as an honored guest, and the hosts shared food and tobacco even if they had little for themselves. When their guests came to trade, they began negotiations with gift giving. If a gift was considered inadequate, however, the receiver might perceive it as a slight or insult.

Since the Wabanaki had no police, no court of law, and no prisons, punishment for a crime was decided in council, or by the sagamore of the village. Punishment was meant to fit the crime. In Penobscot oral history, "We are told that in cases of murder, the family of the victim assumed the right to pursue and take the offender. Then they tortured him to death. The right to such transaction was given by the chief, after he had been informed of the crime and the intended retaliation."[7] The offender could also make restitution if that was acceptable to the victim or the victim's family.

In Abenaki, the word for medicine man is "mdawleno," in Penobscot it is "mətéwələno," and in Passamaquoddy-Maliseet it is "motewolon" or "ptewolon." For simplicity's sake, the term medicine man will be used here.[8]

Councils were presided over by a sagamore, the leader of the community. The position was usually passed from father to son, though the honor was not automatic. A sagamore had to earn it. He had to prove himself in battle, be an expert hunter, or an eloquent speaker, skills that were highly valued. If he was also a medicine man (someone who had a connection through his dreams with the supernatural world of good and bad spirits) then he was even more respected. If a sagamore proved unsuitable for the job, or if his people lost confidence in him, the position was given to someone more worthy.

As a result, a sagamore who remained in power tended to be greatly respected and revered by his people. His words carried more weight in council meetings, and he made the final decision after the council had deliberated on a matter. He set the tone for relationships with neighboring communities, either friendly or confrontational, which could mean the difference between an alliance or war. As a young boy, Samoset undoubtedly studied his father and the most respected leaders of his village, wishing for the day when he would be invited into the Wawenock council. Perhaps he dreamed of becoming a sagamore one day.

For now, he could enjoy the last days of summer without the cares that came with adulthood. As the nights began to turn colder and daylight hours grew shorter, the Wawenock knew they needed to make the most of summer's gifts and prepare for fall.

4
FALL

Cool temperatures of early fall come as a relief from the summer heat. Clean, crisp air energizes a body after the languid days of summer. Nights can be surprisingly cold, and frost comes early in the north. Then there is the color. Trees are painted in red, orange, and yellow, a magnificent contrast against the usual green. But it is fleeting, and therefore precious; heavy rain and wind can wipe out the beautiful canvas in a day.

For Wabanaki people who grew their own food, fall was harvest season. After the women gathered the corn, they selected the best ears to use as seeds for the next year's crop. Then they removed the husks and cut the kernels off the remaining cobs and dried the kernels in the sun so they would not rot in storage over the next several months.

Keeping their food safe from pests was a constant battle. Woodchucks, raccoons, birds, and bears were a continual nuisance, so Samoset's mother dug holes in the ground or on the side of a hill and lined them with bark or clay to store their food. Into these "storage bins" she put dried corn, beans, nuts, and berries, as well as smoked and dried fish and meat—whatever surplus food she was able to put aside. She used clever tricks to disguise the holes, pouring water over the ground that had been disturbed, or building a fire on top of the pit.[1] She was hiding their stores not only from animals, but also from more determined thieves—other people.

These were coastal raiders from the north, possibly Wabanaki people who lived in what is now northeastern Maine and eastern Canada. In the 15th to 17th centuries the world was in the midst of the Little Ice Age, when temperatures were a few degrees colder than today and the growing season was even shorter than it is now. Crops did not grow well in the colder climate, so these raiders came south after the harvest and took what they wanted by force.

People in the north survived off what they could hunt and gather for food, but sometimes that was not enough. A wet fall could prevent them from getting to beaver lodges and the beaver meat and skins they depended on. A winter with little snow made it harder to hunt because there were no footprints to follow or deep snow to slow down their prey. French explorer Samuel de Champlain described how the First People (the Canadian term for Indigenous people) along the St. Lawrence River often lived on the edge of starvation. 'All these tribes suffer so much from hunger that sometimes they are obliged to live on certain shell-fish, and to eat their dogs and skins with which they clothed themselves.'[2] So, people in the north did what anyone else would do—they went in search of food, and people who grew corn lived in fear of them at harvest time.

Though the raiders' actions were reprehensible, they were impressive. They may have traveled hundreds of miles by ocean to rob their neighbors' food stocks. They learned how to sail small European boats, called shallops, which they obtained by trade, scavenge, or plunder.[3] But shallops would have been scarce, and many must have made the trip down the coast by canoe. Then they had to make the return trip home heavily laden with their booty, an achievement that rivals the Viking raids of Europe.

Not only were they able seamen, but they must have been fierce fighters as well. Their attacks completely altered the lives of the coastal Wabanaki, according to Champlain, who sailed the coast in 1605: "[T]hey told us that the savages who plant the Indian corn dwelt very far in the interior, and that they had given up planting it on the coasts on account of the war they had with others, who came and took it away." Champlain also mentioned the fortifications of the large village of Saco: "The savages dwell permanently in this place, and have a large cabin surrounded by palisades made of rather large trees placed by the side of each other, in which they take refuge when their enemies make war upon them."[4]

As a result of never knowing when the next attack might come, the people of Pemaquid had to be prepared to fight or flee at a moment's notice. Practically speaking the men were always prepared, since their hunting skills directly correlated to fighting skills. Samoset learned from a young age to move quietly through the forest to sneak up on prey, set ambushes, run long distances, and shoot accurately at a moving target, skills he could use against prey or foe.

Another reason the raids were so dreaded was that they usually happened in the fall during prime hunting season. If Wawenock men had to stay home to protect the village then they could not hunt, which was crucial to their survival. They needed meat for the protein it provided, furs to keep themselves warm in the winter, and skins for clothing. Hunting territories were fiercely guarded for this reason. One Penobscot hunter asked his medicine man to lay "a curse on his hunting territory against anyone who might invade it, by declaring that such a person would be found floating there dead."[5]

> **Champlain did not identify the raiders by name, so we do not know exactly who they were. One possibility is that they were the Mi'kmaq of present-day Nova Scotia, who had a long history of animosity with the coastal people of Maine that finally erupted in war in 1607.**

Therefore hunting territories had to be clearly divided and marked. Maine has many natural boundaries with its rivers, lakes, and mountains, so most territories were set between those geologic formations. To avoid confusion (or poaching), it was common practice to mark territories using family symbols. "Likenesses of the animal eponyms [symbols] were painted or carved on landmarks such as trees and rocks, or represented by birch-bark cut-out silhouettes posted here and there on the borders of the hunting ranges."[6] The forest was clearly marked by signs—if you knew how to read them.

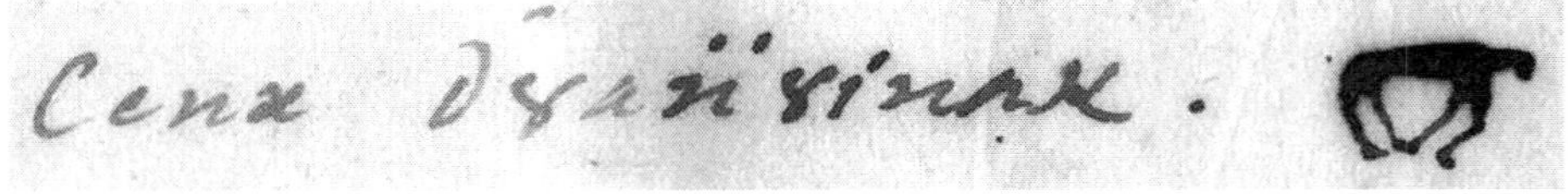

Wabanaki communities identified themselves with an animal or a bird symbol such as a sturgeon, bear, deer, moose, fox, or turtle. They might mark their territory with their symbol, or in later years, use it as a mark to sign a treaty or a land deed. This is the Wawenock "signature." Its shape is a mystery. DETAIL COURTESY OF THE MASSCHUSETTS ARCHIVES[7]

Hunting territories were large, covering more land than hunters could walk in a day. It was more efficient to set up temporary camps, so they did not have to return home each day, and the Wabanaki used simple, clever ways to leave a

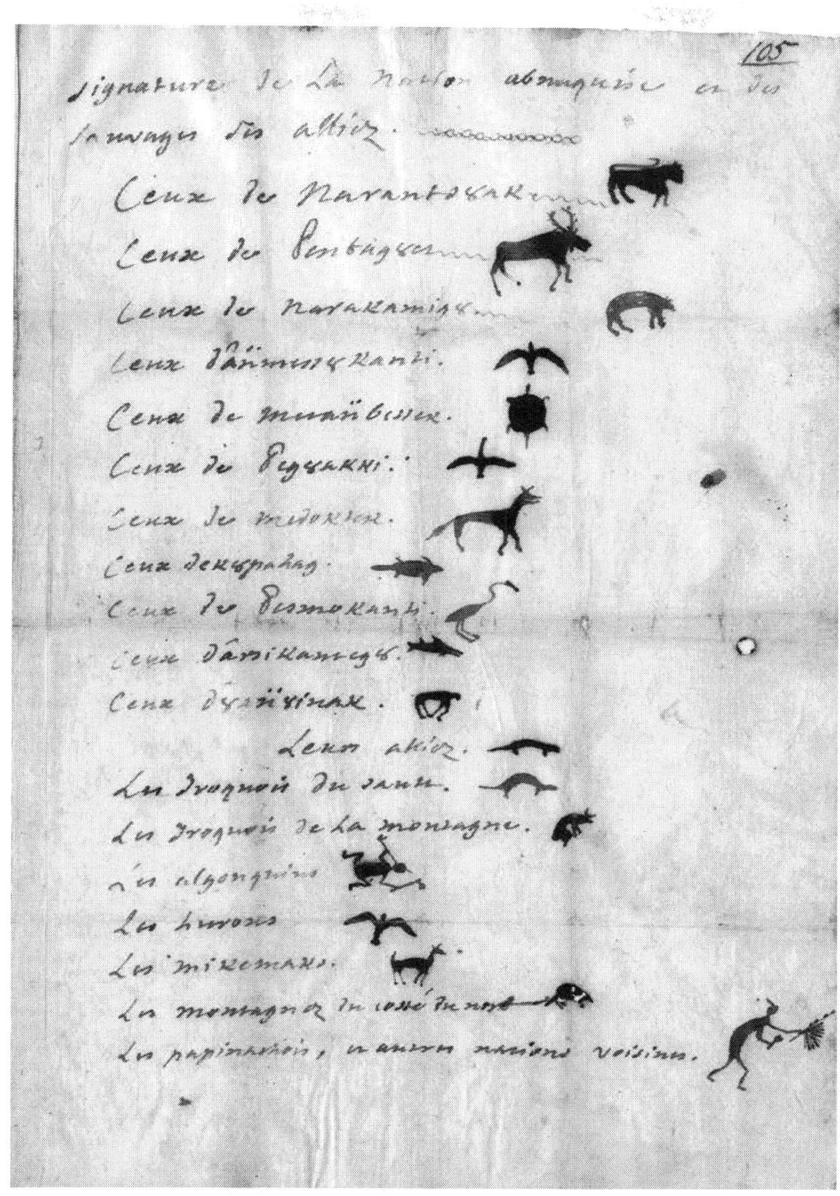

105

signature de la nation abenaquise et des sauvages ses alliez.

Ceux de Narantsouak

Ceux de Pentagoet

Ceux de Narakamigou

Ceux d'Anmissoukanti.

Ceux de Muanbissek.

Ceux de Pegouakki.

Ceux de Medoktek.

Ceux de Kwapahag.

Ceux de Pesmokanti.

Ceux d'Arsikantegou.

Ceux d'Ouanaouinak.

Ceux alliez.

Les Iroquois du Sault.

Les Iroquois de la montagne.

Les algonquins

Les hurons

Les mikemaks.

Les montagnez du costé du nord

Les papinachois, et autres nations voisines.

Above are "signatures" of nineteen Indigenous communities from the northeast, including Canada, from a letter written in July 1721. The Wawenock symbol is eleventh from the top.
Courtesy of the Massachusetts Archives[7]

message for their families. If they wanted to let them know which direction they had gone, they put a stick in the trail pointing in the direction they were headed. Another method was to cut a slit in the bark of a tree and put a stick in the hole pointing in the appropriate direction. Sometimes the message was more elaborate, like the example shown here etched into a piece of birch bark.

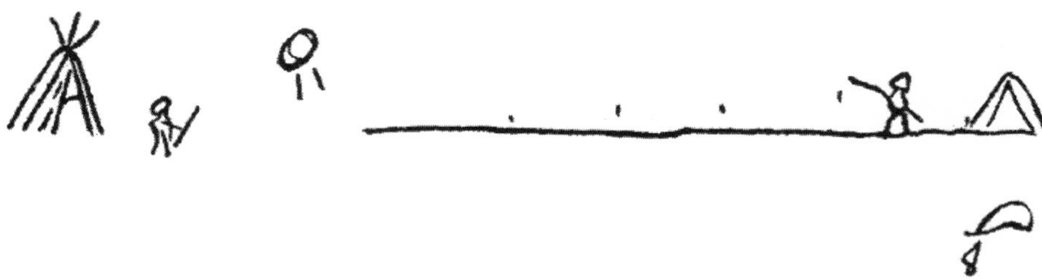

"This is a drawing of a wigwam on the left, then a man facing to the right, meaning that the writer is about to leave home, then the sun with two marks beneath it, meaning that he will be gone two nights, then a long line, the sign of his journey, or the path, then himself again, facing to the left, that is the hunter returning and the little temporary camp he is leaving. Underneath at the right is the beaver house where he is going to trap, and the small mark beneath this is the trap. The whole thing interprets: 'I am going to leave here to go to my small beaver camp... where I shall remain two nights trapping; then I shall return.'"[8]

Hunters had to take advantage of the remaining good weather before animals hibernated or went dormant for the winter. They had many tricks to make their work a little easier. They used special calls to attract turkeys and baited beaver traps with castor, an oily substance that beavers secrete to attract a mate. Fall is mating season for moose, and Wabanaki men learned to imitate a cow moose in heat to lure in a bull moose, sometimes from miles away. When the amorous bull arrived on the scene and did not find a cow, the hunter had to be a good shot or deal with the disappointed lover.

Birds that were migrating south stopped to feed on nuts dropping from trees, and the most plentiful of these by far was the passenger pigeon. Passenger pigeons are now extinct, but once they flew in such large numbers that they literally darkened the sky according to eyewitness accounts. It could take several hours for one flock to fly by, even though the birds flew at an estimated 60 miles per hour. They were an abundant source of protein for the Wabanaki, who would wait for them to roost in trees at night, then track them by torchlight and, while they slept, club them to death.

Slaughter of passenger pigeons really took off in the mid-1800s. Hunters could simply go to their roosting sites and shoot them or club them by the thousands. They were mostly sold for food, but sometimes they were simply killed and disposed of because they were such a nuisance to farmers. The pigeons could not adapt to the loss of their forest habitats which had been cut down for lumber or firewood or to make way for houses or farms. As their numbers dwindled they also had difficulty adapting to living in smaller groups. The last passenger pigeon, Martha (named for Martha Washington), died in the Cincinnati Zoological Garden in 1914. Americans had managed to completely exterminate a species. The one positive consequence is that their extinction spurred a conservation movement and laws that protect other species from the same fate. Reprinted with permission from Smithsonian Institution Archives[9]

Eels and ducks were important sources of food as well. Eels migrate from lakes and rivers to the ocean in the fall to spawn (like alewives, only in reverse), so fall was the best time to harvest them. Ducks sleep at night in rivers or salt marshes, so hunters would "drift in quietly in canoes, light torches to cause sudden confusion among the birds, and knock them down with clubs or paddles. Then a specially trained canoe dog, sitting in the bow, would jump into the water and retrieve the game."[10] As a boy, Samoset would learn all of these skills from his father and other men in the village.

After a good season of harvesting and hunting, the Wawenock had a supply of dried corn, meats, fish, nuts, herbs, and fruits to take with them to their winter camp. The move inland was necessary because there was more game there to hunt and trap. The villagers would break up into small groups to avoid encroaching on each other's hunting grounds.

Thus they made preparations to leave Pemaquid. They paid close attention to the weather because they could not risk the river freezing; it was their highway to the interior. As Samoset's mother packed up the dried provisions and household goods, his father readied the boat and gathered his tools and weapons. They would need all of these things to survive Maine's long, challenging winters.

5
WINTER

The first snow of winter is magical. Perfect, one-of-a-kind ice crystals fall from the sky as if to prove there is a grand design in nature. Light snow, which forms in the coldest temperatures, squeaks underfoot and sparkles when the sun strikes it. Winter can be a test of endurance, with its long dark nights and bitter cold and storms that restrict all movement. It can also be a time of rejuvenation, a chance to slow down and enjoy the serenity of a world made quiet by snow.

When Samoset and his family arrived at their winter camp, around 20 to 30 miles inland or as far as they could go by river, they set up their wigwam, gathered firewood, and buried their cache of dried provisions. Samoset's social circle was much smaller this time of year. He spent the season with his parents and siblings, if he had any, and maybe extended family and close friends. He probably kept company with a dog or two, since most Wabanaki kept them on hand to hunt and to alert them of anyone approaching their camps.[1]

This season of forced family intimacy was a time for bonding. Winter daylight is short in the north, so they would have spent a lot of time in their wigwams. Perhaps that is why they became such accomplished storytellers.

Storytelling has a long tradition in Wabanaki culture. Myths, history, religion, and life's lessons were passed down from generation to generation through oral storytelling. Winter nights were the perfect time to gather around the fire and share stories. Their favorite subject was Gluskabe (also written as Glooscap, Gluscap, Koluskap, etc.), a cultural hero. Gluskabe is so beloved that these stories continue to be popular today.

In addition to Gluskabe, Wawenock people believed in the existence of

François Neptune, the last known speaker of the Wawenock dialect (1912)[2]

two other deities, Squanto and Tanto, the first good and the second malevolent. They attributed their good luck to Squanto and their bad luck to Tanto. But above all was the supreme deity, the Creator of all life. The following story was told by François Neptune, the last known speaker of Wawenock, translated into English and paraphrased here. We see how the Creator (here translated as the Owner) made the earth and the first man, and then according to Wawenock legend, Gluskabe made himself. In an amusing twist, the Creator puts Gluskabe in his place when he shows off a little too much.

The Owner made the first man, and with the earth left over, Gluskabe created himself. That is why he was so strong. As he sat up, the Owner saw him and said with astonishment, "How did you get here?" Gluskabe answered, "I formed myself from the earth left over from first man." And the Owner told him, "You are indeed a very wonderful man. Let us roam about together." So they went up a hill, then up a mountain, and from the top of the mountain they gazed all around. They could see a great distance, see all the lakes, rivers, and trees in the country. The Owner said to Gluskabe, "Look at this, my wonderful work. The earth, the water, the ocean, the rivers, the basins, the lakes. What have you made?" And Gluskabe answered, "I have not made anything. But perhaps there is one thing I could do. Perhaps I could make the wind." The Owner encouraged him, and told him to be as powerful as he could be. Gluskabe made the wind, and it began to blow. Then it blew harder and increased in strength until it tore the trees out by their roots and blew them over. "That is enough," said the Owner. "I have seen what you can do. Now I will make a wind." Then the wind began to blow, and it grew stronger and stronger until they could not stand up without being blown over. Then it blew so hard that it tangled all the hair on Gluskabe's head. When he tried to smooth it down with his hand, the wind blew all the hair off his head. And that is the end of this story.[3]

In general Gluskabe appears as a kind and loving god who teaches humans the survival skills they need to live in their hostile environment. Animals figure very prominently in these tales, due to the close relationship the Wabanaki had with them. They were keen observers of animal behavior because their lives depended on being able to predict it.

Their relationship with the natural world went even deeper. When Samoset's father killed an animal, he thanked it for giving up its life to feed his family. Wabanaki people believed in a spiritual life force, sometimes known as "gitchi manitou," (gitchi meaning "great" and manitou meaning "spirit") that could be anywhere and live in anything. This powerful spirit lived in a beaver, a rock, or a river. "To the Indian the whole creation was replete with powers: the sun, the moon, the four winds, thunder, rain; in his own person, the heart, the lungs."[4] Therefore, Samoset's father both respected his prey and feared it, because gitchi manitou could manifest itself as good or evil.[5] It was potentially dangerous to disrespect or waste any part of the animals he killed, because their souls could come back to haunt him.[6]

The Wabanaki never took for granted the gifts the earth gave them. Showing gratitude helped keep the world in balance. They did not take more than they needed to survive, and always made sure there would be more for another day—they were early practitioners of sustainability, and it was fundamental to their culture.[7] In contrast, Europeans often hunted or harvested a commodity until they had completely exhausted the supply. It was a practice with devastating consequences.

Hunting and fishing in winter was a little different than in other seasons. In order to fish, the men had to cut a hole in the ice. As for hunting, the animals that hibernate in the winter were safe from the hunter. Not the moose. The heavy moose becomes easy prey because it has difficulty walking through deep snow. It breaks through any top crust and wades through snow that might be chest deep. All the while it is leaving tracks that are easy to follow.

Detail of moose in winter[8]

The Wabanaki solved the problem of walking on snow by using snowshoes. Like the canoe, snowshoes were an ingenious invention that allowed them to move efficiently in their environment. One European visitor described them this way: "In the winter when the snow will bear them, they fasten to their feet their snow shoes which are made like a large racket we play at tennis with, lacing them with deer-guts and the like."[9] Making snowshoes was a joint effort of men and women. The men would make the frames by steaming and bending ash wood, then the women did the lacing, typically using rawhide.

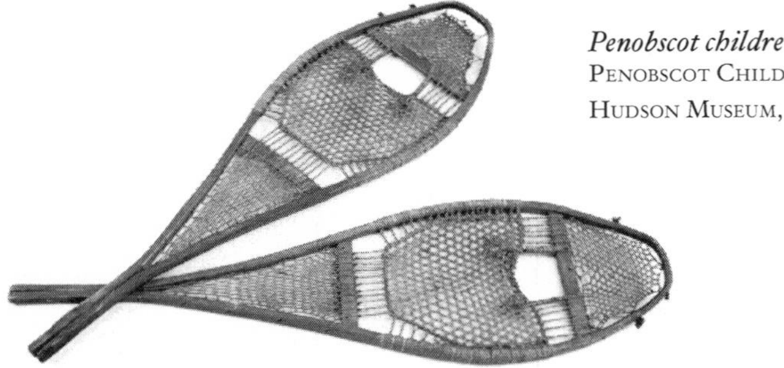

Penobscot children's snowshoes. HM7028 PENOBSCOT CHILDREN'S SNOWSHOES C. 1900. HUDSON MUSEUM, UNIVERSITY OF MAINE[10]

Many animals, like the beaver, were more desirable prey in the winter because they put on extra fat and their fur becomes much thicker. The Wabanaki preferred these pelts because they provided extra warmth to survive the cold winters. When Europeans arrived and began trading for beaver furs, they quickly learned that a winter-caught beaver was worth more than a summer-caught beaver.

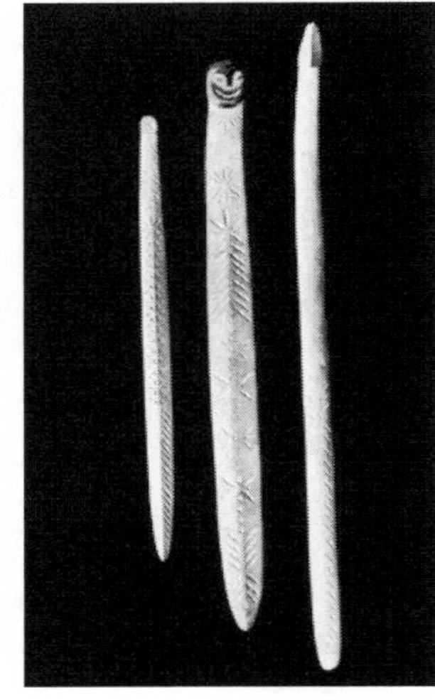

To play snowsnake, a player needed to carve sticks three to six feet long in the shape of a snake. Then when a group of players was gathered, they would "select a slope and make a track by dragging a log down its snowy incline. When they could not find a log, they would grab a small boy by the heels and drag him down the slope! Icing the track by throwing water on it came next. When it was frozen, the players in turn would scale one of their sticks down the chute."[11] They would mark their spots by jamming their sticks upright in the snow, and the player whose stick went the farthest would collect all the sticks from that throw. COURTESY OF THE PEABODY MUSEUM OF ARCHAEOLOGY AND ETHNOLOGY, HARVARD UNIVERSITY, 2004.24.1835[12]

It was the job of Samoset's mother to skin any game that her husband killed, and also to cut up the carcass and bring the meat back to camp. It could be quite an ordeal; sometimes the hunt went on for days and the kill happened far from camp. This is where the toboggan, an invention of the First People of present-day Canada, came in handy. If she had to transport the heavy cargo a great distance, it was easier to drag it over the snow than carry it on her back. She then had the arduous task of preparing the hides to use as clothing, shoes, and a multitude of other things.

Though there was always work to do, the Wabanaki made time for fun too. They went sledding on their toboggans and played ice shinny on the frozen lakes and rivers. Perhaps their favorite game, however, was snowsnake, something people of all ages could play.

The snowshoe and toboggan were innovations that helped the Wabanaki survive the challenges of winter. They have endured for hundreds of years and are used for recreation by millions of people today. Even with these tools, winters were a hard time for the Wabanaki. There were good years and bad years, but thanks to their ingenuity—learned from their benefactor Gluskabe—they survived and thrived, passing this knowledge from one generation to the next.

And then the Europeans came.

How to Prepare a Hide to Be Made Into Clothing

"To prepare a deer hide, for example, the usual practice was to place the skin under water in a running brook, one with a clay bottom preferred. This loosened the hair so that it could be readily removed. Next, a paste, perhaps of liver and brains, was spread on the flesh side to soften the hide. A stone gouge, followed by a piece of polished wood, was worked back and forth by hand to break the fibers, making the skin flexible. If a dark color was preferred, the hide was smoked in a damp fire fed with oak bark. One skin could be waterproofed and left pliable, another dried hard as a board, and a third worked as soft as chamois. If the hair was to remain, oil and hand manipulation of the skin were the means for making it supple."[13]

6
THE EUROPEAN INVASION, 1492–1604

Christopher Columbus had no idea that he had stumbled across a "new world" when he made landfall in the Bahamas in 1492. He was looking for a faster route to China, India, and Southeast Asia (or the "Indies" as they were sometimes called) to trade for goods that Europeans coveted, like tea, spices, porcelain, and silk. The overland trade route they had been using for hundreds of years, known as the Silk Road, had been cut off by the Ottoman Turks after they conquered Constantinople (now Istanbul) in 1453. This meant that Europeans had to take to the sea on a very long and dangerous route down the west coast of Africa, around its southern tip, and up its east coast into the Indian Ocean, a voyage that took two years. Columbus was convinced he

Detail of statue of Christopher Columbus in Barcelona, Spain[1]

could find a shorter route to the Indies by sailing west. Even though Norsemen had built a small settlement in Newfoundland around the year 1000 and mariners from Europe had already found their way to the shores of Canada, those discoveries were not widely known.[2] As far as most people in 1492 were concerned, the world consisted only of Europe, Asia, and Africa.

Columbus commented in his journal that the Taino people he met in the Bahamas were "intelligent, for I observed that they quickly took in what was said to them," yet he and his men labeled them "savages" and "heathens," or by their definition uncivilized human beings without religion.[3] These labels dehumanized Indigenous people, making it acceptable in Europeans' minds to kidnap, enslave, rape, torture, and murder them, all of which they did over the course of Columbus's time in the Americas. As Viceroy and Governor, Columbus was responsible for these atrocities. His legacy is tainted by the brutality of the Spaniards and the genocide they committed. Given the fact that he shipped hundreds of Indigenous people to Spain to be sold as slaves, Columbus can also be considered the founder of the slave trade in the Americas.

In recent years there has been a movement to remove the honor given to Columbus by changing the name of the Columbus Day holiday. In October 2019, the State of Maine joined five other states and many cities and towns in replacing the name with Indigenous Peoples' Day.[4]

Dehumanizing and enslaving people was nothing new, and not unique to Spaniards. Slavery was practiced throughout Europe, and had been for more than 1,000 years. The fact that the zealous Christians of Europe—the same ones who launched several bloody crusades to the Middle East to Christianize the "barbaric" Muslims—could engage in such an unchristian and barbaric practice is tragically ironic.

Unlike previous adventurers like the Norsemen or early fishermen who had been to the Americas, Columbus broadcast the news of his "discovery" far and wide. This set off a wave of exploration to the west. It quickly became apparent to others that what he had found was not a new route to the Indies, but a whole new world (though never to Columbus himself, who went to his grave believing that he had found a westward passage to the Indies). The term "new," of course, was the European term; the Indigenous people who had lived there for thousands of years—or since time began—would not have considered their world "new." Nor could they possibly have foreseen the epic collision of very different civilizations that was in the making.

By the 16th century many Europeans had attained a decent standard of living. They were well past the medieval period, a time when religious fanaticism and intolerance was at its height. People lived in less fear of the bubonic plague, known as the Black Death. Though there were still periodic outbreaks, the disease hit its peak in the 14th century and death rates had generally decreased. Science, music, and art were flourishing during what came to be known as the Renaissance. So why sail west now, when the quality of their lives was improving? What were they looking for—or running away from?

Mariner's astrolabe, an instrument used to determine latitude at sea[5]

In the first place, they went because they could. Long journeys across oceans were now possible because of improvements in ship design and navigational technology. Ships were being constructed with covered decks, no longer open from top to bottom to the weather, making the sailor's life more comfortable. Square sails were supplemented with lateen (triangular-shaped) sails that enabled better maneuverability, especially in windy conditions. Navigation techniques improved; magnetic compasses and astrolabes—instruments used to determine direction and latitude, respectively—were common equipment on board ships by the 15th century. Now navigators could more safely set a course out of sight of the coast and have a better chance of finding their way home again.

Even with these improvements, sailors' lives were difficult and dangerous. They lived at the mercy of the weather and unseen hazards like rocks, reefs, and shallows. Shipwrecks were common. Climbing to the top of the yard to furl a sail in rolling seas, with no footropes or handholds, could prove deadly.

In addition to the hazards of working on board, living conditions were pretty dreadful. Many men had only one set of clothes and bathing was rare, so the discomfort of the wretched mate, and those around him, was undoubtedly great. They were tormented by rats, cockroaches, and lice. Until 1596 when hammocks were introduced to the Royal Navy (an invention of Indigenous people of the Caribbean), sailors slept wherever they could find a spot on the floor.[6] Scurvy, a disease caused by a lack of vitamin C in the body, was common and could lead to a long, slow, painful death. A well-financed voyage was stocked with plenty of provisions, but food and water often spoiled on a long voyage, which could leave sailors with little to eat or drink until they made their next landing.

Caravel in the style that would have been popular in the 16th century for the cross-Atlantic voyage[7]

Discipline on board had to be strict because mistakes could be deadly. Carelessness with fire was disastrous on a wooden ship and falling asleep on watch might result in being dashed upon rocks. Therefore, punishments for infractions were severe. They included flogging, dunking in the sea, keelhauling (being dragged under the ship), and abandonment. Mutiny and insubordination were often punished by death.[8] On a voyage to New England in 1638, one passenger reported that a young servant was "whipped naked at the capstan, with a cat with nine tails, for filching nine great lemons out of the surgeon's cabin, which he eat rinds and all in less than an hours' time," which was harsh but necessary as the passengers and crew needed the lemons to prevent scurvy.[9]

Despite these hardships, living a life on the open ocean was better for some than a life of poverty back home. Many sailors were running away from debt or a criminal past. Whatever drove them to the sea, they certainly did not lack courage. The first sailors to cross the Atlantic, not just captains like Columbus, were brave to make the journey. The lowly deckhand took the same risks as his captain, though he did not share in the riches or the glory.

Debtors and criminals were not the only ones running away from the motherland. The Church of England did not make room for people with dissenting religious views, so finding a place to practice religion without interference was the principal motivation for many. Half of the Plymouth colonists were fleeing religious intolerance and outright persecution. Puritans, Catholics, Quakers, and other non-Anglicans also sought safety and freedom.

But the greatest motivation to sail west, by far, was money and the pursuit of a better life. Wealthy investors with an adventurous streak gambled that they could make huge profits from commodities in the "new" world that were ripe for the taking. Expeditions across the Atlantic were expensive and risky, but if successful were extremely lucrative. And for those at the bottom of the economic ladder, who had little chance of breaking the cycle of poverty and becoming landowners at home, going west meant they could escape the oppression of their social class by potentially becoming landowners in a new land.

Spain had given the rest of Europe a tantalizing glimpse of the riches that might be found in the Americas. There were vast deposits of gold and silver in the Caribbean, Mexico, Central America, and South America, and Spanish conquistadors brutally exploited Native people to obtain them. Within a few short decades they conquered the Aztecs in Mexico and the Incas in Peru, then expanded into the southern part of what is now the United States. The Spanish built our nation's first permanent European settlement at St. Augustine, Florida in 1565. Spain became the wealthiest and most powerful empire in Europe in the 16th century by enslaving millions of Indigenous people—and then Africans—and forcing them to mine precious metals, which the Spanish then shipped back to Europe. Portugal was having its own success in Brazil. The English, French, and Dutch wanted to expand their empires as well with the hope that they would discover such riches. While Spain jealously guarded its territories, other kingdoms fought over what was left.

Though gold and silver did not pan out for those realms, it quickly became clear that there were plenty of other goods in North America that *could* make a man wealthy. The land and its waters could supply Europe with many valuable commodities that were being rapidly depleted at home, due to a growing population and increased demands. And of course, there was the land itself.

In England, the population was rebounding after the bubonic plague killed almost one third of its inhabitants in the 14th century. The population of London rose from about 70,000 at the end of the 15th century to around 250,000 by 1600.[10] All of these people had to be fed, clothed, and sheltered, and England—restricted to a small island—had limited resources that were quickly being exhausted. The English used so much whale oil in their lanterns that they had nearly wiped out the European whale populations. They stripped their forests for fuel and timber to build houses and ships. Trees were being cut down so fast that tall, straight trunks used for ships' masts had to be imported. Sassafras trees were also a dwindling commodity. They were used to make medicine to cure syphilis, a new disease thought to have been introduced by Columbus's men, a souvenir of their travels to the Americas. The same practice was happening throughout Europe.

So, when the next explorer to follow Columbus to the Americas discovered one of the richest cod fisheries in the world, Europeans took notice. Though he was an Italian (like Columbus), John Cabot sailed for the Crown of England in 1497. He chose a more northern route than Columbus, also hoping to find a passage west to the Indies. When he landed in what is now Newfoundland, Canada, he claimed the territory for England. Then he chanced upon the Grand Banks, where the cod were allegedly as big as a man and so plentiful they could be scooped up in baskets.[11] It was a windfall. Cod was very popular, especially on holy days when Christians could not eat meat, and it had been overfished to near extinction in Europe. Cabot's discovery not only added to the map of the Americas and gave England a claim to North America, it also paved the way for fishermen, and they came in droves.

The fishermen's goal was to fill their ships with fish as quickly as possible and make it back home safely, but they did sometimes interact with the local people. They went on shore to dry their catch, preserving it for the long voyage home, and to gather firewood and water. At other times the local people came to them, paddling their canoes out to meet the foreigners. When Europeans saw what Indigenous people were wearing, they knew they had found more manna from heaven: furs.

It is strange to think that Samoset's world was turned upside down by a fashion craze, but that is how it began. Beaver felt hats were all the rage in Europe, and like so many other resources, Europeans had harvested the beaver to near extinction. Beaver fur can be felted, a process that includes removing the outer coarse fur to get to the softer fluff underneath, which is then made into felt. It became the favorite material for making hats starting in the 1550s and continued to be popular for almost 300 years thereafter. Everyone from royalty to the man on the street wanted a beaver felt hat; women wore them too. So fishermen and explorers started bringing "trinkets" with them to offer in trade, items that Indigenous people had never seen before—metal knives, copper kettles, woven cloth—and beaver trapping soon dominated the lives of the Wabanaki.

Beaver felt hat in the style worn by the settlers at Plymouth.

Now that the secret was out about North America's riches, there was no stopping a very determined class of "merchant adventurers," as they called themselves, from beating a path to America to exploit them. Columbus and Cabot had swung the sticks that broke open the piñata and several greedy European empires now came rushing in to scoop up the prizes.

Before long the merchant adventurers decided that trading for a few pelts from the decks of their ships was not enough. They needed permanent bases in America—colonies even—to maximize their profits. European monarchs encouraged this exploration and trade by promising large land grants to the adventurers, since it was a no-lose proposition for them. The entrepreneurs risked their own capital to send ships to America, and a percentage of their profits went straight to the national treasury. This in turn helped to finance the nearly constant wars European kingdoms fought against each other. Pope

Alexander VI had legitimized the practice with the papal bull of 1493, the Inter Caetera, which led to the "doctrine of discovery," essentially declaring that any Catholic kingdom could claim as its own any lands that were not inhabited by Christians. It has been over 500 years, and the Inter Caetera has never been revoked.[12]

Although Europeans did not abandon the search for a westward passage to the Indies, they were now drawn to North America for its riches. Samoset and other Native people just happened to be living in their treasure trove. As far as many, if not most, Europeans were concerned, Indigenous people could either help them get what they wanted or be pushed aside—and if necessary, eliminated.

The Penobscot described their first sighting of a European ship as a "swan towards the rising of the sun."[13] It seems that the sails of the ship, coming from the east, looked like the great white bird to them.

Word of such a curiosity would have spread far and wide. As more foreigners arrived on their shores, tales of strange men in huge canoes would have been confirmed, but sightings and interactions with non-Natives were still rare in Samoset's homeland in the 16th century. Chances are he did not see his first European until he was a teen.

To understand the steps that led to the first English settlement in present-day Maine and the events that brought Samoset into contact with the English, we have to go back well before his birth to 1567. That was the year that sailor David Ingram shipped out from England with the crew of Captain John Hawkins, a famous privateer and a pioneer in the English slave trade. After picking up slaves in West Africa and selling them in the Caribbean to sugar plantation owners, Hawkins ran afoul of the Spanish in the Gulf of Mexico. Being on the losing end of that battle, he had to abandon Ingram and 100 other men on the coast of present-day Mexico.[14] Ingram and two companions determinedly made their way to what is now Nova Scotia, Canada, mostly by foot but with an occasional lift by the locals. There they were able to find passage back to England aboard a French ship.

For years Ingram made a living telling the tale of his travels to anyone who would pay to hear it. As he went from tavern to tavern, no doubt consuming copious amounts of ale, his stories grew more elaborate. We can discount his claims of seeing elephants and other fantastic creatures, and kings who wore rubies that were six inches long, but he also spoke of things that were quite true, like the fact that the northern people wore their beaver skins "hairy side being next to their bodies in winter."[15]

Sir Humphrey Gilbert Courtesy of the Gilbert family at Compton Castle[16]

Ingram's sensational stories caught the attention of fellow Englishman Sir Humphrey Gilbert. An adventurer who hoped to set up a trading colony in America, he heard Ingram's descriptions with undisguised interest. He was especially intrigued by a place called Norumbega, a city or region in Wabanaki territory that had begun to take on mythic status like El Dorado, the legendary city of gold. Sir Humphrey's heart probably skipped a beat when Ingram told him he found 'gold nuggets as big as his fist.'[17] Gilbert had to see this place for himself.

It just so happened that Sir Humphrey Gilbert was a favorite of Queen Elizabeth I, as they had known each other since childhood. He convinced her to grant him letters-patent, a wide-sweeping charter that would allow him 'to discover, search, find out and view such remote heathen and barbarous lands countries and territories not actually possessed of any Christian prince or people.'[18] The date was June 11, 1578, about twelve years before Samoset was born. This charter, the first given to any English colonizer, gave him such encompassing privileges that he could settle almost anywhere on the coast of North America, sell parcels of the territory for profit, and 'take and surprise' any vessel that sailed the coast. The charter also set the precedent for all English colonists who followed. Even though they might live in America, colonists would still retain their rights and privileges as Englishmen and be subject to English laws. It was a remarkably generous gift.

Sir Humphrey, it turned out, was more successful at charming queens than heading up expeditions. After several setbacks, both in time and finances, he managed to send out two ships tasked to look for Norumbega, one in 1579 and another in 1580. Though his scouts did not find the mythical Norumbega, they did find a country blessed with an abundance of timber, plants, wildlife, and safe harbors—a good place to set up a colony. Based on this information, Gilbert was determined to investigate America for himself, even though Queen Elizabeth wished he would not go, saying he was 'a man of not good happ [luck] by sea.'[19] She was right. He did not survive the trip.

Sir Humphrey set sail with a fleet of five ships in 1583. His goal was to sail to Newfoundland and then continue south to the coast of present-day Maine and set up his colony there. One of the ships had a problem and turned back almost immediately. When he and the rest of his fleet arrived at St. John's, Newfoundland, they found 36 ships fishing there: Portuguese, Basque, French, as well as English. Even at this early date, St. John's was a bustling international fishing port. Sir Humphrey went ashore and dug up a shovelful of dirt, as was the custom, and claimed Newfoundland for the English crown. Though John Cabot had done this in 1497, the English had apparently forgotten, and Sir Humphrey claimed the credit anew.[20]

Things went badly from there. Many of the crew were sick, and he had to send them home on one of the ships. Then, his supply ship ran aground and sank. Only twelve out of a crew of one hundred men survived the wreck.[21] With little choice due to their lack of provisions, Sir Humphrey made the difficult decision to return to England. His colony would have to wait.

Sir Humphrey sailed for home on his favorite but rather unseaworthy vessel, the *Squirrel*. The *Squirrel* and the other remaining ship hit heavy seas off the Azores, close to Portugal, and the *Squirrel* ran into trouble. Even so, he refused to transfer to the other ship, a larger and safer one. He was reportedly seen sitting on deck reading Sir Thomas More's *Utopia* while the *Squirrel* floundered. At the last, the crew of the surviving ship heard him exclaim over and over, "We are as near to heaven by sea as by land!"[22] That night, the ship went down with all hands.

Though Sir Humphrey never made it to the coast of Maine, his story is significant for two reasons: his charter from Queen Elizabeth I set the precedent for how land in any future English colony would be granted and how the colonists would be governed; and his ambition to set up a colony in Maine lived on in others, including his son, Raleigh, whom Samoset would meet twenty-four years later.

The failure of Sir Humphrey Gilbert's expedition and his resulting death were no doubt shocking to English high society, but the tragedy did little to dampen interest in colonizing North America. Queen Elizabeth transferred the charter to Sir Humphrey's half-brother, Sir Walter Raleigh, one of England's more flamboyant and famous adventurers and the Queen's favorite at the time. Sir Walter bypassed Maine and chose to build a settlement in present-day North Carolina instead, the now famous Lost Colony of Roanoke (1585–1590). Roanoke's settlers disappeared in a mysterious chapter in this country's early history. Over a decade would go by before English explorers returned to America, and this time they were coming to Samoset's homeland.

PART II

Meeting Europeans, 1605–1625

7
THE KIDNAPPING, 1605

It was late in the spring, past the time of clearing fields and planting seeds, and the Wawenock were visiting their neighbors to the east in Muscongus Bay. Samoset was around 15 years old, not quite a man but much more than a boy. He had almost reached the age where he could grow his hair long, a privilege reserved for grown men.[1] He was tall, with a lean runner's body. A young man his age would be preparing himself to run long distances to hunt. It was also the age for him to undergo the rite of passage from boy to man.

Reverend William Morrell, who lived in New England in 1623, wrote about the ritual used to train each male child "to make him fit for arms." "He is constrained to drink a potion made of herbs most bitter till turned to blood with casting, whence he's fitter." By drinking an herbal concoction that would cause him to vomit over and over until he spit up blood, Samoset would experience "the worst... of what may hurt him most."[2] If he could endure that he could endure anything, and would now be ready to face his enemy in war. It was training that would help him deal with many future ordeals in his life.

The Wawenock had likely traveled east to participate in the alewife run and spring games. As a teen, Samoset was undoubtedly excited to test his physical skills against fresh opponents, as well as get a look at the eligible young women. It was a typical spring.

Then a ship came.

It first appeared on the horizon, then it sailed boldly into the bay. Though few of them had probably seen one before, they knew what it was from the stories passed down. Word spread through the camp quickly, and they may have sent messengers throughout the area to alert other villages and to inform their sachem, or great leader. It would have been the custom for the sagamores to meet with their councils and deliberate over what to do about the strangers. Should they prepare for war? Should they try to make contact, and if so, whom should they send? Meanwhile, they stayed on high alert.

Finally, after eleven days (they may have been waiting for a directive from their sachem), it was decided. They would make contact.

In a stroke of luck, the encounter between the English and the Indigenous people in Muscongus Bay was recorded and preserved. Since this was Wawenock territory they were presumably Wawenock, though it is possible that some were visiting from nearby Penobscot territory. James Rosier—who documented the whale hunt and ceremony mentioned earlier—was a member of the expedition and wrote an account, *A True Relation of Captain George Waymouth his Voyage, made this present year 1605; in the Discovery of the North part of Virginia.* It is one of very few accounts that we have from the period, and the earliest that describes Wawenock people. Although it is a one-sided record of events, it includes important details about the area, the people, and their interactions with the English. Captain George Waymouth (or Weymouth), sailing the *Archangell,* was on a mission for his wealthy patrons to find commodities to export and a suitable place to build a colony. Given that one of the backers of the expedition was a staunch Catholic, the plantation may have been meant for Catholics, who were out of favor with the Protestant Church of England.

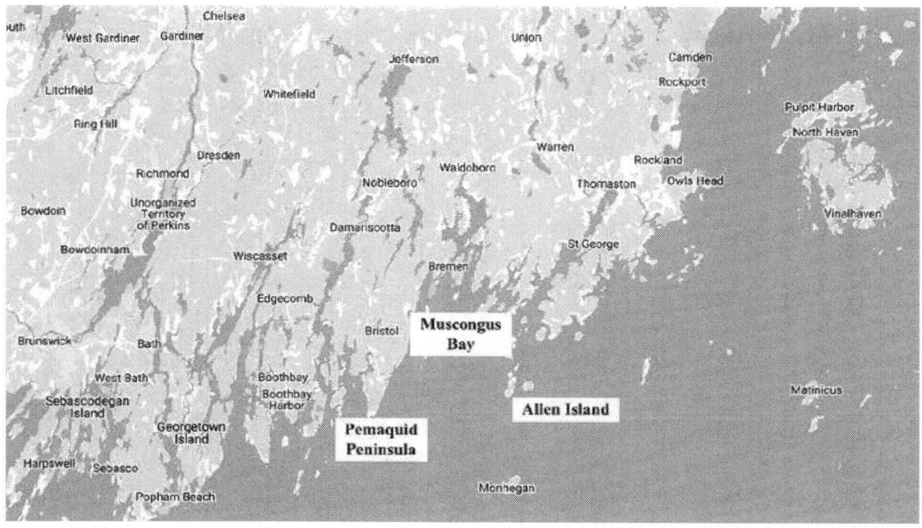

According to Rosier they left England on March 31, 1605, and had an uneventful passage to America. They first spotted land off the coast of Cape Cod (present-day Massachusetts) in mid-May. Strong winds then blew the ship north to Monhegan Island, about twelve miles off the Pemaquid peninsula. Waymouth and his 28 shipmates stopped at Monhegan for one night to replenish their supply of water and firewood, then continued to a cluster of islands closer to the mainland. Most historians agree that they dropped anchor in what is today called the Georges Islands, somewhere between Allen Island and Burnt Island in Muscongus Bay. They most likely went ashore on Allen Island, the largest of the five islands. They dug wells for fresh water, built a small boat to be used for exploring (they had brought the pieces with them as a "kit"), sowed seeds to see how they would grow, took stock of the resources on the island, and erected a cross to let the world know this was now Christian territory that belonged to England. They liked the area so much that many in the crew wished to stay permanently.[3] Eleven days later, they had their first visit from the Wawenock.

> This day [May 30], about five o'clock in the afternoon, we in the ship espied three canoes coming towards us, which went to the island adjoining, where they went a shore, and very quickly had made a fire, about which they stood beholding our ship: to whom we made signs with our hands and hats, [waving] unto them to come unto us, because we had not seen any of the people yet. They sent one canoe with three men, one of which, when they came near unto us, spoke in his language very loud and very boldly: seeming as though he would know why we were there, and by pointing with his oar towards the sea, we conjectured he meant we should be gone.[4]

Thus began the earliest recorded meeting between Europeans and Wawenock people. There may have been misunderstandings from the very start. Rosier jumped to the conclusion that the Wawenock were telling them to leave—as if he were expecting the locals to be hostile. But who is to say that the man was not simply pointing out to sea to ask if that is where they had come from?

Captain Waymouth had gone off exploring in the smaller boat, so Rosier took charge of this meeting. He was anxious to make contact with Native people and enticed them with gifts: "bracelets, rings, peacock-feathers, which they stuck in their hair, and tobacco pipes."[5] That seemed to break the ice. Gift

Granite cross erected in 1905 on Allen Island to commemorate the 300th anniversary of Waymouth's voyage.

giving was important in establishing good relations in Wabanaki culture, so Rosier's gesture was well received. From that point on, the Wawenock pursued a relationship with the strangers, visiting their ship, sharing food and tobacco with them, and inviting them to their camp on one of the islands.

Not all journal writers provided a detailed physical description of Indigenous people, but thankfully Rosier did. It is the earliest firsthand description of Samoset's people.

> The shape of their body is very proportionable, they are well countenanced, not very tall nor big, but in stature like to us: they paint their bodies with black, their faces, some with red, some with black, and some with blue.
>
> Their clothing is beavers skins, or deer skins, cast over them like a mantle, and hanging down to their knees, made fast together upon the shoulder with leather: some of them had sleeves, most had none: some had buskins [leggings] of such leather [tied]: they have besides a piece of beavers skin between their legs, made fast about their waist, to cover their privities.

> They suffer no hair to grow on their faces, but on their head very long and very black, which those that have wives, bind up behind with a leather string, in a long round knot.
>
> They seem all very civil and merry: showing tokens of much thankfulness, for those things we gave them. We found them then (as after) a people of exceeding good invention, quick in understanding and ready capacity.[6]

Rosier painted a vivid picture. He described the Wawenock as "not very tall nor big," but we know from the Plymouth settlers' description of Samoset that he was tall, so he may have been exceptional. We do not know why they painted their bodies and their faces, nor what the different colors or markings meant. Frank G. Speck, an anthropologist who spent a great deal of time with Penobscot people in the early 20th century, wrote about the practice of face and body painting: "The men regarded painting as a formality intended for war, dances, and festivities...Before ceremonies, the men, one by one and alone, went into the wigwam where the paint was kept, and decorated themselves...Warriors also painted their naked backs to indicate exploits."[7] Meeting non-Natives for the first time would certainly qualify as a special occasion. Of course, Speck interviewed Penobscot people living 300 years after these events, and customs could have changed during that time.

Rosier went on to complain that although the Wawenock were friendly, they were not willing to extend that courtesy to their women. "One of their canoes came not to us, wherein we imagined their women were: of whom they are (as all savages) very jealous."[8] Jealousy of their women was a preconceived notion not backed up by experience—had Rosier gotten this idea from talking to other explorers who had been to America, or perhaps from their journals? If there were indeed women nearby, then this was probably not a war party. Men planning an attack would not bring women into harm's way.

The description of Wawenock clothing made from animal skins is similar to what we know about the clothing of other Native people in the northeast. Their garments were constructed in separate pieces (sleeves, leggings), so that they could add or take off pieces as needed, which was very practical. The comment about facial hair is also consistent—the men did not have beards. The detail about only married men wearing their hair up in a knot is curious—did Rosier later witness a wife do this for her husband?

They found the Wawenock were not only civil, but also smart, quick learners, and inventive. It was a pleasant surprise for the English who "little expected any spark of humanity."[9] Horrific stories circulated in England that Indigenous people were "not content to kill, they delight in tormenting people in the most bloody manner possible."[10] The English carried this misconception with them, and it biased their perceptions. Given this is what they expected, it is surprising they found any common ground at all.

Rosier cheerfully took up the task of documenting the Wawenock's culture and language. They did not eat raw meat or fish and loved the sugar candy he gave them. They disliked "aqua vitae" (most likely a type of grain alcohol), but liked the Europeans' other beverage, which was probably beer or cider. They laughed when they saw their reflections in a mirror for the first time. Rosier tested the strength of their bows and was greatly impressed by the craftsmanship. They were fascinated by metal goods such as kettles and helmets and were terrified of guns "and would fall flat down at the report of them."[11] Firearms were almost certainly new to them.

The Wawenock quickly realized that the markings Rosier was making on paper helped him remember the names of things. It was undoubtedly their first exposure to writing, and they were enthusiastic about teaching the English their language. "Then on the shore I learned the names of diverse things of them: and when they perceived me to note them down, they would of themselves, fetch fishes, and fruit bushes, and stand by me to see me write their names."[12]

On the third night of their acquaintance, Waymouth invited two Wawenock men to the ship to dine with him at his table to see how they would behave. The men impressed him, "neither laughing nor talking all the time...neither would they eat or drink more than seemed to content nature; they desired peas to carry a shore to their women, which we gave them, with fish and bread, and lent them pewter dishes, which they carefully brought again."[13]

Initially the English went out of their way to treat the Wawenock well. They gave them gifts, shared their food, and traded and socialized with them. They restrained their dogs, which were probably mastiffs, because they frightened the Wawenock who were unaccustomed to such large and aggressive canines. (Mastiffs became a weapon in the English arsenal and accompanied most voyages.) Rosier explained that since they found the area to be highly suitable for a colony, "we used the people with as great kindness as we could devise."[14] It was all part of a plan to earn the Wawenock's confidence, learn as much as they could from them, and ultimately take some of them back to England.

That same evening new visitors, perhaps from a different village, arrived bringing tobacco, and the English were ceremoniously invited to the island where they were camping for a smoke. Now the Wawenock reciprocated with their own hospitality. They spread deerskins on the ground next to the fire for their guests and joined them in a friendly, bonding smoke. The Wawenock must have begun to relax around the foreigners, for Rosier finally got a close view of some of the women and children. He guessed the women's curiosity finally won out. The women "were well favoured in proportion of countenance, though coloured black, low of stature, and fat, bare headed as the men, wearing their hair long" and the two little boys were "very fat and of good countenances, which they love tenderly, all naked, except their legs, which were covered with thin leather buskins [leggings], fastened with strops to a girdle about their waist, which they gird very straight, and is decked round about with little pieces of red copper."[15] The leggings were probably meant to protect the babies' tender legs when they crawled on the ground. Overall, Rosier noted that they were a healthy, well fed population; the term "fat" was meant as a compliment.

The English hoped to entice some of the Wawenock to sleep on board the ship—an invitation that made the cautious Wawenock uncomfortable. They said no. They may have been aware that other Indigenous people had been forced onto European ships and were never seen again. Europeans underestimated the extent to which Indigenous people traded and shared information between communities, and thought they were dealing with naïve people who knew nothing about foreigners and their ways. This refusal no doubt surprised Waymouth.

In their diplomatic way, the Wawenock came up with a solution so that their new friends would not be offended. After all, it was in their best interests to stay on good terms with the foreigners. They could gain a lot from an alliance. For one, they would be able to trade directly for European goods without having to go through middlemen from the north, which was their usual method of procuring them. In addition, they recognized that the Europeans, with their huge ship and terrifying guns and dogs, would be a powerful ally against their enemies. So after conferring, a delegation paddled out to the ship and offered a compromise: three men would stay on board if the English would send one of their men to stay on shore.

Waymouth readily agreed. He sent Owen Griffin, and this was the night that the Wawenock held a ceremony (described earlier in detail), perhaps to be hospitable to Griffin, or in celebration of their new friendship with the English. Either way, being willing to share such a sacred ceremony suggests they were quick to embrace their new friends.

The next morning the men were exchanged, and several canoes full of Wawenock men came to the ship expecting another day of trading and socializing with the English. But Rosier sent them away. It was Sunday, the holy day of the week when Christians did not work or engage in business. Rosier tried to explain why he was sending them away, but in all likelihood the meaning was lost on them. How does one describe the Sabbath with hand gestures?

They probably felt rebuffed and wondered what they had done to offend their new friends, so that evening they tried again. They paddled back to the ship and brought tobacco, making a point to give some to Waymouth and Rosier, the two leaders. The English offered "bread and peas" in return, and relations appeared to be back on track. Later the Wawenock returned to the ship to invite the English back to their campsite for another smoke, an invitation they accepted. Rosier wrote that they used the short claw of a lobster as their pipe and they served red berries of a type unknown to him in cups made "very wittily of bark."[16]

Birchbark container, made in the style of his ancestors, by Penobscot Barry Dana.

Etiquette satisfied, they got down to the business of trade. The Wawenock offered fish for bread, but Rosier refused. He drove a hard bargain. They tried to trade four young goslings for four biscuits, and Rosier gave them two. The Wawenock were satisfied, but Rosier wanted more tobacco and furs. They had no more, they claimed, but indicated that their leader, Bashabes, was on the mainland with plenty of furs and tobacco to trade. Would the English come to the mainland to meet him?

Bashabes (or Bessabez, Bashaba) requires an introduction. He was the sachem for a vast territory that covered over half the coast of what is now Maine, which the Wabanaki called Mawooshen. It extended from the Saco

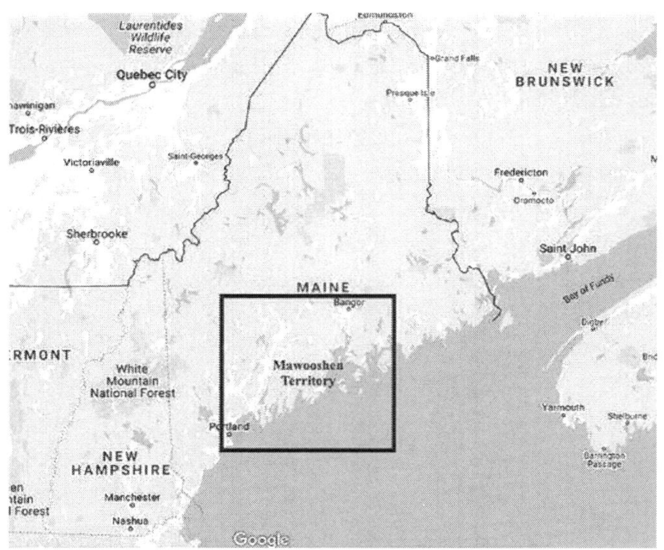

Scope of Mwooshen territory on present-day map of Maine.

River to the present-day Union River in Ellsworth, with several distinct groups in the territory, the Wawenock and Penobscot being just two. Bashabes may have lived in what is now the city of Bangor, located about forty miles up the Penobscot River from Penobscot Bay.[17] Samuel de Champlain met him there in 1604 and as it was the largest village in the region he guessed it was the great city of Norumbega that David Ingram mythologized. It is even possible that Bashabes met Ingram—Bashabes could certainly have been alive in 1569 when Ingram passed through the area. By 1605 he was a greatly revered leader who played a large role in the early contact period.

That night they agreed to exchange more men, and this time two English sailors stayed on the island while three Wawenock slept on the ship. The exchanges were getting more equal and more comfortable. The next morning, Monday, June 3, the 5th day of their acquaintance, Captain Waymouth agreed to meet Bashabes.

Waymouth manned the small boat, now called a "light horseman" because they had reinforced the sides with extra wood against a possible attack, with 15 men. Two canoes went on ahead, presumably to alert Bashabes that they were coming, while the three Wawenock men who had slept on the ship guided Waymouth in their canoe. Rosier was impressed that even with eight of their men rowing, the three Wawenock were able to paddle circles around the English.

The Wawenock guided them to a point of land in what is thought to be present-day Cushing. Waymouth was understandably cautious, not knowing what was waiting for him on shore. He offered to send Rosier, whom he trusted to "take a view of them, and what they had to traffique [trade]" in exchange for a man who appeared to be one of their sagamores.[18] However this man flatly refused (Rosier would in future refer to him as *he who refused to stay as a pawn*). Was the sagamore offended that this exchange was beneath his station? Was he suspicious of the foreigners' intentions? Or perhaps involved in some plot against the English?

They had come this far and the English did not want to leave without the furs, so a compromise was reached; a young Wawenock was exchanged for Owen Griffin, who was told go ashore and report back to Waymouth. While Waymouth and the others waited for Griffin, one of Waymouth's officers, Thomas King, spent the time engraving his name on a rock along the shore. Shortened to Tho. King, he added a cross and the date 1605.[19] This engraving is the only known physical piece of evidence of Waymouth's time spent in America, and beyond doubt places him in Muscongus Bay.

Rubbing of Thomas King's engraving.
Reprinted with permission from David Morey[21]

When Griffin returned to the boat, he had startling news. He had counted 283 men, all with bows and arrows, and "their dogs, and wolves which they keep tame at command, and not anything to exchange at all."[20] He was told that the furs, and their great leader Bashabes, were just a little way up a small river. He had not gone to verify this, and who could blame him. Such a large party of armed men would certainly have been alarming.

Waymouth and Rosier had heard enough. They concluded they had been betrayed by these "very treacherous" people, and resolved "so soon as we could to take some of them, least (being suspicious we had discovered their plots) they should absent themselves from us."[22] Did the Wabanaki really plan to attack them? And did the English hatch this scheme to abduct some of the Wabanaki only *after* they thought they had been betrayed, as Rosier's comment implies?

Of course, we cannot know what the Wabanaki planned to do. The English saw the large force of armed men as a threat and concluded they had been betrayed. It must have seemed odd, too, that the Wabanaki insisted the English go to this particular place to trade, rather than bring the trade goods to them at Allen Island. Then there was the sagamore who refused to stay in exchange for Rosier—was that because an attack was imminent?

The men that Griffin counted must have come from several Wabanaki villages throughout Mawooshen territory, because there was no single village in the area with a male population that large. However, the fact that no arrow was shot, nor did they attack Waymouth's men, casts some doubt that this was a war party.

But why so many Wabanaki? Several things might explain it. Since there was always a risk of raids from the north, Bashabes may have traveled with a large entourage of bodyguards due to his high status. There are other historical accounts of important sachems who traveled with large forces—Ousamequin (whose name has come down through history as Massasoit), for example, arrived in Plymouth for his first meeting with the colonists with sixty armed men. Another possibility is that the surrounding communities may simply have come together to honor their great leader, whose visit would have been an important event, and they were understandably curious and wanted to see the foreigners. Finally, they may have wanted to show the English, with whom they hoped to make an alliance, that they would be a strong ally. A show of numbers and weaponry would impress them. Perhaps it was a combination of these reasons.

Whatever happened that day, the consequences were clear: there would be fear and mistrust between the Wabanaki and the English in the future. It was a lost opportunity for them both, and now Waymouth was motivated to complete his mission and get on his way.

The next morning they started preparations for the journey home, loading the ship with water and firewood from one of the islands. By 10:00 a.m., they had visitors—six men from Pemaquid in two canoes. These men could not know it, but their lives were about to change forever. Two of them boarded the ship and went below deck to warm themselves by the fire. Rosier tried but could not entice the other four aboard. He gave them peas and bread which they took to one of the islands.

One of the four went back to the ship almost immediately to return the food container, and stayed on board. This one the English were especially glad to have, "he being young, of a ready capacity, *and one we most desired to bring with us into England, had received exceeding kind usage at our hands,* and was therefore much delighted in our company" (author's emphasis).[23] This young man had been treated with special attention from the beginning of their relations because they knew they wanted to bring him back to England. Here is proof that they planned the kidnapping from the start. That left three men on the island. Waymouth and Rosier hatched a plan to lure them in.

> We manned the light horseman with 7 or 8 men, one standing before carried our box of merchandise, as we were [accustomed] when I went to traffique [trade] with them, and a platter of peas, which meat they loved: but before we were landed, one of them (being too suspiciously fearful of his own good) withdrew himself into the woods. The other two met us on the shore side, to receive the peas, with whom we went up the cliff to their fire and sat down with them, and while we were discussing how to catch the third man who was gone, I opened the box, and showed them trifles to exchange, thinking thereby to have vanished fear from the other, and drawn him to return: but when we could not, we used little delay, and suddenly laid hands upon them. And it was as much as five or six of us could do to get them into the light horseman. For they were strong and so naked as our best hold was by their long hair on their heads: and we would have been very loath to have done them any hurt, which of necessity we had been constrained to have done if we had attempted them in a multitude, which we must and would, *rather than have wanted them, being a matter of great importance for the full accomplishment of our voyage* (author's emphasis).[24]

They were prepared to use force, and do the men harm, rather than go back to England without them. Waymouth's mission would not have been fulfilled without Native hostages. The Wawenock must have felt terribly betrayed. Their friendship with these strangers had been false from the beginning.

We do not know the identity of the man who escaped, and there is no evidence that it was Samoset. But it could have been.

Considering that the five other men were from Pemaquid, as Rosier later tells us, the odds are strong that the sixth person was as well. Samoset was about

15 years old at the time, perhaps around the same age as the young man "they most desired to bring to England," and possibly old enough to be included in the trading party. Also, given the fact that he later became a sagamore of the Pemaquid area, Samoset probably held some status—either through his family or because of some superior skill—that could have entitled him to be included. So he may have been the one who got away.

Whoever it was, he must have been suspicious before Rosier's party even landed. He surely witnessed the abduction, given that the islands are small and two struggling men would have made a lot of noise. He may have feared that the English would come back for him and that he would suffer the same fate as the others. He assumed they were murdered. Since the English took both canoes and all the bows and arrows from the beach, he would have been stranded on the island with no way to get off and possibly no weapon with which to hunt or defend himself. The mainland was five miles away across open ocean, too far to swim. His best chance of escape was to hide or swim to one of the nearby islands and hope the English would not look for him there.

Days went by, and the English stayed moored in the harbor. They had to realize that the captured men would be missed, but they did not seem worried about retaliation. They took their time. The day after the kidnapping they continued to gather wood and water. The next day they stowed the canoes they had stolen below deck—both to secure them from damage and to hide them from view, presumably, in case other locals came on board. On day four Waymouth took the light horseman and coasted all around the islands, charting the depths and looking for fresh water sources. Despite their treacherous behavior, the English planned to come back to this spot in the future and they were making detailed notes about the surroundings. Waymouth may have also been searching for the man who had escaped.

On that same day, June 8, they had their first visit from the Wabanaki since the abduction. Seven men in two canoes came from the east, the opposite direction from Pemaquid which lies to the west of the Georges Islands. They may have been Penobscot, since Wawenock territory did not extend east of the St. George River. As this was the first mention of any canoes in the area since June 4, we must assume that the one who got away was still hiding on one of the islands and had not been able to alert anyone of the kidnappings. Of the seven, all were new faces, with the exception of the sagamore who had refused to be exchanged for Rosier (*he who refused to stay for a pawn*) at the aborted meeting with Bashabes.

The delegation was in full regalia, with fresh face paint in black, red, and blue. They wore "jewels in their ears, and bracelets of little white round bone, fastened together upon a leather string" (probably wampum, a decorative form of shell bead).[25] These men had been sent by Bashabes, and Rosier seemed relieved when they made no sign that they knew about the kidnapped men. They had come to invite the English once again to meet with Bashabes, promising that he had furs and tobacco to trade. Was this really a trade delegation or an ambush? After the last meeting, Waymouth expected treachery, but even with the risk he was tempted to trade given the profit he would make. So he informed the Wabanaki that Bashabes would be welcome on his ship, but he would not meet him on shore. Then he gave them some token gifts and quickly sent them on their way. Three days went by with no word from Bashabes. He had now been rebuffed twice by Waymouth, and as the supreme leader of Mawooshen, this could only be seen as an insult.

On June 11, Waymouth pulled anchor and went exploring up one of the rivers—likely either the St. George or Penobscot. Finding large, navigable rivers was another goal of their expedition. Boats would be more protected from wind and waves in a river than anchored on the open ocean, and a river would give the English access to the interior of the country. Their wishlist also included rich farmland, a good supply of trees for firewood and building, sources of fresh water, and plenty of game. They found evidence of all of these.

On June 12, four days after their most recent encounter with the Wabanaki, the English received their final visit. Here he was yet again, *he who refused to stay for a pawn*, with two others. The persistence of this man is remarkable; Waymouth and crew were now more than 20 miles north of the Georges Islands, and he had presumably paddled all this way to meet them again. He asked Waymouth to send one of his men to stay the night with Bashabes on shore, who was waiting nearby. (If this is true, then Bashabes had now traveled to three different locations in an attempt to meet with the English.) Waymouth said no.

Rosier finally offered a clue that might explain why *he who refused to stay for a pawn* so doggedly pursued them: "[W]e had one of his kinsmen prisoner, as we judged by his most kind usage of him being aboard us together."[26] One of the prisoners was a family member or a close friend, and by now he knew about the abduction. It is both heartwarming and heartbreaking to know that he followed Waymouth all that way in the hope that the men were still alive and on board the ship. But Waymouth did not soften, and simply ignored their request.

On June 16, the English sailed away from the coast for good, carrying the five Wawenock prisoners with them.

Word had now spread about the men from Pemaquid. French explorer Champlain happened to be cruising the coast on his way back from Cape Cod when he heard about the incident. The Wabanaki told him that men on a ship "had killed five savages of this river, under cover of friendship." Champlain guessed by the description that the guilty party was English.[27] Naturally the Wabanaki had no way of knowing that these men were still alive and being held prisoner on Waymouth's ship, so they presumed the worst. Champlain was understandably disturbed by this news; bad behavior on the part of any European could jeopardize all relations with the Wabanaki.

The English felt no remorse about tearing these men from their families and using them for their own purposes. Rosier repeated the prevalent—and profit-oriented—thinking of his people when he called the Natives "a purblind [blind or dimwitted] generation, whose understanding it hath pleased God so to darken, as they can neither discern, use, or rightly esteem the valuable riches in the midst whereof they live."[28] The "valuable riches" were not only furs, timber, fish, and other commodities, but the land itself. In Eurocentric fashion, Rosier felt that the English were justified in taking land from Native people, who did not appreciate it or use it like the English would. To an Englishman, land should be owned, divided, planted, harvested, grazed, and built upon...or it was wasted. If Wabanaki people were not "improving" the land, then they ought to forfeit the right to use it. This ideology conveniently provided the rationalization they needed to take Wabanaki land.

The English planned to use their prisoners "to give us further instruction... of their governors, and government, situation of towns, and what else shall be convenient, which by no means otherwise we could by any observation of ourselves learn in a long time."[29] They would be back, and they would be armed with knowledge gleaned from their kidnapped hostages—knowledge that would help them dominate Wabanaki people and take over their land.

8
THE WAWENOCK IN ENGLAND, 1605-1606

After the initial shock of their capture, the five men from Pemaquid became compliant prisoners. Waymouth and Rosier may have secured their cooperation by telling them that they could return home if they did what was expected of them. They had little to gain by resisting, as there was no hope of escape. By the time Waymouth released them from their captivity below deck, they were well out to sea. Rosier described them on board the ship:

> First, although at the time when we surprised them, they made their best resistance, not knowing our purpose, nor what we were, nor how we meant to use them; yet after perceiving by their kind usage we intended them no harm, they have never since seemed discontented with us, but very tractable, loving, & willing by their best means to satisfy us in any thing we demand of them, by words or signs for their understanding: neither have they at any time been at the least discord among themselves; insomuch as we have not seen them angry, but merry; and so kind, as if you give any thing to one of them, he will distribute part of it to every one of the rest.[1]

He identified the five men in his journal as **Tahánedo**, **Amóret**, **Skicowáros**, **Maneddo**, and **Sassacomoit**. He described Tahánedo as a "Sagamo or Commander." Amóret, Skicowáros and Maneddo he labeled gentlemen (a European term) and Sassacomoit a servant.[2] The term servant is unclear.

Wabanaki people did not have servants in the same sense that Europeans did, but they did have social hierarchy in their culture. Sassacomoit may have been of a "lower class," or he could possibly have been a prisoner of war, which would also make him appear to have a lower status.

Rosier used the month at sea to learn as much as he could about the captives. They worked on language, with the Wawenock both teaching him their language and learning English. Since they spoke the Wawenock dialect of Algonquian (the family of languages spoken in a vast area of the northeast), one of the earliest vocabulary lists compiled of North American languages was Wawenock. Rosier originally transcribed between 400 and 500 words but most of them were lost, with less than 100 included in the printed journal.

There are several alternative spellings of the names of the five kidnapped men. Rosier added the accent marks to help with the pronunciation.

Tahánedo: Nahanada, Tehanedo, Bdahanedo, Nahaneda, Dohannida, Tahinda, Dehanada

Amóret: Amooret

Skicowáros: Skidwarres, Scikaworrowse, Skettawarroes, Skitwarres, Sketwarrers, Sketwarroes

Maneddo: Maneduck, Mannido, Manedy

Sassacomoit: Assacomoit, Satacomoah, Assacumet

Rosier was faced with quite a linguistic challenge. Given that his ear was not familiar with the pronunciation or structure of the Wawenock language, it would have sounded very strange to him. The following examples give an idea of what he was up against. In the Abenaki and Penobscot languages, the closest living languages to Wawenock, the word "hand" would not stand alone. The root is *elji* in Abenaki, but the Wabanaki speaker would always qualify it by saying *nelji* (my hand), *kelji* (your hand), *welji* (his or her hand), or *melji* (someone's hand).[3] Also the English alphabet did not correspond neatly to that of the Wabanaki. They did not use *f* or *v* sounds, they substituted *l* for *r*, they swapped *t* and *d*, and did not distinguish between *p* and *b*. To them the words "Penobscot" and "Bemopscot" were the same.[4]

The structure of their sentences is nothing like English. The language is polysynthetic, which means that one word might express the meaning of an entire sentence.[5] This linguistic construct makes for some fantastic words, like *Eda'li-t'wa'kil-a'muk* which means "place where you have to run up hill" and *"ačə́ssahtək^{w}e,"* the Penobscot word for "he who has many colors," or a dragonfly.[6] Place names highlighted a geographic feature or some cultural or historical significance of the location. The melodious name *Pas-sag-as'sa-wau'keag*, for example, means "place for spearing sturgeon by torchlight."[7]

Now add to the mix that the Wawenock dialect differed from that of their neighbors. Samuel de Champlain's Mi'kmaw guide from Nova Scotia could only understand a few words spoken by the people of Saco, even though they all technically spoke a form of Algonquian.[8] If Sassacomoit was indeed a captive from another community, he may have spoken a different dialect than the Wawenock, which would have added to Rosier's confusion. Europeans sailing down the coast would have encountered the same thing. Imagine trying to compile a vocabulary list when the word for "moon" is *gizos* in Abenaki, *nipawset* in Passamaquoddy-Maliseet, and *tepkunset* in Mi'kmaq.[9] Of course, Native people would have encountered the same difficulty when they met Europeans who spoke English, French, Spanish, Dutch, and Portuguese.

One reason why the Wabanaki had different words for the same things was that they described them in unique ways. The Penobscot word for bear is áwehsohs, which can be translated as "it stands upright" or "the beast," and the Passamaquoddy-Maliseet word for bear is muwin, which has been translated both as "the berry eater" and "the black being." All are meaningful descriptions of bears. According to Rosier, the Wawenock word for bear was rogsoo, though we do not know its translation.[10]

These initial exchanges were undoubtedly full of errors and misunderstandings, like when Rosier learned that the Wawenock made butter and cheese from deer milk. Either this was a complete misunderstanding—the Wabanaki did not tame deer and certainly did not try to milk them—or they were pulling his leg (a more fun interpretation). Maybe they were getting a little revenge.

Illustration of London by Claes Visscher published in 1616[11]

When Waymouth returned to England with five Wabanaki men from North America, he created quite a sensation. There had been little exploration since the disastrous failure at Roanoke, and people were curious about the "new" world and its people. Queen Elizabeth I had died in 1603 and her nephew, James Stuart, had been crowned King James VI of Scotland and King James I of England. Though King James was just as reluctant as Queen Elizabeth to *fund* a colony, he encouraged those who wished to invest their own money to go there. Exploration was still in its infancy, however, so seeing a Native person from the Americas was still new for Europeans.

Waymouth and his crew were met in Plymouth, England, by Sir Ferdinando Gorges, the Captain and Commander of the Plymouth Fort. From that moment until his death forty-two years later, Sir Ferdinando was a fervent believer in colonizing the Mawooshen territory and he became intimately involved in its future. Gorges recounted his fateful meeting with Waymouth: "And so it pleased our great God that there happened to come into the harbor of *Plymouth* (where I then commanded) one Captain *Waymouth*...[who]...happened into a river on the coast of *America,* called *Pemaquid*, from whence he brought five of the Natives." (Gorges understandably thought the Wawenock had been captured in Pemaquid since that is where they came from.) And though he condemned Waymouth for kidnapping the Wawenock, he readily admitted "This accident must be acknowledged the means under God of putting on foot, and giving life to all our plantations."[12] With their knowledge of the land and its resources, as well as the strength

of any possible opponents, he hoped these five men were going to be the means of English success in America.

Maneddo, Skicowáros, and Sassacomoit were taken to live with Sir Ferdinando in Plymouth. Tahánedo and Amóret were sent to London, for what reason we never learn. The separation from the others must have been agonizing, as they no doubt feared they would never see each other again. At this point the record falls silent on Amóret. A few historians believe that Amóret was actually Samoset because of the similarity of the names. However, Samoset never once mentioned that he went to England, a detail he was unlikely to omit. Putting that discussion aside for now, Amóret is never mentioned again, unlike the other captives. Since the plague had been rampant in London two years earlier, Amóret may have died of that disease or possibly another.

Tahánedo was housed with Sir John Popham, the Lord Chief Justice of England and the most important man of law in the country. He had been appointed to the post by Queen Elizabeth herself, and also served on the Queen's Privy Council (her board of advisors). When King James succeeded Queen Elizabeth, he retained Sir John in those two positions.

Each of these two men, Sir Ferdinando Gorges and Sir John Popham, played important roles in the history of both England and Maine. The men from Pemaquid were well placed to meet some of the most important people of the time, and witness some remarkable moments in history.

Sir Ferdinando was a military man who had a long history of fighting for the English crown. He loved to tell the story of how the French king saved his life when he was wounded at the siege of Paris in 1589.[13] He was given

Sir John Popham. Courtesy of Harvard Law School Library, Historical & Special Collections[14]

command of the fort at Plymouth and executed his duty with the utmost seriousness, to the point of annoying the royal government with his constant barrage of requests for additional men and supplies. He was loyal to a fault, and his devotion to a former commander nearly cost him his life when he became involved in the Essex Rebellion, a plot to depose Queen Elizabeth and overthrow her government in 1601. Though Sir Ferdinando was eventually absolved of guilt in the affair, his commander, the Earl of Essex, was found guilty of treason and beheaded. The judge who presided over the trial was Sir John Popham.

Sir Ferdinando and Sir John may have initially met because of their roles in the Essex affair, but their association grew strong because of their mutual interest in starting a colony in North America. Their motivation is unclear, but given the troubled state of affairs in England at that time, the prospect of building their own fiefdom from scratch—free from England's rampant poverty and religious and political discord—would have been appealing. Money was certainly a factor. Whatever their reasons, from the moment they met the captives from Mawooshen, their commitment to building a colony there never wavered. Their first attempt in 1607 would be named the Popham Colony after Sir John.

In his memoir written late in life, Gorges took credit for the creation of a document that became known as *The Description of the Countrey of Mawooshen*, an inventory of the rivers, lakes, waterfalls, towns, sagamores, and population of Mawooshen. It was the kind of document that makes historians and anthropologists swoon. The men from Pemaquid supplied the information and the English used it to make plans for their colony.

Mawooshen was partitioned by eleven rivers, with the area around each river "governed" by a senior sagamore and in some cases a junior sagamore as well.[15] Bashabes was the preeminent sagamore, or sachem, and his main home was on the Penobscot River. The Wawenock lived in the area roughly between the Kennebec River and the St. George River, as mentioned before. (Samoset's village of Pemaquid was only one of many Wawenock communities, each located on one of the rivers or bays.) The captives knew a remarkable amount of detail about the other regions of Mawooshen, including how many men lived in each village and how many wigwams there were. This was impressive, because the distance from one end of the territory to the other was over 150 miles. Though we have no way to verify the accuracy of their information, the men from Pemaquid claimed there were approximately 2,930 men living in Mawooshen, with a total population of around 10,000 men, women, and children.[16]

Satisfied that the area suited their purpose, Sir Ferdinando and Sir John began to bring in other investors to help fund their colony. But first, and most importantly, they needed the endorsement of the King to make it legal. That proved to be quite easy, since he would not be risking any of the crown's money. Colonies were to be developed with private resources, and he was free to give away the land because the charter that Queen Elizabeth I had granted to Sir Humphrey Gilbert in 1578 had been declared null and void.

When Sir Humphrey went down at sea, his half-brother, Sir Walter Raleigh, inherited the charter. However, Sir Walter had fallen out of favor after Queen Elizabeth's death. He was accused of treason, with rather tenuous evidence, and found guilty in 1603—his case presided over by Sir John Popham. Thus, the charter was revoked and could be reallocated. It makes one wonder if Sir John was really impartial in the case, since he had a personal interest in some of the land in Sir Walter Raleigh's charter.

With strong encouragement from wealthy noblemen and merchants, King James created The First Charter of Virginia in 1606, named after Elizabeth, the "Virgin Queen." The charter created two separate companies, London and Plymouth. The London Company, with backers in London, had the right to inhabit the land and develop the resources in the southern half of the Virginia territory, from latitude 34 degrees to latitude 41 degrees, or roughly from North Carolina to New York. (The London Company would establish a colony at Jamestown in present-day Virginia in 1607. It would

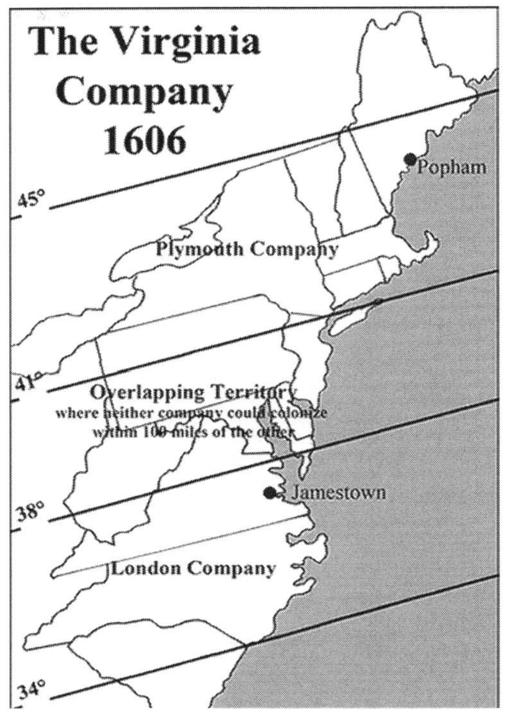

The Virginia Company 1606. Reprinted with permission from Pat Higgins[17]

survive and become the first permanent English settlement in America.) The Plymouth Company, with backers from Plymouth, Bristol, and Exeter, had the same privileges from latitude 38 degrees to 45 degrees, or roughly from Virginia to Maine. The overlap, from latitude 38 to 41 degrees, was available to both, with the proviso that the second company to get there could not develop within 100 miles of the first.

Being a devout Christian, the King included terms for converting Native people to Christianity in the charter. He dictated to those who ventured to Virginia to bring "Christian religion to such people, as yet live in darkness and miserable ignorance of the true knowledge and worship of God, and may in time bring the Infidels and Savages, living in those parts, to human civility, and to a settled and quiet government."[18] King James's view, that Indigenous people were "Infidels and Savages" who needed to be tamed and saved, was shared by his subjects. So, when faced with actual Native people such as the five from Pemaquid, the English were often surprised to find them well-mannered and civil. Perhaps the Wawenock would not have thought the same of the English.

English life in 1605, especially in London, ranged from utter opulence at court to wretched poverty in the streets, and the Wawenock may well have witnessed both extremes. The country was still recovering from the bubonic plague of 1603 when more than 37,000 people died in London alone, or 17 percent of the population.[19] Plague was spread by fleas living on rats, which fed on raw sewage and garbage thrown into the street in the poorest sections of the city.

Though the large number of deaths may have eased the overcrowding somewhat, living conditions for the poor had not improved.

The historical record is silent on what the five men from Pemaquid did or saw while they were in England. Still, we can make a few assumptions based on how other Indigenous captives taken to Europe were treated. Between 1500 and 1776, approximately 175 Native men and women were transported to England alone. As early as 1501 King Henry VII had an audience with three men 'taken in the New found Ile land' [Newfoundland]. The English thought them uncivilized because they wore animal skins and ate raw fish; two years later two of the men were spotted attending a ceremony in Westminster Palace wearing English clothing. In 1603 there was a staged demonstration of Native men paddling a canoe on the Thames River in London, an event that drew hundreds of spectators.[20] Many unlucky captives were sold as slaves or displayed as curiosities for a fee. Most did not return home.

The men from Pemaquid were likely treated well because they were never intended to be slaves, but instead were meant to be guides and interpreters. The English wanted them to act as liaisons with the people of Mawooshen, both to keep the English safe from attack when they went back to colonize the area, and to set up a trade network. The captives may have even become celebrities, like some others experienced:

> British crowds, especially in London, ogled them on the streets and in public parks; kings and queens entertained them at court; leaders of church and state consulted them at formal and informal meetings; merchants feasted them at elegant restaurants; less reputable Britons plied them with drink. Newspapers and magazines reported the Americans' attendance at courts and castles, at theatres and fairs. English authors—Ben Jonson, William Shakespeare, Alexander Pope, Daniel Defoe, Joseph Addison, Richard Steele, Jonathan Swift, Elkanah Settle, Oliver Goldsmith, and James Boswell—wrote visiting Americans into plays and essays.[21]

Presuming the Wawenock were not kept in complete isolation, what they saw would have astounded them: densely packed cities with buildings taller than trees; bridges that spanned the width of a river; not just one, but fleets of huge ships; people with skin color as black as night; horses, so tame men could ride

King James I of England and VI of Scotland[22]

on their backs; glass windows, brick chimneys, feather beds, clocks, eyeglasses, books, buttons—none of these things existed in their world. They would have been witnesses to daily English life, as well as important moments in English history. Tahánedo, in particular, would have had a front row seat to one of the most memorable events of the century: *The Gunpowder Plot of 1605*.

Queen Elizabeth I had been a very popular sovereign, ruling with a firm but loving hand over her people, yet the country stagnated at the end of her long reign. King James was expected to bring youth and vitality back to the throne. Many of England's citizens hoped that their lives would improve under new leadership but none more than the Catholics, who had been persecuted and prohibited from practicing their faith during Elizabeth's reign. The fact that James had a Catholic wife, Anne of Denmark, gave them great hope. But that hope turned out to be false when, rather than offering concessions to the Catholics and Puritans who asked him to make changes to religious laws, James dismissed their requests outright. Things quickly went downhill from there. The King was vain and frivolous, preferring to hunt and leave state affairs to others. He and his courtiers became notorious for their negligence, drunkenness, and promiscuity, as well as for running up enormous debts; over a period of five years he bought almost 2,000 pairs of gloves which he could not possibly wear.[23] He detested the English people and did not bother to hide it, and was known to swear or call a pox or a plague on them when they flocked around him.[24] By 1604, only a year into his reign, some of his subjects decided to assassinate him.

It was a bold plan that involved killing the King, his family, and all the Members of Parliament with one stroke—by blowing up Parliament on opening day. The conspirators were Catholic noblemen. The only non-aristocrat was Guy Fawkes, who was recruited because of his knowledge of gunpowder and his ability to procure it. The plot was uncovered, only just in time, when Fawkes was discovered in the basement of Parliament, guarding the gunpowder that he was supposed to ignite the next day. When asked why he had brought in so much ammunition, more than enough to blow the building sky high, he answered that he wanted to 'blow the Scottish beggars back to their native mountains.'[25]

King James, his family, and the Members of Parliament were saved. Under torture authorized by James himself, Guy Fawkes named other conspirators, all of whom were eventually caught or killed during their capture. The survivors were sentenced to be hanged, drawn, and quartered—the punishment for high treason and a particularly gruesome death. The judge who presided over the trial was Lord Chief Justice Sir John Popham.

Tahánedo was living with Sir John while he presided over this extraordinary case. It seems likely that it was the talk of the household, and that Sir John would have shared his thoughts about it with Tahánedo. What would Tahánedo have thought about a country where the subjects tried to murder their leader? The Wabanaki, Rosier observed, "show great reverence to their king, and are in great subjection to their governors: and they will show a great respect to any we tell them are our commanders."[26] Perhaps this was because the Wabanaki chose their leaders based on merit, not on birth. In England there had been two attempts to overthrow the monarchy in a span of four years—the Essex Rebellion and the Gunpowder Plot. Thanks in part to the depravity and arrogance of King James, the English were entering into a period of tremendous political instability. Samoset's adult life corresponded with the reign of King James and his son, King Charles I, and his life would be affected by their actions.

Despite the political turmoil in England, Sir John Popham was not deterred from his resolution to build a colony in Mawooshen, and plans moved forward quickly. With the aid of his son, Sir Francis Popham, who became Treasurer of the Plymouth Company, and Sir Ferdinando Gorges, who was working on the venture from his base in Plymouth, Sir John and the Plymouth Company solicited funds, hired crews, gathered supplies, and outfitted ships. By April 1606, they had a charter. By September, after a year in England, Tahánedo was headed home.

9
THE RETURN TO PEMAQUID, 1606–1607

Both Tahánedo and Skicowáros returned home to Pemaquid. Their reunions with the Wawenock must have been extraordinary, especially as they were presumed dead. How could they begin to describe the things they had seen in England? Amóret's fate is unknown, as previously noted, and he probably did not survive. Maneddo and Sassacomoit were also not so fortunate. Their stories took a darker turn.

In 1606 the Plymouth Company outfitted two ships to sail to the northern part of Virginia, as they called the new territory. Provisioned for up to 12 months, they were prepared to set up a small colony "if any good occasion were offered," and to further explore the Mawooshen region.[1] They had notes and maps from Waymouth's expedition to help them navigate, and Wawenock guides to help them find a favorable location for their settlement.

First out of the docks in August was the *Richard*, a ship sailing under the command of Captain Henry Challons from the port of Plymouth. It was followed a month or two later by the second ship commanded by Captain Thomas Hanham and Master Martin Pring from the port of Bristol. Hanham was Sir John Popham's grandson, and Pring was an experienced captain in his own right with an expedition to North America already to his credit.

Maneddo and Sassacomoit were aboard the first ship with Challons, and Tahánedo shipped out with Hanham and Pring. Presumably Skicowáros was kept as a hostage or to guide an expedition the following year. The two ships were supposed to meet at Pemaquid, or thereabouts, but the *Richard* never arrived. It was captured by the Spanish in the Caribbean Sea.

The *Richard* was not supposed to be there. Sir Ferdinando Gorges warned Challons not to take the southern route to America, "commanding them by all means to keep the northerly gage, as high as [Cape Breton, Nova Scotia]."[2] It is not clear from later testimony of the crew exactly why they ended up in the Caribbean—whether by the whim of the winds, incompetence, or willful disobedience of orders (perhaps in the hope of doing some plundering, as English crews often did). But that is where they found themselves one foggy morning, surrounded by eight hostile Spanish ships. No matter that war between Spain and England had ended two years earlier; these Spaniards were tired of being attacked by English pirates and had a score to settle.

The pilot of the *Richard*, John Stoneman, described the scene when the Spanish boarded their ship:

> And forthwith the Admiral [of the Spanish fleet] came on board of us, with two and twenty men in their ships boat with rapiers, swords, and half-pikes. We being all in peace stood ready to entertain them in peace. But as soon as they were entered on board of us, they did most cruelly beat us all, and wounded two of our company in the heads with their swords, not sparing our Captain nor any. Also they wounded Assacomoit [Sassacomoit], one of the Savages aforesaid, most cruelly in several places in the body, and thrust quite through the arm, the poor creature creeping under a cabin for fear of their rigor: and as they thrust at him, wounding him, he cried still. King James, King James, King James his ship, King James his ship.[3]

Stoneman knew Sassacomoit because he had been on Waymouth's expedition the year before. Sassacomoit could not understand why this was happening. The English had not tried, or perhaps had not been able, to explain to the Wawenock their long warring history with Spain. So when he invoked King James's name, it probably only fueled the Spaniards' anger.

Somehow Sassacomoit survived his wounds. The English captives, along with Maneddo and Sassacomoit, were taken to Spain and thrown into the brutal Spanish prison system. If Sassacomoit was indeed a captive of the Wawenock, then this was the third time he had been captured and taken prisoner—first by the Wawenock, then by the English, and now by the Spanish. When Sir Ferdinando Gorges learned that some of Challons's crew had been imprisoned, he immediately started a letter-writing campaign to the King, asking for the government's intervention to get the prisoners released. He kept up the pressure for over a year with special entreaties to save the "savages" because they were so valuable, even calling for war with Spain.[4]

Their case was so consequential that it was debated in Parliament, for it came at a very delicate time in English-Spanish relations. Who really had the rightful claim to settle North America? The treaty of 1604–1605 that had ended the war between England and Spain apparently was inconclusive on that point. The Spanish thought they did, because they already had a successful settlement in Florida. The French were busy trying to establish settlements in Canada based on their explorations there. The English had tried and failed to establish a colony in Roanoke, North Carolina, but felt they could still claim that territory and all the land north to Newfoundland as a result of the explorations of John Cabot and Sir Humphrey Gilbert. The English did not want to stir up trouble with Spain now that they had just achieved peace, but they desperately wanted to stake a claim in America. The verdict from Parliament was that the English would not give up their claims in North America, but conceded that if English vessels sailed to the Caribbean, which was undisputedly Spanish territory, then they were there at their own peril.[5] The Crown would not be sending help to the prisoners in Spain.

Meanwhile, the men languished in prison month after month. Captain Challons, who was not a prisoner but stayed in Spain to work on their release, wrote to Sir John Popham on June 26, 1607 that after six months of captivity, one man was dead, another had been fatally stabbed, and *the Indians had been taken away and made slaves* (author's emphasis).[6] He did not say why Maneddo and Sassacomoit were singled out to become slaves, or what type of slavery they were forced into. Most likely they were chained in a galley ship and forced to row day and night, a common sentence for slaves and criminals in Spain at the time.

On July 3 Challons wrote again, and in the span of one week there were now "three men very sick, several dead, their bodies inhumanly and shamefully treated, himself under severe penalties *not to speak with the Indians, whom they are striving to convert to their religion even by processes of starvation*" (author's emphasis).[7] The Spanish had separated Maneddo and Sassacomoit from the English and were using starvation to try to convert them to Catholicism. Their situation was desperate. Challons asked for speedy relief, before it was too late. After this we hear no more of Maneddo, so perhaps for him it was already too late—he may have starved to death.

Relief from England never came, but somehow Sassacomoit survived the ordeal. We know from Sir Ferdinando's memoirs that he made his way back to Sir Ferdinando's household by 1611, but after that his fate is unclear.

Tahánedo fared much better than Maneddo and Sassacomoit. The ship he sailed on left England in September or October 1606 and took the northern route, avoiding any trouble with the Spanish. The voyage was successful, and we know that Tahánedo returned to Pemaquid because there is a record of him being there the following year. Sir Ferdinando wrote later that according to Pring's report the fertility of the Mawooshen region surpassed their expectations. This was certainly good news, coming on the heels of the seizure of the *Richard* and the arrest of its crew. The investors needed reassurance that the venture could still be successful.

Sir Ferdinando Gorges, Sir John Popham, and Sir Francis Popham (Sir John's son) quickly got to work organizing the next expedition. This time they would be better prepared. They would send two ships out together with strict orders to take the northern route to Canada and down the coast to what is now Maine. They would be fully provisioned to build a fortified settlement, and Skicowáros would be their guide. Sir John's nephew, Captain George Popham, was chosen to lead the expedition and be president of the colony. Raleigh Gilbert, the youngest son of Sir Humphrey Gilbert, was second in command. Both choices turned out to be poor ones.

George Popham, in his late fifties, was described by Sir Ferdinando as "old Captain Popham" who "was well stricken in years before he went, and had long been an infirm man."[8] It seems short-sighted to send a man of questionable vigor to do such a rigorous job, but family ties may have won out. Also, George Popham was an experienced military man, and there had been rumors—probably passed along by Hanham and Pring—that the French were in the area and they might attack any settlement too close to their own. The colony needed a leader with his military qualifications.

Raleigh Gilbert, on the other hand, was youthful and energetic, but he lacked experience and maturity. He also harbored ambitions and prejudices that may have led to the colony's eventual downfall.

The two ships left England on May 31, 1607 with around 100 men destined for the colony. Popham commanded the *Gift of God* and Gilbert was at the helm of the *Mary and John*. Almost immediately they were separated when Gilbert ran into trouble with a Dutch ship, and Popham either did not see, or chose *not* to see (a matter of debate), his distress signal. After this rocky start and possibly the beginning of hard feelings among the men, they both had uneventful voyages and convened on August 7 at the designated meeting spot, the Georges Islands where Waymouth had anchored two years before.

Once again, we are fortunate to have some documentation of the venture. Robert Davies (or Davis), the pilot aboard the *Mary and John*, kept a journal during the outward voyage and the first two months of the colony's existence.[9] Besides documenting the usual navigational information, he included details about the local people and their interactions with the colonists. There were tensions from the very start.

Around midnight on the day he arrived at the Georges Islands, Raleigh Gilbert set out for Pemaquid in a small boat with thirteen others, including Skicowáros. Why they could not wait until morning is a mystery, but the weather was fair and the sea was calm so perhaps they were just taking advantage of good conditions. They rowed the ten miles by moonlight and arrived early the next morning. At Skicowáros's direction they landed at present-day New Harbor on the eastern side of the peninsula because it was safer to walk across land than row a small boat around treacherous Pemaquid Point. Davies remarked, however, that Skicowáros brought them there *much against his will* (author's emphasis), a curious reaction after two years away from home.[10] Skicowáros told Gilbert that the Wawenock would be away from the village, which was not true. It was August and he knew they would be living at their summer camp in Pemaquid. Gilbert insisted they would not leave until they had spoken with the Wawenock. Skicowáros must have anticipated what happened next.

The men walked two miles in the early morning light over the well-worn trail from New Harbor to the Wawenock village. As soon as they arrived, a "howling or cry" went up and the whole village rushed at them armed with bows and arrows. They were obviously not expecting visitors. It must have been a tense moment, and could very well have resulted in a deadly skirmish. Gilbert had not really thought this through.

Skicowáros called out in their language (Wawenock), Davies wrote, and "when Nahanada [Tahánedo] their Commander perceived what we were he caused them all to lay aside their bows & arrows and came unto us and embraced us & we did the like to them again."[11] The Wawenock put down their weapons, the moment of danger passed, and a happy reunion followed. Gilbert and his men stayed with the Wawenock for two hours and were invited into their wigwams. Once they got over their shock at the intrusion, the Wawenock were gracious hosts.

Illustration of Tahánedo embracing Skicowáros at Pemaquid.[12]

It is unfortunate that Davies included only a few details about the Wawenock and their village, because his narrative is the only surviving firsthand description of Samoset's village during his lifetime. Davies noted that there were about a hundred men, women, and children living in the village, which matches the figure in the Mawooshen document. But what was the village like? What did they eat? How did they treat each other? Davies was a sailor after all, not an ethnohistorian, and he was more inclined to note the depth of the harbor than what the local people were doing or wearing. After their visit Skicowáros returned with Gilbert and company to the ships anchored at the Georges Islands, apparently still under their command.

Two days later the English went back to Pemaquid, in greater force this time. Captain Popham loaded his shallop with 30 men and Gilbert brought 20 in his small boat, for a total of 52 men, including Skicowáros. They sailed and/or rowed around Pemaquid Point this time and made their approach directly up the Pemaquid River to the Wawenock village. With so many men it must have looked like an invasion, for "Nahanada [Tahánedo] with all his Indians with their bows and arrows in their hands came forth upon the sands" and would not let them land.[13] Tahánedo's first priority was to protect his people, and his actions suggest he did not trust these Englishmen.

Popham and Gilbert were oblivious to how their behavior would be perceived. Skicowáros was called upon once again to speak to Tahánedo, and convey that they "tended to no evil towards himself nor any of his people."[14] Tahánedo had learned through hard experience that there were some Englishmen he could trust and some he could not. He was right to proceed with caution.

Eventually he agreed to let some of the men land, but not all. Ten or twelve of the "chief gentlemen" were allowed to go ashore, and after a while they convinced Tahánedo to let the others disembark. Davies described the encounter as "all landed we using them with all the kindness that possibly we could. Nevertheless after an hour or two they all suddenly withdrew themselves from us into the woods and left us."[15] The Wawenock were friendly to the English for an hour or two, and then for no reason that the English could fathom, all the villagers left. They did not appear to flee in panic. Skicowáros stayed behind with the English, but offered no explanation.

It was late in the day and apparently the Wawenock were not coming back, so the English decided to retire to the other side of the harbor for the night. Skicowáros did not go with them this time. Davies wrote he "was not desirous to return with us. We seeing this would in no sort proffer any violence unto him by [bringing him by force, and allowed] him to remain and stay behind us. He promising to return unto us the next day following but he held not his promise."[16] Skicowáros was not "desirous" to go with them and they let him go. It was probably the plan to free him eventually, as they had done with Tahánedo, but they were reluctant to do so yet because they still needed him. All the same, they could not use force and risk a confrontation with the Wawenock because they also needed their cooperation. A big part of their mission was to find Wabanaki trading partners to supply them with furs and other trade goods.

When Skicowáros did not come back the next day, breaking his "promise," the English returned to their ships at the Georges Islands to prepare for the next part of their mission—finding a site and building a colony.

10
THE POPHAM COLONY, 1607-1608

On August 12, 1607, the *Gift of God* and the *Mary and John* set out for their ultimate destination: the mouth of the Kennebec River, known as Sagadahoc. Hanham and Pring, who had explored the area the previous year, must have recommended it for the colony because Davies wrote "we weighed our anchors and set our sails to go for the river of Sagadehock."[1] They knew exactly where they were going and had directions to get there. The Kennebec River is less than 20 miles west of Pemaquid and is much larger than the Pemaquid River. It appeared to be a good choice for a site.

According to Fannie Hardy Eckstorm, who studied Maine's Indigenous place names, the word Sagadahoc meant "to pour forth." In this case it referred to the mouth of the Kennebec River, where it "poured forth" into the sea. The English mistakenly called the river the Sagadahoc.[2]

The trip there should have been uneventful but weather on the Maine coast can be unpredictable and they were hit with a massive summer storm. Davies, who was not prone to exaggeration or fearfulness in his journal, described the experience as though they were fighting for their lives: "[A]bout midnight there arose a great storm & tempest upon us which put us in great danger and hazard of casting away of our ship & our lives by reasons we were so near the shore."[3] The storm raged all night and three times they had

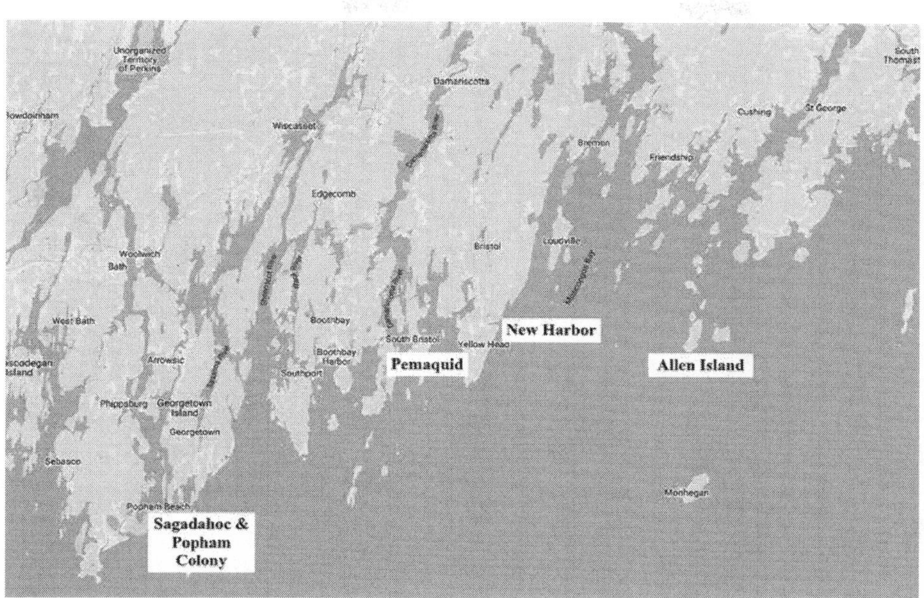

to save the ship from being dashed on the rocks. During a break in the storm they dropped anchor near a small island where they found "4 savages & an old woman" who had also been forced to take refuge from the weather.[4] Finally, four days after leaving the Georges Islands, they made it safely to Sagadahoc.

Over the next few days they explored the Kennebec River. Davies found the river "most gallant," and the colonists were satisfied that it was broad and deep enough for ships to navigate. They chose a high, flat site at the mouth of the river for their settlement, one with a good vantage point for defense. After hearing a sermon on shore, they read aloud their patent with the orders and laws that would govern the colony—an act required by law to make their taking of the land "legal" by English standards.

By now it was already the third week of August and they probably did not realize that they were racing the calendar. Summer in the Dawnland is short. Few crops will grow when started so late in the year, and the first frost is often in September. They had much to do so they divided the labor and got to work. In addition to a garden they needed a fort for protection, a storehouse for their provisions, and buildings for shelter, so those were the top priorities. The plan was truly ambitious; it called for approximately fifty "houses," though how many

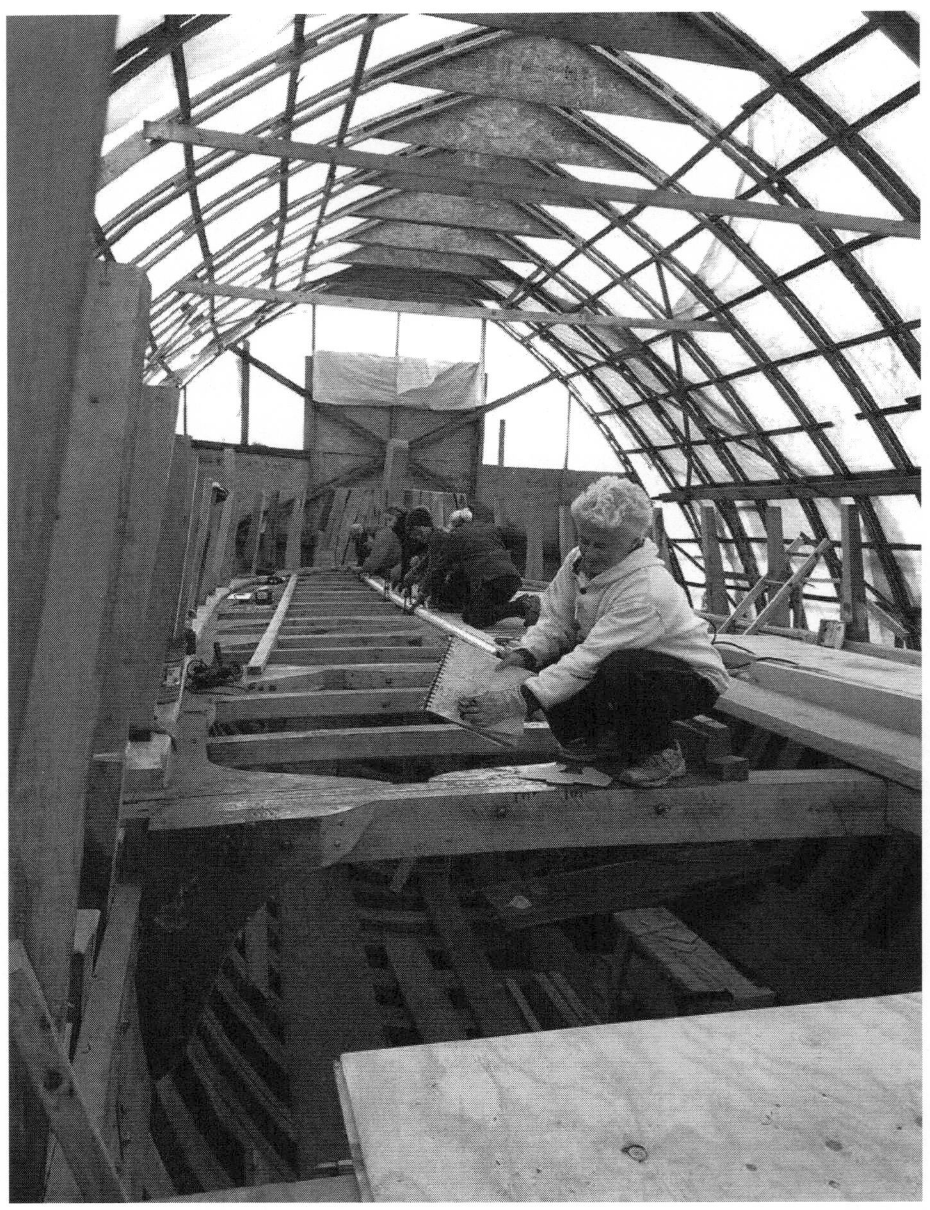

Volunteers with the organization Maine's First Ship at work on a replica of the pinnace Virginia. After a decade of research and hard work, the ship will be ready for launch in 2022.

were actually completed is hard to say. There were to be private residences for President George Popham and Admiral Raleigh Gilbert, a chapel, a munitions house, a kitchen, a bake house, a blacksmith shop, a cooper shop, a "buttery" for storing wine and liquor, houses for several other officers, and barracks for the rest of the men. They built a large garden, a trench on three sides, and an earthwork barricade around the colony's perimeter that was over 1,100 feet long.[5] They named the fort St. George after the patron saint of England.

They had brought with them a shipbuilder from London named Digby, whose task was to build a ship on site. Waymouth's crew had built a small boat on Allen Island back in 1605, but they had brought all the materials with them for the job in the form of a partially constructed kit. What made Digby's task unique was that he was to build it from scratch using trees and materials harvested on site (with the exception of the ship's metal fittings). Sir John Popham, Sir Ferdinando Gorges, and the other merchant adventurers wanted to show the world that shipbuilding could be a profitable venture in their new colony. As a result, the ship that Digby built, the pinnace *Virginia*, was the first English-built ship in North America using local materials. Four centuries later, Maine's shipbuilding tradition continues to thrive on the Kennebec River and includes Bath Iron Works, one of our nation's preeminent shipbuilders for the U.S. Navy.

A detailed map of the plan of Fort St. George has miraculously survived. John Hunt, one of the colonists and an expert draftsman, drew a meticulous bird's eye view of the fort, though it is admittedly a polished rendition of what they actually built. The map was probably meant to be presented at court to show off their accomplishments and keep their investors happy. It may have also been used to impress their enemies (note the fortified walls with cannons).

The Virginia Monument at the site of the Popham Colony. The Virginia was the first ship built by the English in North America using materials harvested on site.

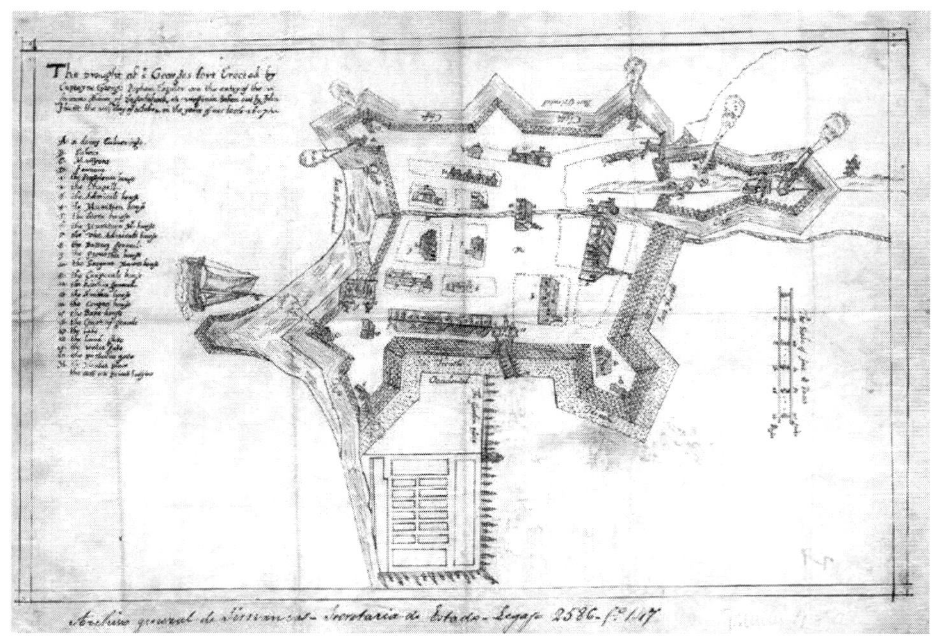

Drawing of Fort St. George by John Hunt, 1607. Collections of Maine Historical Society, 7542 [6]

Modern historians had no idea that John Hunt's map existed until it was discovered in the Spanish archives in 1888.[7] The Spanish Ambassador to London in 1607, Don Pedro de Zúñiga, probably had a hand in pilfering it. He was sending regular reports to King Philip III of Spain about the two Virginia colonies (Popham and Jamestown), imploring him to find a way to destroy the new settlements before they could take hold. In a letter dated December 6, 1607 he wrote: "As to Virginia, I hear that three or four other ships will return there. *Will your Majesty give orders that measures be taken in time*; because now it will be very easy, and quite difficult afterwards, when they have taken root, and if they are punished in the beginning, the result will be, that no more will go there."[8] If the Spanish had acted on Zúñiga's recommendation and eliminated the upstart English settlements, this nation's history might well have turned out very differently.

The work on the fort was progressing well, and after a few days Captain Popham felt confident that he could leave to do some exploring. He was under an obligation to find goods that the colony could turn into a profit, anything from fish, furs, and timber to sarsaparilla, a plant that was used like sassafras to cure everything from syphilis to headaches. The holy grail would be precious metals. So, he and his men needed to scout the surrounding area before winter limited their movements.

On August 22, Captain Popham set out with a small group in his shallop to explore the river of "Pashipskoke," as Davies wrote it. It was most likely the Sheepscot River which lies just east of the Kennebec.[9] Davies did not go with Popham on this excursion and what a pity, for we would have benefitted from his firsthand description of an encounter they had with some local men. From his journal: "Saturday the 22nd August Captain Popham early in the morning departed in his shallop to go for the river of Pashipskoke. There they had parley with the Savages again who delivered unto them that they had been at war with Sasanoa & had slain his son in fight. Skidwares and Dehanada [Skicowáros and Tahánedo] were in this fight."[10]

Popham had a chance encounter with the Wawenock, and in the 12 days since they had parted company, the Wawenock had been at war. Samoset was now 17 years old and considered a man, and would have joined in the fight. We know that it was the Wawenock since Davies wrote that Popham spoke with the Savages *again*. These were people they had met before, the Wawenock from Pemaquid. Moreover, without Tahánedo or Skicowáros there to translate, the English could not have understood the details that were included in the journal.

The Wawenock were returning from a battle with Sasanoa (or Sasinou, as the French called him), a sagamore of the Kennebec River people. Sasanoa was a member of Bashabes's Mawooshen alliance when Samuel de Champlain first heard of him in 1605, and now the Wawenock had killed his son.[11] Popham and his men were unknowing witnesses to the beginning of the Mi'kmaq War, a conflict that would last for years and would ultimately end with Bashabes's death and widespread devastation for Wabanaki people in the northeast.

Soon after, the Wawenock and English met again on September 5 in a more pleasurable encounter when nearly half of the Pemaquid villagers paid a visit to the colony. Davies counted nine canoes and approximately forty people. Tahánedo and Skicowáros were there, and Samoset most likely joined the party. What is notable is that they brought women and children with them, a sign that they had begun to trust the English. Maybe Tahánedo and Skicowáros's stories about the English and their great inventions had aroused the curiosity of the Wawenock and they wanted to witness the wonders for themselves. They would have seen a large storehouse and the ship *Virginia* under construction, a garden, earthwork fortifications, and perhaps other buildings as well.

Captain Popham was a good host and treated them kindly, feeding all forty of them. They remained a couple of hours but would not stay the night at the fort, instead choosing to paddle across the river and camp there. Skicowáros and "one more of them" stayed longer, until evening. Then Skicowáros insisted on joining the Wawenock for the night. His allegiance was firmly with his own people and he seemed wary that he might be held captive again. Raleigh Gilbert and two others offered to take the two men across the river and "remained amongst them all the night."[12] This was out of the ordinary. Unless the wind was against them, they could easily have rowed back to the ship and slept in their own bunks rather than camp out with the Wawenock. Were they culturally curious, or was there another reason? Gilbert was described as a man "desirous of...a loose life, prompt to sensuality" by Sir Ferdinando Gorges.[13] And there were women just across the river. Perhaps after a few months with no female companionship he was hoping to win the favor of one of the Wawenock women. Davies did not speculate about it, however.

Early the next morning the Wawenock departed for Pemaquid, promising Gilbert that they would accompany him to the Penobscot River and introduce him to Bashabes. It appears that one of the objectives of their trip to Sagadahoc had been to set up a meeting between Bashabes and the English. Two years before, Bashabes had tried to meet George Waymouth three different times, and now he was making another attempt. It turns out, he had a very good reason. Gilbert arranged to meet the Wawenock at Pemaquid in two days' time, and together they would travel to the Penobscot from there.

On the morning of September 8, Gilbert and 22 men loaded their boat with "diverse sorts of merchandise for to trade" and set out to meet Bashabes, but once again the weather proved uncooperative.[14] Contrary winds kept Gilbert at bay for three days. When he and his men finally arrived at Pemaquid on the 11th, there was not a soul there. The Wawenock, they presumed, had left for the rendezvous with Bashabes. If that was the case, it was a perilous journey. The trip from Pemaquid to the mouth of the Penobscot River is over sixty miles by water, and September tends to be hurricane season in Maine. To make that journey with the entire village, babies and elderly included, was arduous in the best conditions, and Davies tells us that there were strong winds during that time.

Gilbert set out for the Penobscot River but could not manage to find it.

For two days they sailed and searched, but without a guide they were unsuccessful (some might say incompetent, but the conditions may have been against them). Their food supply was running low, so they had to turn around and head back to Sagadahoc. It was another missed opportunity for the English to meet Bashabes.

For the next few weeks, the colonists worked around the fort. They finished the storehouse, unloaded supplies from the ships, and then set to work on other buildings. On September 23 Gilbert embarked on a small expedition with the goal of making it to the head of the Kennebec River. Near present-day Augusta he and his men had an encounter with some Wabanaki people, probably Kennebec—the same people who were now at war with the Wawenock. Through a series of misunderstandings and perceived rudeness on the part of Gilbert (who showed contempt for the trade goods that the Kennebec offered) the encounter quickly became unfriendly. Two things are noteworthy: the Kennebec in the Augusta area spoke a little English, in spite of the fact they lived over forty miles from the coast where most encounters with Europeans took place; and they knew that the English needed fire to make their matchlock muskets work. During the hostile exchange, one of the Kennebec grabbed the firebrand (in this case, a burning stick) that the English used to ignite their gunpowder and threw it into the river, thereby disarming them. It was a critical piece of information to know. The reach of European culture was long by 1607, and the Kennebec were already well informed.

Gilbert and his crew made it back to the fort safely, no doubt boasting of their brave exploits. A few days after their return, on October 3, Skicowáros reappeared at the fort. He paddled up to some of the men who were fishing on the beach and asked them to tell President Popham that Tahánedo and Bashabes's brother were on the other side of the river and would visit him the next day. Skicowáros may have been giving advance warning of their visit to make sure that Popham would be prepared to entertain Bashabes's brother with the respect he deserved.

The diplomatic delegation arrived the next day in two canoes, and included Tahánedo and his wife, Skicowáros, Bashabes's brother, and another sagamore named Amenquin. Amenquin, we know from the *Description of the Countrey of Mawooshen*, came from "Apponick," which is thought to be the Damariscotta River, just west of Pemaquid.[15] Popham treated them with respect befitting their status. He "feasted, and entertained with all kindness both that day and the next, which being Sunday the President carried them with him to the place of public prayers, which they were at both morning and evening, attending it with great reverence & silence."[16]

The visit was a success. Bashabes had evidently not given up on the English and had sent his brother to open a diplomatic dialogue. Popham made a promise to visit Bashabes at his home on the Penobscot River, and though he did not keep that promise he did many things right. He gave each of the visitors gifts of "copper beads, or knives, which contented them not a little" and sent gifts to both Bashabes and his wife.[17] This was proper etiquette as far as Wabanaki people were concerned. For their part, the Wabanaki showed a great deal of trust and respect for their hosts. They dutifully sat through not one, but *two* religious services which impressed the pious colonists. The fact that Tahánedo brought his wife is intriguing. Her presence at this meeting was unusual, because women were not normally invited to diplomatic councils. Was she merely a curious bystander, or did she come along to participate and advise?

Davies's journal ends at this point. Everything else we know about the Popham Colony comes from letters, court proceedings, and two books written years after the events (Samuel Purchas's *Hakluytus Posthumus or Purchas his pilgrimes* and William Strachey's *The historie of trauaile into Virginia Britania),* whose authors had access to journals that have since been lost.

Four days later, Davies sailed the *Mary and John* back to England, arriving in Plymouth on December 1. It was the plan from the start to send one ship back to England with news of their safe arrival and hopefully a hold full of treasure. Davies brought letters for Sir John Popham and a list of supplies the colony needed, but no treasure. He also brought with him John Hunt's map of Fort St. George and his journal of the first four months of the expedition.

Sir Ferdinando Gorges, having been debriefed by the returning colonists, immediately wrote to inform the King that they had found a fertile country with gallant rivers and stately harbors, and "a people tractable" who would be easy to control. He raved about the plentiful fish, infinite and various trees, excellent grapes that would generate wine as good as they made in France, high quality furs (if they could keep the Frenchmen at bay), and the existence of precious metals (according to the Wabanaki). He then had to make excuses for the fact that they had not brought back any of these things with them—i.e. they were there such a short time, there were so few of them, and they had so much to accomplish. Then he could not stop himself from criticizing some of the colonists for "the defect and want of understanding" to perform their duties, which was leading to confusion and a split into competing factions among the men.[18]

Sir Ferdinando then wrote a second report, probably after debriefing the men a bit more, which was even more troubling. He claimed that though Sir John Popham was himself honorable, he had been deceived; the men he had employed were not of suitable character and in fact were "childish...ignorant timorous, and ambitious persons" who had created instability and discord.[19] On top of that, the supplies were insufficient. These were serious problems, especially the lack of supplies. Having arrived so late in the season, they were dependent upon the supplies brought from England to get them through the winter.

Amenquin lives on in history because of an amusing anecdote. Apparently much taken with the English, he stripped off the beaver skin clothing he was wearing, leaving nothing but his loincloth, and gave "the skin off his back" to Popham in exchange for a straw hat and a knife. He stayed on after the others left and offered to go to England, or so the story goes, though there is no record that he actually went.

Next, he condemned the leaders of the enterprise. "For first the President himself is an honest man, but old, and of an unwieldy body, and timorously fearful to offend, or contest with others that will or do oppose him, but otherwise a discreet careful man. Captain Gilbert is described to me from thence to be desirous of supremacy, and rule, a loose life, prompt to sensuality, little zeal in religion, humorous, head-strong, and of small judgment and experience."[20] It was a damning portrait of the two men in charge. Raleigh Gilbert, who was apparently a self-indulgent man with poor judgment, was trying to take charge, and Captain Popham was not standing up to him. It sounded as if they had split the loyalties of the men, and the colony was suffering as a result.

Those who had returned on the *Mary and John* warned Sir Ferdinando that there was more trouble afoot: Gilbert was trying to get the charter for Virginia reinstated to his family. Gilbert argued that his father, Sir Humphrey Gilbert, had received the charter through an Act of Parliament, and that the King did not have the authority to reissue it. He was purportedly sending letters to friends back in England asking them to help him reclaim the charter. It had the earmark of a coup in the making.[21]

Sir Ferdinando concluded with a request to take on more responsibility for the affairs of the Plymouth Company. Never shy in his ambition with regard to the colony, he may have felt the need to fill a leadership void because the colony had lost its greatest benefactor, Sir John Popham. Sir John had died on June 10, 1607, ten days after the *Gift of God* and the *Mary and John* left for North America. He had been the driving force and the largest investor in the Plymouth Company, and his support was greatly missed. Gorges and Sir Francis Popham were still committed to the enterprise, however, and managed to find the means to outfit three supply ships to send back to the Popham Colony the next year, despite waning support from the merchant adventurers who were helping to finance the venture.

Notwithstanding the disquieting news from the colony, things were generally going according to plan. Then winter came, and it was colder than they could possibly have imagined. Hastily built shelters offered little protection from the cold, and the men suffered. They were running low on food. Huge ice floes came hurtling down the Kennebec River and damaged the *Gift of God*, so they decided to send the ship back to England. Half the men would sail home on her since there was not enough food to sustain all of them through the winter. That left only 45 men at the colony. They were vulnerable to attacks without the help of their ship and the extra men, but they had mounted twelve cannons in the fort, and it would have to be enough. On December 16, 1607, the *Gift of God* left Fort St. George and sailed home to England.

She arrived in Plymouth by February 7, 1608 after a difficult journey. Captain Popham could not spare much food for their voyage, so he and his council directed them to stop at the Azores west of Portugal and sell off thirty ship's masts that they had managed to harvest, as well as a cannon and anything else they could spare, in order to buy enough food for the rest of the voyage home. John Havercombe, who was responsible for the ship's provisions, later testified in a court case that the men were reduced to drinking contaminated water and that "diverse of the said company died for lack of food."[22] His testimony was verified by two others that three men died on the voyage home. These were the first confirmed deaths among the Popham settlers.

The news of the *Gift of God*'s troubles and the latest reports from the colony were certainly worrisome. Sir Ferdinando Gorges again wrote to the King with a full account, and he did not sugarcoat the problems. They were suffering a harsh winter with thin clothing and poor diets. So far, they had remained healthy, which was fortunate since the only doctor on the expedition had returned to England on the first ship. Gorges continued to assure the King that there were many "wonders" to be had from the country, but he accused the settlers of being too lazy to procure them. He speculated that he would have to send over better men to do the work necessary for the colony's success. The breakdown into factions had worsened, and now they "disgraced each other" in front of the Wabanaki.[23] The locals were getting caught up in the trouble.

A passage in Sir Ferdinando's letter to the King suggests that relations with the Wawenock had deteriorated since their last visit to the colony on October 4. It might be one of the most important pieces of evidence to explain the failure of the Popham Colony. Gorges implied that Tahánedo and Skicowáros, who had previously helped promote relations between Bashabes and the English, were now sabotaging the colonists' attempts to trade with the Wabanaki in the area. "They show themselves exceeding subtle and cunning, concealing from us the places where they have the commodities we seek, and if they find any [Wabanaki], that hath promised to bring us to it, *those that came out of England* instantly carry them away, and will not suffer them to come near us anymore" (author's emphasis).[24] *Those that came out of England* could only be Tahánedo and Skicowáros. What had changed? Why had they turned against the English?

A clue in Samuel Purchas's version of events might explain their change of heart. Purchas had access to Raleigh Gilbert's journal (and others) before they were lost. He suggested that the Wawenock feared retribution from Tanto, the evil spirit which haunted them every moon. Tanto "commanded them not to dwell near, or come among the English, threatening to kill some and inflict sickness on others, beginning with two of their Sagamore's children, saying he had power, and would do the like to the English the next moon."[25] Reading between the lines, it may be that two children had fallen ill (perhaps Tahánedo's children, since he was a sagamore) and their medicine man—who interpreted Tanto's message through his dreams—blamed the illness on their friendship with the English. If so, the interpretation would not have been far off the mark. The Wawenock had brought their children to the Popham Colony, and because of their susceptibility to European germs they could easily have caught a disease from the English. If Tahánedo believed that his children or his people would become sick or die as a result of their association with the English, then naturally he would do everything in his power to keep them apart.

We must also remember that the Wawenock were now at war with the Kennebec. If they were trying to trade with the colonists, then the Wawenock would naturally want to disrupt that relationship. They would not want the Kennebec to profit from an such alliance, nor could they risk that the English would give them firearms or other weapons.

This left the English in a precarious position. They were counting on being able to trade for furs that they were not able to hunt or trap themselves. And with their food supplies running low, they looked to the Wabanaki to supplement their provisions. Like most other early colonial ventures, they had not come fully prepared for the difficult first year. If the colonists could not engage with the local people, then the venture would likely fail, and the men could even starve.

The signals coming from the Wawenock were certainly contradictory, but George Popham was only willing to see the positive. He informed King James by letter that the King was greatly admired by the people of Mawooshen, because "Tahinda [Tahánedo], one of the natives who has been to Britain, has broadcast your praise and your fine qualities to them here." Popham assured the King that the locals had given up their own gods to worship the only true God, and that "they would willingly give military service under his authority and command."[26] Popham also declared that the Wawenock claimed there were "nutmegs, mace and cinnamon in these parts" along with many other valuable goods. His claims were frankly hard to believe, and in the case of the spices, impossible. Popham may have been susceptible to Wawenock flattery or he misunderstood the translation, or perhaps he was embellishing his report to impress the King and gain his support for the colony.

Popham's letter to King James marks the end of any surviving documents from the Popham Colony. After that the historical record is nearly nonexistent, with only a few remaining details from the Purchas and Strachey accounts. Sometime during the winter Raleigh Gilbert's house, with all its contents, burned down, and possibly the storehouse as well.[27] The worst blow came when

George Popham died on February 5 of unknown cause and Gilbert took over as president of the colony. Given his previous insensitivity dealing with the Wabanaki, and his "small judgment and experience," this did not bode well for relations with the local people.

Somehow, in the midst of these events, the colonists managed to obtain some furs and sarsaparilla to send back to England. In March 1608 Gorges sent two supply ships to the colony carrying the news of Sir John Popham's death. The ships returned to England with the furs and sarsaparilla and the news of George Popham's death. There is no mention that any new colonists were delivered to the colony, so they were apparently still managing with the 45 men who had wintered over.

Though it had been a rough winter with a multitude of challenges, the colony was still viable at the beginning of 1608. The death knell came, however, when Robert Davies, our journal writer, returned to the colony that summer as Captain of the *Gift of God* with the news that Raleigh Gilbert's elder brother had died. Gilbert had inherited the family estate and was needed back in England. No one stepped into the leadership vacuum, so the remaining colonists packed everything into the two ships, the *Gift of God* and the new pinnace *Virginia,* and returned to England. The Popham experiment had failed.

The Wabanaki were glad to see them go and took credit for driving them away. When a French Jesuit missionary visited the ruins of the abandoned colony in 1611, the locals told him that after George Popham died, English behavior toward the Wabanaki changed. 'They drove the Savages away without ceremony; they beat, maltreated and misused them outrageously and without restraint; consequently these poor abused people, anxious and dreading still greater evils, in the future, determined to kill the whelp ere its teeth and claws became stronger.'[28] The story went that when some of the colonists were fishing offshore, the Wabanaki attacked and killed eleven of the men and the English left soon after.

Two other stories about the Popham Colony were passed down in Wabanaki lore. The first comes from the Norridgewock people, a northern group on the Kennebec River: "There was a tradition amongst the Norridgwalk [sic] Indians, that these planters invited a number of the natives, who had come to trade with them, to draw a small cannon by a rope, and that when they were arranged on a line in this process, the white people discharged the piece, and thereby killed and wounded several of them."[29]

The second story was still circulating decades after the English abandoned the colony. According to this legend, a quarrel broke out between the English and the Wabanaki and some Englishmen were killed. The English then left and the Wabanaki were satisfied that they had driven them away. When they went to scavenge the remains of the fort, they found barrels of gunpowder left behind; not knowing what it was, they carelessly scattered it around. It caught fire and caused an explosion that wounded and killed many people. The Wabanaki took this to mean that the great spirit was angry with them for killing some of the English. True or not, the Wabanaki believed these stories and passed them down for generations. They had long memories and harbored anger and resentment against the English for these alleged misdeeds.

There is some archaeological evidence that might corroborate the story of the explosion. It appears that the storehouse burned *after* the English left—charred remains have been found but few artifacts were discovered, suggesting that the fire happened after they had removed everything for the return voyage.[30]

In the end, there were too many things working against the Popham Colony for it to succeed: the climate was more harsh than they expected; there were no precious metals in the area to generate enthusiasm among the merchant adventurers; and the deaths of Sir John Popham, George Popham, and Raleigh Gilbert's brother were tremendous hurdles. Most importantly, the English colonists never established good relations with the Wabanaki. Yet in spite of these setbacks, Sir Ferdinando Gorges and Sir Francis Popham would have continued to support it. If they had been able to shift their efforts to harvesting fish and timber, they might have started a profitable trade. If they had found a suitable leader, one who respected and worked with the local people, the colony might have been saved. But it was dismantled before they had a chance. The Popham Colony lives on as a mere footnote in history because it failed. Its sister colony, Jamestown, earned the honor of being the first successful English colony in America. It would take another twelve years before the English would build another colony in present-day New England. That one, in what is now Plymouth, Massachusetts, would falter but take hold. In the meantime, Sir Ferdinando and Sir Francis never lost sight of the value and possibilities of Mawooshen.

It is easy to see why the Wabanaki took credit for driving the English out of Mawooshen. Why else would they have left? To their thinking the English—even with their powerful weapons, their advanced technologies, their supposedly mighty King and superior God—were no match for the Wabanaki who had tenaciously lived on the land for thousands of years.

It may have been the last time the Wabanaki felt so powerful. They were entering a decade that would see their numbers diminished by up to 75 percent, the Mawooshen alliance toppled, and their faith in their own beliefs terribly shaken. Samoset's world was about to come crashing down.

11
FISHING AND WAR, 1607–1615

When Raleigh Gilbert and the Popham colonists returned to England in the fall of 1608, it was clear that the enterprise was finished. Sir Ferdinando Gorges wrote years later "all our former hopes were frozen to death," invoking the insufferably cold winter of 1607–'08. The merchant adventurers financing the venture gave it up as a lost cause, and many threw their lot in with the southern colony in Jamestown. Not Sir Francis Popham, who "continued to send thither several years after in hope of better fortunes."[1] Rather than focusing on building a colony, however, Sir Francis scaled back the operation to fishing and trading in the area around Pemaquid.

Sir Ferdinando, never discouraged for long, was quick to follow. As a devout man he believed God would support his endeavors because God would want Christians to go to a heathen world and prosper. So, with divine confidence he bought his own ship and sent it to Mawooshen to engage in fishing and trade. He, too, had tempered his ambition for the moment, but the irrepressible man would take up the pursuit of colonization before long.[2] Those he sent to fish and trade were also scouting for a more favorable location to set up a permanent colony than the Popham settlement had proven to be.

The next few years were dedicated to seasonal fishing excursions. Monhegan Island was popular because the fishing ten miles off the coast was better than close to shore. Another island to the west, Damariscove, became a favorite destination as well. Sir Francis based his operation at either Pemaquid or New Harbor. A "lead cloth seal with the date '1610' embossed on its surface" was found in New Harbor in the late 19th century, a tangible piece of evidence of the early use of that harbor.[3] In those early days, the fishing crews in all likelihood did not live on the mainland. They would have slept on board their ships and gone ashore mainly to process the fish, resupply their firewood and water, and do some hunting and foraging to supplement their diet of dried meat and fish.

The Wawenock seemed to settle into a comfortable relationship with the itinerant fishermen. Somehow, they got past their distrust—perhaps the children recovered from their illness or the fishermen treated them with more consideration than Gilbert and his men. Since the English made no signs of building a permanent settlement like the Popham colony, they apparently saw no harm in trading with them. After all, everyone was getting something out of the exchange. Trading for furs made the fishing trips more profitable for the English, and the Wawenock were getting direct access to European goods. Samoset would have gotten used to seeing Englishmen around his home. He began to learn their language and customs and, as we will see, was not shy about enjoying their food or company.

Word was spreading throughout Europe about the good fishing in the Gulf of Maine, and the waters began to fill with an international assortment of fishermen and explorers. Henry Hudson (for whom the Hudson River and Hudson Bay are named) notably stopped in Penobscot Bay in the summer of 1609 and stayed a few days to repair one of his ship's masts. Though Hudson was English, he sailed under the banner of the Dutch East India Company, looking for a passage west to Asia. While anchored somewhere near the St. George River, presumably not far from Allen Island (the site of the Waymouth kidnappings), he encountered some Wabanaki. "At 10 o'clock two boats with six of the savages of the country came out to us, seeming glad of our coming. We gave them trifles and ate and drank with them. They told us there was gold, silver and copper mines close by and that the Frenchmen do trade with them. This is very likely for one of them spoke some words of French."[4] The Wabanaki had apparently put Waymouth's treachery behind them or had at least decided that trading with Europeans was worth the risk. It is worth noting that they told Hudson there were gold, silver, and copper mines close by, which was not true. By 1609 they knew what Europeans were looking for and tried to entice them with the promise of these riches. Even though the Wabanaki were friendly, Hudson wrote rather ominously, "*we could not trust them*" (author's emphasis).[5] Assuming he did not know that the Wabanaki were lying about the mines, his mistrust seems unfounded.

The fishing, on the other hand, was excellent. Hudson noted in his journal that one of his crew caught twenty-seven cod in two hours, and they found a shoal teeming with lobsters. A couple of days later, they saw two French shallops "full of Indians" enter the harbor; these were probably Mi'kmaq hoping to trade for "red gowns." Red fabric was a popular commodity; the Mi'kmaq treasured it and asked the French to give them some to wrap the body of one of their deceased kinsmen.[6] Hudson wrote that they were already used to trading with the French for "red tunics, knives, hatchets, copper, kettles, trivets, beads and other trifles."[7] They were also becoming proficient at sailing European ships.

Still in Penobscot Bay a few days after, Hudson casually wrote in his journal, "In the morning we manned our scout with four muskets and six men, took one of their [Indian] shallops and brought it aboard. Then we manned our scout and boat with twelve men and muskets, two stone pieces or murderers [small cannons], and drew the savages from their houses and robbed them, as they would have done to us."[8] Just like that. He gave no rationale for the attack, other than the Wabanaki could not be trusted. They were "savages," according to Hudson—no justification needed. The attack probably came as a complete surprise to the Wabanaki.

Monhegan Island was the scene of another violent episode two years later, in 1611. Captain Edward Harlow, who had been a member of the Popham expedition, returned to the area and kidnapped three men, presumably Wawenock.[9] One managed to escape and led the Wawenock in a counterattack. Harlow slipped away with the other two captives and sailed south, first to Nantucket, then on to Capowack (now called Martha's Vineyard) in present-day Massachusetts. In the process, he kidnapped three more Indigenous men, including one named Epenow. Epenow was sent to live with Sir Ferdinando Gorges and Sassacomoit, the captive from Pemaquid who had survived prison in Spain. Nine years later, Epenow would reappear in Samoset's story.

Despite these incidents, trading between Europeans and the Wabanaki continued. Sir Francis Popham sent his fishing boats to the Pemaquid area year after year, and a certain degree of familiarity and trust was established.

Maybe the Wawenock also had a grudging respect for the hardworking fishermen. Working usually in crews of four, the men would leave the harbor early in the morning in a small shallop and spend the day baiting a line of hooks with mackerel or herring or cod entrails, lowering the lines weighted with lead over the side, and hauling hooked fish into the boat. A successful haul was 200–300 fish per man per day.[10] After an exhausting day on the water, they still had to process their catch. Using a gaff, they hauled the fish on shore, then up to the splitting table. Here the "throater" would cut the throat of the fish, make an incision along the belly to the anus and loosen the backbone, then hand the carcass to the next man. He, in turn, would rip out the entrails to be saved as bait, throw the liver into one barrel to ferment into cod liver oil, and toss the roe, or fish eggs, into another to be processed and sold as caviar.[11] After that he would break the neck and tear off the head, which he threw back into the sea. Next it was the splitter's job to cut the flesh back and de-bone the fish.[12] At that point the fourth man on the crew salted the fish. A day later he rinsed and drained them and laid them on flakes, or platforms built as drying racks.

Flakes, or drying racks, used to dry out fish before transporting them to Europe.[13]

Drying the fish was a tricky process that required keeping a vigilant eye on the weather; if it was hot and sunny, the fish had to be turned regularly to keep them from cooking in the sun; if it rained, the fish had to be covered to prevent them from rotting. On a hot, sticky summer day, all of this must have been tedious work. In the cold of winter, their hands would suffer terribly from being constantly wet. The putrid smell of rotting fish parts that the tide could not quite clear away would have been a constant annoyance. It was hardly delicate work, to say the least, but the men were usually rewarded by sharing in the profits of the catch.[14]

Fish drying flakes at Colonial Pemaquid State Historic Site.

These were the men with whom Samoset and the Wawenock shared their homeland, a rough and tumble bunch most likely, quite unlike the staunchly religious Puritans who would later come to epitomize colonists in the northeast. These poor, mostly uneducated men came to work with no thoughts of settling down, just making the most of a short fishing season. To relax they smoked, drank, and probably did a little gambling on dice or cards. Beer was a staple since water was considered harmful to one's health, and this was probably when Samoset developed a taste for it.[15] They came to know each other through their trade interactions, and the Wawenock began to do more hunting and trapping so they could acquire more European goods.

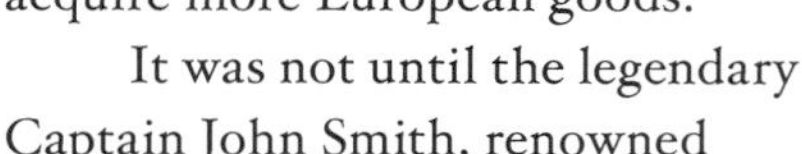

It was not until the legendary Captain John Smith, renowned colonizer of Jamestown, traveled to Monhegan in 1614 that interest in building a colony in the area was revived. Smith was a polarizing figure who believed in strict discipline, telling the Jamestown colonists in the midst of their starving time that "He that will not work shall not eat."[16] Whether or not Pocahontas famously saved his life when he was captured by the Powhatan is open to question, and Smith was probably not above embellishing his life story in the books he wrote about his adventures. But he carried the lessons of Jamestown with him when he ventured to Monhegan.

Smith's goal for the voyage was "to take whales and make trials of a mine of gold and copper. If those failed, fish and furs were then our refuge."[17] He arrived at "Monahiggan" in April with two ships outfitted by London merchants. Whaling turned out to be harder than he expected; they spent "much time in chasing them but could not kill any." The gold was only a fool's errand, concocted to get funding for the venture. So they turned to fish and furs, but after wasting so much time trying to catch whales they had nearly missed the fishing season. By June, the fishing failed. In July and August, the catch improved, but not enough to defray their costs. Even so, in that short amount of time they were able to catch and process 47,000 fish.[18]

While his crew fished, Smith took eight or nine of his men exploring. For "trifles" he traded for "near eleven hundred [beaver] skins, one hundred martins, and near as many otters."[19] He had poor luck trading east of Monhegan because the locals were used to trading with the French, who were offering more generous terms. And "right against us in the main," referring most likely to New Harbor, "was a ship of Sir Francis Popham's, that had there such acquaintance, having many years used only that port, that the most part [of the trade] there was had by him; and forty leagues westward were two French ships."[20]

So we have a picture of the busy nature of fishing and trade on the coast as early as 1614. The French had expanded their range south from the territory they called Acadia, and Sir Francis had a monopoly in New Harbor, so much that other traders bypassed it completely. If Samoset and the Wawenock wanted to trade with someone other than Sir Francis's men, they had to travel outside the area.

Smith continued exploring south as far as Cape Cod and created a detailed map of the area. He labeled the region "New England," and is credited with inventing the term. In the tradition of anglicizing place names, he renamed Monhegan "Barties Isles" and Pemaquid "St. Johns Towne," a name that lives on in Johns River, Johns Island, and Johns Bay (the other two names did not stick).[21] Smith was smitten with New England, proclaiming "of all the four parts of the world that I have yet seen not inhabited, could I have but means to transport a colony, I would rather live here than anywhere."[22] It was easy to see why. According to Smith the air was healthy, the soil was fertile, and the fish, fowl, and fruits were plentiful. There was an inexhaustible supply of trees and plenty of meadowland for grazing cattle. He boasted of planting a garden in May and eating salads from it in June and July.[23] The climate was moderate, he asserted, which was especially important to note because of the area's reputation in England for being too cold.

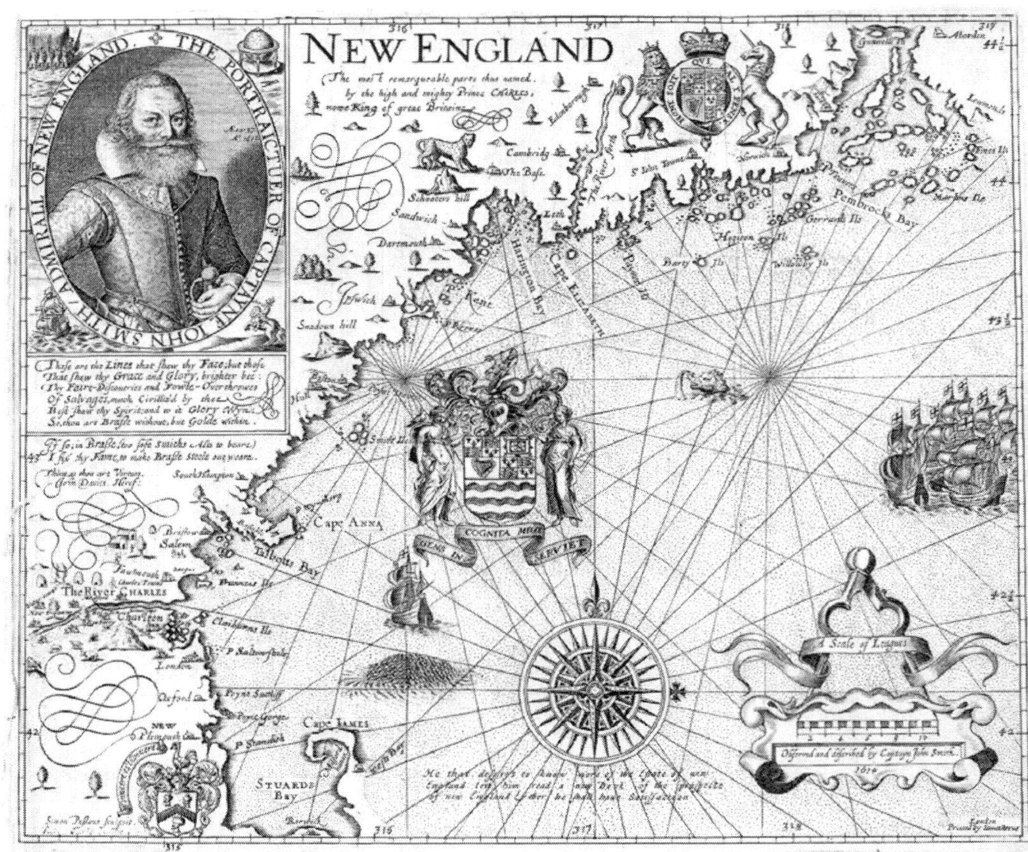

John Smith's 1616 map of New England. Courtesy of the Osher Map Library, University of Southern Maine[24]

Natural resources were not the only ones Smith had in mind to exploit—there were also the people. He described them as "goodly, strong and well proportioned"; in other words, a ready-made work force.[25] "Now, young boy and girl savages, or any others...may turn, carry, and return fish without either shame or any great pain; he is very idle that is past twelve years of age and cannot do so much, and she is very old that cannot spin a thread to make engines to catch them."[26] He was describing how to put Wawenock children to work. And if the locals did not cooperate? "[I]f they should be untoward, as it is most certain they are, thirty or forty good men will be sufficient to bring them all in subjection."[27] Smith's philosophy was simple—try to buy the local people's cooperation for a few trifles, and if that did not work, use force. Luckily for the Wawenock, Smith was never able to carry out his plans. He made two more attempts to return to Maine (hired by Sir Ferdinando Gorges, no less) but due to various difficulties —a broken mast, French pirates, and lack of wind—he never succeeded.

Surprisingly, while Smith was at Monhegan he found an ally: Tahánedo. The last interaction between Tahánedo and the English at the Popham settlement in 1607 or 1608 may have been confrontational; Sir Ferdinando thought he was trying to sabotage the English settlers' relationship with the local people. But things had changed over the intervening six years. The Wawenock now needed their help. Smith wrote:

> The main assistance next God I had...was my acquaintance among the savages, especially with Dohannida [Tahánedo], one of their greatest lords, who had lived long in England. By the means of this proud savage I did not doubt but quickly to have got that credit with the rest of his friends and allies, to have had as many of them as I desired in any design I intended, and that trade also they had...With him and diverse others I had concluded to inhabit and defend them against the Terentynes [Tarrantines] with a better power than the French did them, whose tyranny did enforce them to embrace my offer with no small devotion.[28]

He was referring to the war with the Mi'kmaq, or as the English called them the Tarrantines. The conflict they were engaged in back in 1607, when George Popham happened to come upon Wawenock warriors as they were returning from a battle, was still raging. The war must have been going badly for them since they were now ready to throw their lot in with the English.

Almost everything we know about the Mi'kmaq War comes to us from the French. They had befriended the Wabanaki when they built a settlement in Mi'kmaq territory in present-day Port Royal, Nova Scotia. War had engulfed the people from there to the Saco area, and the weapons that the French supplied to the Mi'kmaq were influencing the outcome. The Wawenock had no choice but to seek help from the English, with their guns and steel swords, to neutralize their enemy's advantage.

Conflict among Wabanaki people was not new. They had disagreements with their neighbors long before Europeans arrived on their shores, just as all people do. But the *way* they fought each other after Europeans got involved changed dramatically, causing much greater loss of life. To begin with, warfare was not a way of life and most Wabanaki conflicts were settled with small-scale raids or skirmishes. It was the custom to avenge a wrong, where retaliation was carried out as a matter of honor. But there was no intention of annihilating their enemy; that was a European concept.[29] In fact early English chroniclers wrote contemptuously of how Indigenous men waged war, calling their fighting 'feeble' and mocking that 'they might fight seven years and not kill seven men.'[30]

The European way was to wait for the light of day, dress in bright colors, outfit the commander in a uniform that easily distinguished him as the leader (which also made him a highly visible target), cluster in large groups (which were also easy targets), and meet the enemy on an open battlefield. Then, when both sides politely agreed to begin, they would march forward at their leader's command and shoot at each other like "true gentlemen." Good aim mattered little; if they pointed their muskets in the general direction of the crowd, they were likely to hit someone. Generally, the battle was not over until the enemy had been slaughtered.

Very early accounts of Native warfare were written by observers in Canada and southern New England—north and south of Maine—but Wawenock men likely used similar tactics. The Europeans could not understand the Indigenous way of war, which was conducted with stealth and surprise and resulted in few casualties. One English soldier wrote that their fighting seemed 'more for pastime than to conquer and subdue enemies.'[31] They might set up an ambush in the woods along a well-established path, then strike "without warning when

It would take the English decades to adopt Indigenous war tactics. When they began to form alliances and fight on the same side as Native people, they learned the practicality of fighting 'Indian-style.'[32] During King Philip's War, for example, English Captain Benjamin Church asked some of his Native soldiers how they '*got such advantage often of the English in their marches thro' the woods?*' The answer, though obvious to Native people, had never occurred to the English. Native warriors always 'took care in their marches and fights, not to come too thick together. But the *English* always kept in a heap together, that it was as easy to hit them as to hit an House, [and] that if at any time they discovered a company of *English* soldiers in the woods, they knew that there was all, for the *English* never scattered; but the *Indians* always divided and scattered.'[33] It was techniques like these, learned from Indigenous people, that helped the fledgling revolutionary soldiers defeat the more experienced and professional British soldiers during the American Revolution.

their victims passed by."[34] Sometimes they used one of their own men as a decoy, leading their enemy into a trap. They fought with bows and arrows and a tomahawk for close fighting. High ranking warriors, like the sagamores, may have also used spears.[35]

Wabanaki men were experts in woods warfare, employing the same skills they used to hunt animals. Their clothing made of animal skins blended in with the colors of the forest and the moccasins they wore on their feet allowed them to step quietly and run fast. They were accustomed to traveling long distances and subsisting on little food. Dried corn ground into a fine powder, called nocake, was a staple of the warrior's (and the hunter's) diet because it was lightweight and nutritious and could simply be mixed with water. Even better, it did not require cooking over a fire, which might alert the enemy. In battle they used trees and rocks as cover and were skilled at shooting a moving target. They were also skilled at dodging arrows when they saw them coming.[36]

They also used the advantage of surprise raids. The best attack is one that your enemy is not expecting. Native men knew they would find families in their wigwams at night or taking cover from a wild storm or thick fog, making it a good time to strike. Storms and fog also helped cover any noise they made when they approached. So Native people learned to be prepared for battle—or flight—at all times, day or night and in all types of weather. We saw this when Raleigh Gilbert insisted that Skicowáros take him to Pemaquid early in the morning. Skicowáros knew what to expect. The Wawenock heard them coming—the English always stomped loudly through the woods alerting everyone to their presence—and rushed at them armed with bows and arrows, alert and well prepared against a potential raid.

There were certain ritual preparations that Native men performed before going into combat, like painting their faces to make themselves appear more terrifying to their enemy. Hoping to invoke the great spirit, warriors counted on their medicine man to perform ceremonies to bring them victory.[37] These might include dances, incantations, and speeches. In some communities, men abstained from sex for three days before an engagement in order to "purify" themselves and not deplete their energy. They were convinced that if they did not observe these rites, they risked misfortune or even death by angering their gods.[38]

Women also made preparations in case of attack. They made ready to pack up what they needed and flee at a moment's notice. They ground corn into nocake and stockpiled and hid food that would sustain them if the enemy raided their stores. And they undoubtedly did what they could to bolster the confidence of their men.

The beginning of the Mi'kmaq War was vividly immortalized by Marc Lescarbot, a Frenchman who lived in Port Royal at that time, in an epic poem titled "The Defeat of the Armouchiquois Savages by Chief Membertou and His Savage Allies, in New France, in the Month of July, 1607." Armouchiquois was the French word for Indigenous people living in southern Mawooshen territory and New England, and Chief Membertou was the Mi'kmaw sagamore in the Port Royal area.

According to Lescarbot there was an ancient discord between the Mi'kmaq and the people of Mawooshen, but all-out war began with the Battle of Saco in July 1607. Several events precipitated the battle, beginning with a diplomatic mission by the Mi'kmaq to Saco in 1606, during which they felt insulted by gifts that were inferior to their own. The first blood was spilled that fall in a separate incident when Mi'kmaq warriors killed some men in Bashabes's territory, presumably Penobscot. The spark that lit the powder keg was when the Mi'kmaq carried off women as prisoners, then murdered them.[39] We do not know what prompted these violent acts, but harming women was particularly offensive. The Penobscot swiftly retaliated by killing a Mi'kmaq trader, who happened to be a relative of Chief Membertou.

Membertou was livid. Bashabes tried to apologize and smooth things over, but there was no stopping the escalation. Membertou would have his revenge and would lead the charge himself, even though he was rumored to be over one hundred years old. The Mi'kmaq and their allies traveled the 400 miles from Port Royal to Saco in an armada of shallops and canoes. Membertou's plan was simple and clever; he took a small delegation to meet with the leaders of Saco and convinced them that he had come to end the hostilities and restore their trading partnership. Then, on the next day when they were distracted by looking at his trade goods, at a pre-arranged signal his full force attacked from two fronts, catching the people of Saco by surprise.

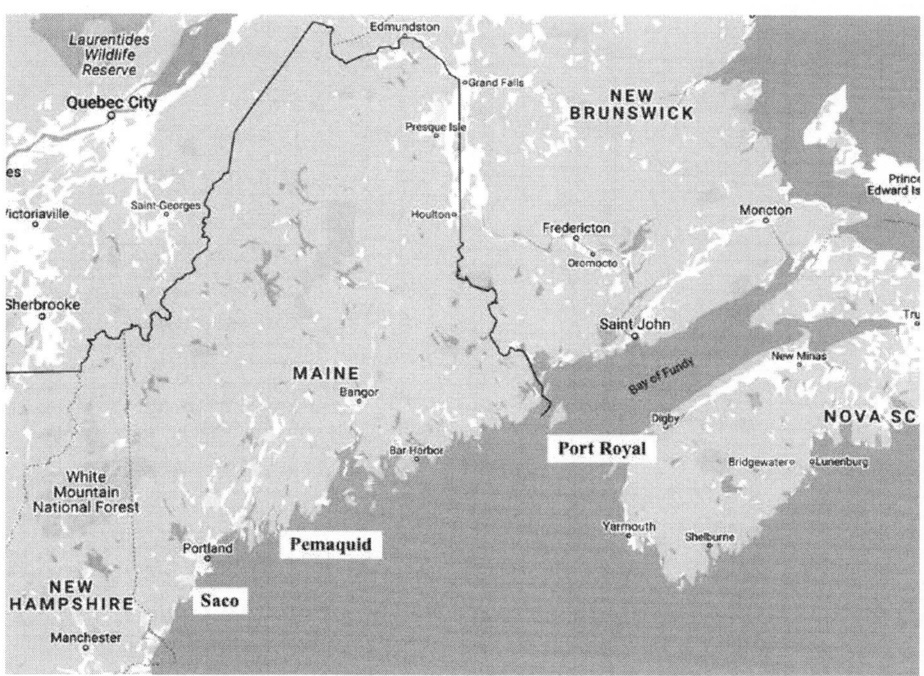

Map showing distance from Saco to Port Royal. Copyright © 2021 Google

The Mi'kmaq had the early advantage, but the people of Saco rallied. They even gained the upper hand, but then Membertou pulled out his secret weapon: muskets.

The French had provided the Mi'kmaq with guns, along with swords, cutlasses, and steel-tipped arrows, and by doing so they were choosing a side in the conflict. This cemented a French- Mi'kmaq alliance that would last for over a century. The Mi'kmaq and their allies shot ten Mawooshen men and frightened off the rest. The battle was over. With their deadly weaponry, Membertou's warriors inflicted many mortal wounds on their enemy. Until then, battle wounds were common but not often fatal. Twenty men in total were killed in Saco—not one was Mi'kmaq. Wabanaki warfare changed forever as a result of this battle.

An archaeological excavation done by Helen Camp at the Colonial Pemaquid State Historic Site in 1965 uncovered two early graves located in the heart of the settlement. These remains, presumed to be of three Indigenous people, were dated to approximately 1630 (plus or minus 90 years). In one grave lay the skeleton of an adult, whose sex could not be determined. In the second, the skeleton of an infant, perhaps only a few days old, had been placed on the chest of a woman. She had suffered blunt force trauma to her back and the back of her head, possibly injuries sustained in a Mi'kmaq raid.[41]

While Membertou and the Mi'kmaq celebrated their victory, word of the battle at Saco quickly spread up the coast. Though there is no evidence that Samoset or the Wawenock took part in the battle, all the villages in Mawooshen territory were called on to avenge the deaths of their allies in Saco, and the cycle of bloody retaliations continued. According to Sir Ferdinando Gorges the war "consumed the Bashaba [Bashabes], and the most of the great sagamores, with such men of action as followed them."[40]

Revenge started with one of their own. Sasanoa, the Kennebec sagamore whose people lived just north of the Popham Colony, took part in the Battle of Saco. But he fought on the side of the Mi'kmaq and was credited with shooting and killing three Mawooshen sagamores.[42] There are no clues to explain why Sasanoa turned against his former allies. In August 1607, one month after the battle at Saco, Tahánedo, Skicowáros, and the Wawenock killed Sasanoa's son in retaliation. Again, from Davies' journal: "they had been at war with Sasanoa & had slain his son in fight. Skidwares and Dehanada [Skicowáros and Tahánedo] were in this fight."[43] Sasanoa was soon dead too, killed by the kinsmen of the sagamores he had shot.[44]

The war continued for at least eight more years. The Mawooshen allies were at a tremendous disadvantage without European weapons. Now it is clear why Bashabes was so anxious to establish a relationship with the English at the Popham Colony in the fall of 1607—he had already seen the destruction European weapons caused, and he could not ask the French for help because they supplied weapons to his enemy.[45] The Wawenock, too, turned to the English, whom they spurned before, in hopes of getting guns and swords. When John Smith said of the Wawenock that he could "have had as many of them as I desired in any design I intended," there was a hint of the Wawenock's desperation. Tahánedo was swallowing the bitter pill of making an alliance with the English so they could arm themselves against the Mi'kmaq.

The view from Hatchet Mountain in Hope, Maine. According to local legend it was here that delegations from the Mawooshen alliance and the Mi'kmaq met to bury the hatchet to end the Mi'kmaq War.

By the time John Smith left Monhegan Island in July 1614, Samoset would have been a battle-hardened warrior. Though there is no firsthand account of how the war ended, legend has it that Bashabes was killed in battle by the Mi'kmaq sometime between 1615 and 1617.[46] The war ended with a Mi'kmaq victory. Hatchet Mountain in present-day Hope, located halfway between Pemaquid and Bashabes's home on the Penobscot, is supposedly where the two sides "buried the hatchet" to end the war.[47]

The people of Mawooshen never fully recovered from this decade of war and disruption. They lost many men who were in their prime years. The balance in their world had been upset by the introduction of European weapons; they now had to accept these foreigners and their deadly technology into their lives in order to fight off aggressors who were better armed. They had probably suffered from widespread famine as well, for while the men were off fighting, they could not hunt or fish or help at home; when families were displaced by raids, the women were not able to tend their gardens. Living in a state of constant alertness and fear was stressful and exhausting.[48] All of these factors led to them being highly vulnerable when a new enemy appeared, this time a microscopic one. The war had weakened them, but the epidemic of 1616–1619 nearly wiped them out.

12
THE GREAT DYING, 1616-1619

No one knows what the disease was. No one knows who the carrier was. But the effect on a population that had never been exposed to the disease before—known as a virgin soil epidemic—was catastrophic.

There were European diseases in the Americas before 1616. The Spanish brought pathogens to South America, Central America, Mexico, and the Caribbean that decimated those populations. French explorer Jacques Cartier reported a disease previously unknown among the Haudenosaunee in Canada (who were called Iroquois by the French) as early as 1535—perhaps Cartier and his men had unknowingly infected the Haudenosaunee themselves. In 1590 the English described an epidemic among the Indigenous people of Roanoke Island in North Carolina, a 'disease also so strange, that they neither knew what it was, nor how to cure it.'[1] Chief Membertou of the Mi'kmaq complained to Marc Lescarbot in 1610 that "'in his youth his people had been 'as thickly planted there as the hairs upon his head,'" but since the French had come their numbers had diminished radically due to disease."[2] This disease—or perhaps diseases, for we cannot be sure it was only one—that infected people along the northeastern coast in 1616 was apparently new to them and spread like wildfire. The death rate has been estimated to be from 67 percent to 98 percent, depending on the location. Native people who lived inland were generally spared because they did not have direct contact with Europeans; the hardest hit were coastal people from Penobscot Bay to Narragansett Bay in Rhode Island.[3]

In Mawooshen territory Wabanaki people were weakened by war and famine, making them more susceptible to illness. Also, if this was a newly introduced pathogen, no one had immunity so everyone would have gotten sick at the same time. That meant there were few people well enough to care for the sick. Mothers would have been too ill to feed their babies or care for their children.

The cultural practices of Native people may have also exacerbated the problem. Not knowing about contagion, "The usual practice whereby family and friends gathered with the pow-wow [medicine man] in a sick person's wigwam could only have served to spread the disease more rapidly."[4] In the Mi'kmaq culture, if a medicine man determined that an illness was fatal, the sick person would stop eating and "their relatives threw water on them to hasten the end."[5] Medicine men and women who were normally in charge of medical care naturally had no idea how to treat the illness. What terrified the population even more was that the medicine men, who were thought to be especially powerful because of their connection to the spiritual world, were dying at the same rate as everyone else.

Very few clues exist to help solve the mystery of the deadly pathogen, but one piece of evidence comes from the Saco area. Sir Ferdinando Gorges sent one of his agents, Richard Vines, along with a crew to Mawooshen in 1616 provisioned for fishing, trading, and discovery. He sent them to "the usual place" where he expected they would receive "the help of those Natives formerly sent over"—in other words, back to the Pemaquid area where he expected they would receive the help of Tahánedo and Skicowáros. He contracted Vines to winter over in the Saco area and test its suitability for a colony. Sir Ferdinando was "forced to hire men to stay there the winter quarter at extreme rates, and not without danger" because of the war that was still going on, and also because the Wabanaki "that remained were sore afflicted with the plague, for that the country was in a manner left void of inhabitants."[6]

Vines and his men witnessed the epidemic firsthand. "Vines and the rest with him that lay in the cabins with those people [the Wabanaki] that died . . . (blessed be God for it) not one of them ever felt their heads to ache while they stayed there."[7] The Englishmen had slept in close quarters with the Wabanaki, who were dying all around them, and yet they did not catch the disease. One interpretation of Sir Ferdinando's comment is that the Wabanaki *did* suffer from headaches, and that may have been a symptom of their illness.

There are only two other known records of the epidemic. The second account was written by Captain Thomas Dermer who traveled from Monhegan south to Jamestown in May 1619: "I passed along the coast where I found some ancient plantations, not long since populous, now utterly void; in other places a remnant remains, but not free of sickness. Their disease the plague, for we might perceive the sores of some that had escaped, who described the spots of such as usually die."[8]

The third case was documented years later by Reverend Daniel Gookin, who lived in Massachusetts and wrote his account in the late 1670s : 'I have discoursed with some old Indians, that were then youths; who say that the bodies all over were exceedingly yellow, describing it by a yellow garment they showed me, both before they died, and afterwards.'[9]

Sores and yellow skin, and possibly headache—scholars have long tried to match those symptoms with a disease that could have had such a high mortality rate. Yellow fever, which turns the skin yellow, seems unlikely in the northeast in winter since it is carried through the bite of a mosquito. Typhoid fever, measles, and chickenpox can produce spots that might be confused with sores, but Vines and his men would have been susceptible to typhoid fever, while measles and chickenpox are not lethal enough to kill up to 95 percent of their victims. Gorges and Dermer called the disease "the plague," but the bubonic plague is carried by fleas living on rats, and rats were not common yet in New England. Most likely "plague" was used as a generic term for epidemic.

The argument for malignant confluent smallpox is compelling. It can cause all of the symptoms described. Vines and his men would have been immune from it if they had smallpox as children, and it could survive the long journey across the ocean (especially in the scabs produced by its victims, which might then be passed along in fabric or other trade goods). It also had a very high mortality rate. The argument against it is that another epidemic swept through the Indigenous population of New England in 1633–'34 which the local people had not experienced before, and that time the epidemic was clearly identified as smallpox by Europeans who knew the symptoms.[10] Considering the number of Europeans who were cruising the coast from Canada to Virginia at that time, there also may have been more than one pathogen at work, each causing different symptoms.

Whatever the cause(s) of the epidemic that began in 1616—and we may never know unless skeletal evidence settles the issue—it is estimated to have killed more than 75 percent of the people in Mawooshen territory.[11] Everyone was susceptible, from babies to healthy adults to the elderly. Some villages were hit so hard that there was no one left to bury the dead and "skulls and bones were found in many places lying still above ground."[12] Leaving bodies unburied went against all Indigenous customs.

The devastation that Native people experienced is nearly incomprehensible, on a scale much greater than the pandemic of 2020. When people died, their knowledge, wisdom, and memories were lost too. Communities were at risk of completely losing their history and culture. Many survivors blended into other Native communities which resulted in massive resettlement, while those still living had to deal with survivors' guilt and the trauma of their loss. This tragic time came to be known as the Great Dying.

Many Indigenous people thought they had somehow angered the great spirit and brought this devastation upon themselves. Europeans reinforced their fears by telling them that their Christian God was striking them down because they were heathens. Could that be true? What else would explain the fact that Native people were all dying and the Europeans were not? Some would come to believe that the foreigners kept the disease buried in the ground and could bring it out and use it like a weapon against them whenever they wanted.[13] The Europeans' seeming invincibility gave them tremendous psychological power over Indigenous people and may explain why some would later embrace Christianity.

For their part, the English felt they had been given a tremendous gift. King James proclaimed to the world that Almighty God, in his great goodness to the English people, had brought 'a wonderful plague' that caused the 'utter destruction, devastation, and depopulation of that whole territory' just so that it could be possessed by the English.[14] It was as if the great hand of God had cleared the way for them. Oddly enough, they did not judge their own devastation by bubonic plague the same way.

After the ravages of the epidemic, there would have been only a few Wawenock left in Pemaquid. There is no further mention of Tahánedo after John Smith met him in 1614. He likely died in the war or in the epidemic. We never hear of Skicowáros again, so he probably did not survive either. If Pemaquid suffered the same percentage loss as the rest of Mawooshen, then Samoset may have been one of only twenty survivors. He probably helped bury the other eighty members of his village, if that many had survived the war. It was during this time that Samoset became the leader of his people.

He either earned the position by default because there was no one else left to take charge, or he had been groomed to take over as sagamore when Tahánedo died. Either way, it was up to him to guide his people through this new, post-apocalyptic world.

In 1614, when Tahánedo met John Smith, the Wawenock were fatigued by war but still in charge of their own destiny. But the epidemic of 1616–1619 changed everything. It shifted the balance of power to the Europeans. Probably only five or six adult men in Pemaquid survived the outbreak. Given that a single European fishing ship had a crew of at least fifteen adult males (some had as many as fifty), and several ships came to the area every year, Wawenock men were suddenly greatly outnumbered by European men. Samoset also had to worry about the possibility of Mi'kmaq raids. Even though the war had technically ended, the Mi'kmaq continued to make incursions as far south as Massachusetts well into the 1630s.[15]

As the leader of his people, Samoset had to make a difficult choice. He could not protect his village with only five men—he needed allies. The other villages nearby had suffered the same loss, so he could not count on them for reinforcement. The French wanted to engage in trade, but they gave arms to the Mi'kmaq so how could he trust them? For several years now the Wawenock had lived and traded peacefully with Sir Francis Popham's men, and possibly other English fishermen, but there had been too many violent kidnappings for them to feel completely secure with the English. His choice was far from clear.

That may be why Samoset felt he had to go south. And as a 29-year-old man, he possibly needed something else—namely, a wife. By age 29 it is likely, in fact almost certain, that he had already taken a wife. He may have had children. But did they survive the epidemic? For some extraordinary reason, Samoset decided to make a once-in-a-lifetime journey after the epidemic abated. Maybe he was searching for allies among his southern neighbors. Maybe he was hoping to find a wife or others who might join him in Pemaquid and help repopulate his community. Maybe he was just doing reconnaissance to see who was left alive. Whatever the reason it had to be compelling because he left his people alone, weak and vulnerable, just after becoming their leader. And he was gone for almost a year. The first time we hear of Samoset, he is walking into Plymouth Plantation.

13
GETTING TO PLYMOUTH, 1619-1620

> About the 16th of March a certain Indian came boldly among them, and spoke to them in broken English, which they could well understand, but were astonished at it. At length they understood by speaking with him that he was not of these parts, but belonged to the eastern country where some English ships came to fish; and with some of these English he was acquainted, and could name several of them. From them he had got his knowledge of the language. He became useful to them in acquainting them with many things concerning the state of the country in the east parts where he lived, as also of the people there, their names and number, their situation and distance from this place, and who was chief among them. His name was Samoset; he told them also of another Indian, whose name was Squanto, a native of this part, who had been in England and could speak English better than himself.[1]

At last, Samoset appears on the historic stage at Plymouth Plantation on March 16, 1621. His whole life had prepared him for this moment. He had the experience of interacting with Europeans, the skill of speaking their language, the confidence of a sagamore, and the temperament to make this first meeting with the settlers a success. He was an ideal ambassador.

How he got from Pemaquid to Plymouth, a distance he himself described as "a day's sail with a great wind, and five days by land," is a mystery.[2] Regrettably he did not say which route he took. It is also a mystery why Samoset was the one chosen to make contact with the English. His association with Tisquantum, whom the colonists called Squanto, may be the key to answering both questions.

In all likelihood, Samoset and Tisquantum met on Monhegan Island. Tisquantum went to Monhegan at least twice, and possibly three or four times. The island had become a hub of English activity, and consequently, a destination for the local Wabanaki people who wanted to trade with them. The odds are high that the two men crossed paths there. It seems more logical that Samoset met Tisquantum on Monhegan and followed him to Massachusetts than if the two randomly met there. But we will take this one step at a time—it gets a bit complicated.

First, let us put to rest the myth that Samoset was kidnapped and taken to England. In the passage above, William Bradford, one of the first governors of the Plymouth colony, said that Samoset learned English from the men who came to "the eastern country" (meaning Maine) to fish—unlike Tisquantum, who had been to England and could speak better English. So Samoset did not learn to speak English in England. He certainly would have told the English if he had been to their country; it was worth bragging about, and he was quick to drop the names of Englishmen he did know. It is clear that Samoset had never been there.

A note about the "Plymouths": Plymouth, England, was Sir Ferdinando Gorges's home city and a large shipping port; John Smith renamed the Wampanoag village of Patuxet "Plimouth," (his spelling of the English city) on his 1616 map of New England; the *Mayflower* colonists made their home at Plymouth, calling it "New Plymouth" to distinguish it from the English city, and eventually the name was shortened to Plymouth. Plimoth Patuxet Museums, the living history center that one can visit today, uses the Plimoth spelling to distinguish it from the original Plymouth Plantation.

In order to make the connection to Tisquantum, we have to go back to John Smith. When Smith departed from Monhegan Island in 1614 to return to England, he left behind his second ship under the command of Thomas Hunt. Hunt was to continue fishing and processing the catch until he had a full shipment to take to Malaga, Spain, where the fish would sell at a higher price than in England. But Hunt made at least two unscheduled stops on the way to Spain; the first was Patuxet, Massachusetts, which appeared on Smith's map of New England as "Plimouth" and became the home of the *Mayflower* settlers. There he kidnapped Tisquantum and several others by first pretending friendship and a desire to trade. Next he continued on to Nauset, now known as Eastham on Cape Cod, where he kidnapped several more people, for a total of up to 27 abductees.[3] Then Hunt took them all to Malaga, along with the fish, where he sold them as slaves.

Sir Ferdinando Gorges condemned Hunt as "a worthless fellow of our nation" for this wicked act.[4] John Smith, also disgusted with his former colleague, was convinced that Hunt abducted the Natives not only out of greed for the money they would fetch, but also to stir up hatred against the English and thwart any plans they had for planting a colony there in the future.[5] He accused Hunt of being in league with certain English merchants who wanted to monopolize the trade for themselves, though how they would benefit is unclear. If Hunt's intent was to stir up animosity among the local people, it worked beautifully. Indigenous people of southern New England were enraged by the kidnappings and became suspicious of all Europeans. For the next several years, their interactions with non-Native people were unfriendly at best, at other times deadly. This hostile climate still existed when the *Mayflower* arrived in 1620.

Tisquantum was eventually rescued by some benevolent Spanish friars and somehow made his way to London, where he went to live with a merchant named John Slaney (or Slanie).[6] Slaney was the treasurer of the Newfoundland Company, which had set up a small fishing and trading colony in Cuper's Cove, Newfoundland in 1610, the first English settlement in Canada.[7] Slaney thought that Tisquantum could be useful to the colony as an interpreter, and sent him there sometime before 1619. Tisquantum was probably eager to go, since it would get him closer to home.

It was in Newfoundland that he met the man who would be his ticket back home to Patuxet (Plymouth). Captain Thomas Dermer had been a member of John Smith's company during both the aborted voyages to New England, and had even been a "guest" of French pirates along with Smith in 1615.[8] By 1618 Dermer had made his way to Cuper's Cove, where he met Tisquantum. When Dermer heard Tisquantum's description of New England, it "drew his affections wholly" and he resolved to see it for himself.[9] To that end he sent a letter to Sir Ferdinando Gorges asking for a commission to explore the area knowing full well that Sir Ferdinando—with his unquenchable desire to build a colony in North America—would not be able to resist. He told Sir Ferdinando that if he would send the commission and a ship to New England, he would meet it at Monhegan Island and perform whatever tasks Sir Ferdinando desired.

Dermer was right, Gorges could not resist. He promptly outfitted a ship under the command of Captain Edward Rocroft (or Rocraft, Rowcroft) and sent it straightaway to Monhegan. Meanwhile Dermer was counseled by the governor of the Cuper's Cove colony to return to England and speak directly with Sir Ferdinando, so there could be no misunderstanding of the commission. Dermer concurred and returned to England, taking Tisquantum with him. This was likely Tisquantum's second voyage from America to Europe; they must have passed Rocroft somewhere in the Atlantic.

Rocroft turned out to be a disastrous choice for the venture. Rather than waiting for Dermer on Monhegan Island as he was ordered, Rocroft inexplicably sailed south for Jamestown. Members of his crew mutinied and conspired to cut his throat, but he uncovered the plot and marooned the would-be assassins in Saco. Those men later managed to make their way back to Monhegan, where they spent a miserable winter (1618–1619), and Rocroft continued on to Jamestown, where he was killed in a quarrel. His part of the mission had been a total failure.[10]

After meeting with Sir Ferdinando and getting a commission to do some exploring, Dermer and Tisquantum sailed to Monhegan sometime before May 1619. They must have taken passage on one of Sir Ferdinando's fishing ships, intending to join up with Rocroft and his crew when they got there, and were disappointed to find that Rocroft had left and was not coming back. This was Dermer and Tisquantum's *first* stopover at Monhegan and Samoset's first opportunity to meet them.

They had to come up with another plan so Dermer requisitioned a pinnace that Rocroft had left behind and set out to explore the coast south of Monhegan. Dermer, Tisquantum, and a small crew left Monhegan on May 19, and he described the journey in a letter which has survived. The first thing he documented was evidence of the epidemic (noted earlier). Tisquantum had been kidnapped before the outbreak, and when he saw death all along the coast, he must have feared what he would find at his home in Patuxet. When they arrived, it was worse than he could have imagined. What should have been an occasion

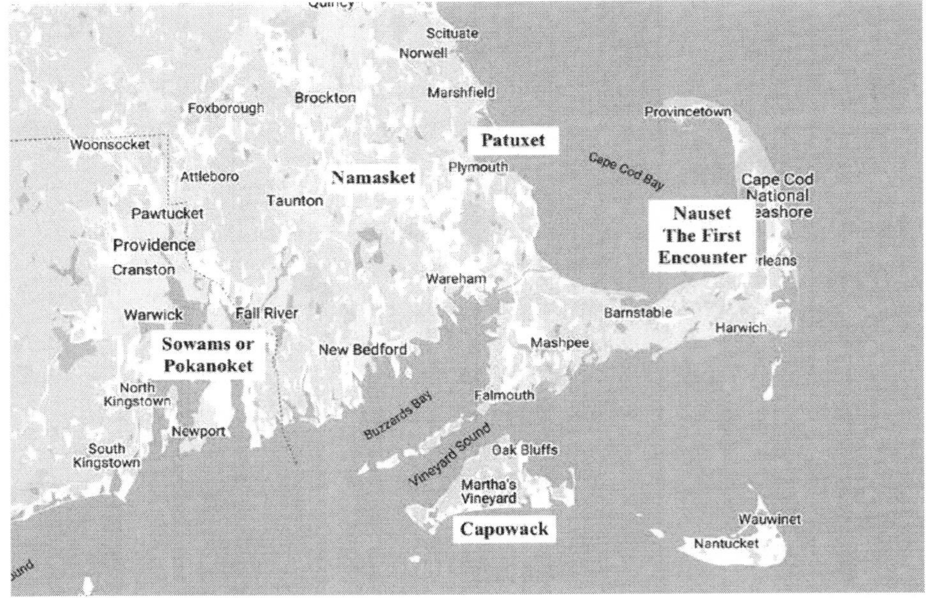

of overwhelming joy at seeing his people after five years' absence was instead a nightmare. Out of a village of approximately 2,000 people, all were gone and presumed dead.[11]

They found survivors at Namasket (the present town of Middleborough, Massachusetts) fifteen miles west of Patuxet, and at Sowams (or Pokanoket, now Bristol, Rhode Island) which is another 25 miles southwest of Namasket. Sowams was the home of the great Wampanoag sachem Ousamequin. The Wampanoag lived throughout what is now southeastern Massachusetts and Rhode Island, including the islands of Martha's Vineyard (known as Capowack or Capawack to the Wampanoag) and Nantucket.

In Namasket "two kings, attended with a guard of fifty men" came to see them; these "kings" were almost certainly Ousamequin and his brother Quadequina.[12] Dermer found out later that they intended to kill him, but changed their minds because Tisquantum "interceded hard for me." They wanted to avenge the act of an Englishman who, "having invited many of them on board slaughtered them with small shot, when, as the Indians say, they offered no injury on their part."[13] We do not know if they were referring to Hunt from five years before, Harlow from eight years before, or yet another Englishman.

Dermer survived his encounter with Ousamequin thanks to Tisquantum, and was even given two French prisoners who had been shipwrecked off the northeastern tip of Cape Cod three years earlier. These unfortunate men had been "sent from one sachem to another, making sport with them and using them worse than slaves" in retaliation for the kidnappings and the murders.[14] Later, when the *Mayflower* first arrived at Cape Cod, the Nauset people of the area believed that the English settlers were colleagues of these Frenchmen and had come to seek revenge. This set the stage for their violent first encounter.

A clarification: Ousamequin, whose name translates as "yellow feather" in English, has been misnamed throughout history. The English settlers heard him referred to as "Massasoit" which means "great chief" and assumed that was his name, an understandable mistake.[15]

Dermer's next stop after his meeting with Ousamequin was an island where he took soil samples to send back to England. This cryptic detail only makes sense if we connect it to Epenow, the Wampanoag kidnapped by Edward Harlow in 1611 who was sent to live with Sir Ferdinando Gorges and Sassacomoit in England. Sir Ferdinando may have sent Dermer on a mission to look for gold, and the paths of Epenow, Dermer, Tisquantum, and Samoset were about to converge.

Epenow is a legendary figure in Wampanoag history. Sir Ferdinando described him as "a person of a goodly stature, strong and well proportioned" with "a brave aspect, stout and sober in his demeanor."[16] Because of his impressive physique, he was shown "up and down London for money as a wonder" and became quite a sensation.[17] Some think he was the inspiration for the line in Shakespeare's *Henry VIII* about the "strange Indian with the great tool come to court" who caused women to "so besiege us."[18] Above all, Epenow was clever. When he perceived how much the English lusted after gold, he told Gorges there was a lucrative gold mine on Martha's Vineyard where he lived, and that he would show them

Coincidentally, the French shipwreck occurred in 1616, the year the epidemic began. Were the French possibly carriers of deadly pathogens?

where it was if they took him back there. Sir Ferdinando bought the story hook, line, and sinker and Epenow got his passage home in June 1614.

Just to be safe Sir Ferdinando sent three armed guards to watch him at all times. Epenow was made to wear long garments so the guards would be able to grab hold of him more easily if he tried to escape—the lesson learned, apparently, from the difficulty subduing the nearly naked men from Pemaquid. Sir Ferdinando did not take into account Epenow's size and strength and his motivation to be free, however. When the ship arrived at Martha's Vineyard, several Wampanoag paddled out to greet it. Imagine their astonishment to find Epenow aboard! He spoke to his kinsmen and planned his escape without the English understanding a word. The Wampanoag promised the English they would come back the next morning with furs to trade.

The next morning they did come back, in much greater numbers. Twenty canoes full of armed men surrounded the ship, and at a signal from Epenow they stood ready to attack. Breaking free from his guards, Epenow jumped overboard and the Wampanoag let fly their arrows. In the ensuing battle men from both sides were wounded and the English claimed to have killed Epenow, though they did not recover his body. The English made a quick retreat, and Sir Ferdinando's hopes of finding gold were once again frustrated.

That brings us back to the undisclosed island and why Dermer collected soil samples to send back to England. It appears that his mission included finding Epenow's gold mine. After this quick stop, Dermer, Tisquantum, and crew headed north to Monhegan, presumably to find a ship heading to England (or meet a prearranged transport) so that Dermer could send the samples and a report to Sir Ferdinando. The date was June 23, 1619, and this would have been Samoset's *second* opportunity to meet Tisquantum and Dermer.

Dermer was anxious to do more exploring and go to Jamestown, where he hoped to find some of Rocroft's men and supplies to bolster his expedition. He left Monhegan with Tisquantum once again and headed south in the open pinnace. Epenow's island, Martha's Vineyard, was one of their intended destinations.[19]

A severe storm hit them somewhere south of Monhegan and they were nearly shipwrecked. They ran aground and had to jettison most of their provisions, leaving them with very little food or drink for the rest of their journey. At that point, Tisquantum left the expedition. Dermer wrote that Tisquantum "desired (in regard of our long journey) to stay with some of our savage friends at

Sawahquatooke [Saco]."[20] It may have been arranged at the outset to drop him there, or else he asked to leave given the dim prospect of surviving the long trip in a small open boat with little food or water. By the look of it Tisquantum was not a prisoner of the English, but rather an employee with the free will to come and go.

To Sir Ferdinando's credit, he treated Indigenous people more like employees than slaves. There is no evidence that he ever directed his explorers to kidnap Native people, though he was quick to take in captives and use them to further his own ends. Tahánedo and Skicowáros were allowed to go free when they returned home to Pemaquid, and Tisquantum may have been promised his freedom as well. The exception seemed to be Epenow. The lure of gold may have proved too strong; perhaps Gorges told him that he could go free once he showed the English where the gold mine was located. And since there was no mine, Epenow had to free himself.

From the moment Dermer left Tisquantum at Saco, he was in trouble. "We had not now that fair quarter among the savages as before, which I take it was by reason of our savages absence...for now almost everywhere, where they were of any strength they sought to betray us."[21] Now that they had no Native guide, the English were under constant attack because of the treachery of Harlow, Hunt, and possibly others. Dermer and his men were taken prisoners on the southern coast of Cape Cod and barely managed to escape. As they continued south, Natives shot arrows at them as they passed by in their open boat. Without Tisquantum or another sympathetic interpreter to intervene on their behalf, their lives were in constant danger.

That is, until they got to Martha's Vineyard, where Dermer found Epenow very much alive. Epenow laughed as he recounted his escape from Sir Ferdinando's men, and gave Dermer "very good satisfaction in everything almost I could demand" except, it seems, the gold mine.[22] He allowed Dermer to continue on his way—this time. It would be Dermer's undoing when he came back a second time.

Eventually Dermer made it to Jamestown, where he and his men became deathly ill. They had probably fallen victim to one of the various diseases brought by new settlers, or the polluted water supply in Jamestown. The drinking water came from the James River, which was contaminated with 'slime and filth' including salt water from the ocean and their own waste. For the first two decades of the colony's existence, a third of the English settlers at Jamestown died each year from typhus, dysentery, or salt poisoning. The colony only managed to survive due to a continuous influx of new settlers.[23] Dermer and his men were fortunate.

By the spring of 1620 they were fully recovered and headed back to New England in their pinnace, which they had fortified against future attacks. Dermer probably intended to meet Sir Ferdinando's fishing ship at Monhegan, since the ship was his means to communicate with Gorges in England. He also needed to get his interpreter back. The last we knew, Dermer had left Tisquantum at Saco. Dermer most likely went to Monhegan either before or after picking up Tisquantum, which would have been his *third* visit to the island. Then he made the fatal mistake of returning to Martha's Vineyard.

Three pieces of evidence shed some light on Dermer's last days: the final letter he wrote on June 30, 1620, which ended up in the possession of William Bradford; Sir Ferdinando's and William Bradford's accounts of his death; and a story that Samoset told the settlers at Plymouth.[24]

Bradford reported that after Dermer wrote his final letter in June, he and Tisquantum went to Martha's Vineyard. Epenow became suspicious when Dermer returned, thinking the Englishman meant to recapture him—so he and his men attacked first. According to Bradford, Dermer "went ashore amongst the Indians to trade, as he used to do, but was betrayed and assaulted by them, and all his men were killed except one who kept the boat. He himself got aboard very sorely wounded, and they would have cut off his head as he climbed into his boat, had not the man rescued him. They got away, and made shift to reach Virginia, where he died."[25] Sir Ferdinando's version included that Dermer received fourteen or fifteen wounds and died in Jamestown "of the infirmities of that place."[26]

But did he go directly to Jamestown after the attack, or back to Monhegan first? Samoset's story suggested the latter. He told the colonists how the Nauset, who were "much incensed and provoked against the English," had killed three Englishmen about eight months earlier, and "two more hardly escaped by flight to Monchiggon [Monhegan]; they were Sir Ferdinando Gorges his men."[27] The similarity between this story and Dermer's is remarkable. The only detail that does not match Dermer's story is that Samoset identified the attackers as Nauset, but they were from Martha's Vineyard. It is possible that Samoset was mistaken about this, given that he was not from the area. As far as we know, Sir Ferdinando did not have any other men in the area at that time, only Dermer.

And the timing is right. The attack Samoset described happened around July 1620, just after Dermer wrote his final letter. Samoset arrived in Wampanoag territory in July, so he may have heard the story just before he left home. If it was Dermer, it was potentially his *fourth* time on Monhegan.

Yet both Gorges and William Bradford said that Dermer died in Virginia, so why would he and his surviving crewman go to Monhegan first? The most logical answer is that it was much closer. Dermer was badly wounded, and it was a very long way to Virginia. They knew there would be several English fishing boats at Monhegan and perhaps even a doctor who could help Dermer, and they could get word to Sir Ferdinando about what had happened. If Dermer was indeed the man in Samoset's story, he must have recovered from his wounds sufficiently to sail to Jamestown where he either died of his injuries or was a victim of Jamestown's contaminated water or some other illness.

This still leaves us with the question of Tisquantum's movements. Unless Bradford was mistaken, Tisquantum must have been with Dermer when he was attacked at Martha's Vineyard. If Tisquantum was left behind there, it could account for why many scholars think he was a prisoner of the Wampanoag when the settlers at Plymouth met him. At first that seems counterintuitive; Tisquantum was Patuxet and therefore also Wampanoag, so why would he be their prisoner? But there may have been a seed of doubt in the Wampanoags' minds as to where Tisquantum's loyalties lay. He had spent many years with the English by then, and later evidence—his betrayal of the Wampanoag and constant friendship with the settlers—lends support to the theory that he was more allied to the English than the Wampanoag. Epenow may have believed that Tisquantum was conspiring with Dermer and delivered him to Ousamequin as a prisoner.

Sir Ferdinando would later credit Dermer with making peace "between us and the savages, that so much abhorred our nation for the wrongs done them by others."[28] It was a decidedly Anglocentric view, blaming the Wampanoags' anger on "others" when in fact the English had done them a considerable amount of wrong. Bradford took a more realistic view of Dermer's accomplishments; writing of the attack and Dermer's death, he declared "This shows how far the natives were from peace, and under what dangerous conditions this plantation was begun."[29]

Samoset's own journey to Wampanoag territory could have happened in several ways. The most simple and obvious answer is that he walked there on his own. However, it is hard to overlook his possible connection to Tisquantum and Dermer. They were on Monhegan twice at least, and Samoset could have met them there or even in Pemaquid. If Dermer went to Monhegan after the attack, Samoset could have joined him on his voyage back to Virginia, getting off at Saco, Patuxet, or somewhere else along the way. The timing of Dermer's last voyage fits Samoset's timeline perfectly. Also, it is hard to shake the idea that Samoset went to Wampanoag territory because of an association with Tisquantum, because otherwise he had no link to the Wampanoag. Did Tisquantum promote his homeland to Samoset, like he had to Dermer?

Some have speculated that Samoset was a prisoner of the Wampanoag. It is not an impossible hypothesis. He could have gone with Tisquantum and Dermer on the final expedition to Martha's Vineyard. If so, he also might have found himself on the wrong side of Epenow's wrath and been branded a traitor, along with Tisquantum, for befriending the English. This scenario, however, does not easily account for Samoset's knowledge that Dermer and his crewman returned to Monhegan after the attack.

Whether his journey was a simple walk or involved a more complex set of circumstances, Samoset arrived in Wampanoag territory in the summer of 1620, eight months before he met the colonists at Plymouth.

14
MEETING THE COLONISTS, 1621

The *Mayflower* arrived in New England in November 1620. Not all of its passengers were fleeing religious persecution; more than half were working class families who were willing to risk the Atlantic crossing for a better life in America. The Separatists (those who chose to separate from the Church of England) who had fled England about a dozen years earlier for asylum in the Netherlands were reluctant to start a colony with these "strangers" given their religious differences, but they needed their numbers and assistance. Though there was tension at times, they pulled together through extraordinary hardships and made it work. Three years into the plantation's existence, the settlers received this encouragement from their backers at home: "Let it not grieve you that you have been instruments to break the ice for others, who come after with less difficulty; the honour shall be yours to the world's end."[1]

The colonists had little financial means, so they were obligated to take on debt to make the voyage. Their sponsors were a group of merchant adventurers of London, whom they hoped to repay by trading with Indigenous people for furs, and also by harvesting and selling goods like sassafras and timber. Hard work was nothing new for them, but they were tragically unprepared for the difficulties that awaited them.

They sighted land at Cape Cod on November 9, after two difficult months at sea. They had a patent from the London Company to settle in the New York area, but because of contrary winds, dangerous shoals, diminishing supplies, and exhaustion of the passengers they decided not to push on and made New

The Mayflower II*, a replica of the* Mayflower[2]

England their home. This meant that their patent, which made their colony legal in New York and included the framework for their government, was now null and void. Consequently two days later the men of the group (women were excluded) signed an agreement later known as the Mayflower Compact, a short contract by which they agreed to make and follow laws and appoint leaders as a "civil body politic." In an age of monarchies, this "early, successful attempt at democracy" was noteworthy.[3] Even during their toughest moments they never broke the contract, and it served as their rule of government until they could obtain a new patent from England.

The Nauset of Cape Cod were the first Indigenous people to encounter the colonists from the *Mayflower*. Even though it had been six years since Thomas Hunt had kidnapped some of their kinsmen, it was not long enough to erase the memory of his crime and they watched the foreigners who came ashore with suspicion and hostility. The English did little to change their opinion.

While they were exploring the area, they dug up Nauset burial sites, pilfered a canoe, robbed their houses, and looted their stock of corn, leaving barely a kernel behind. (To their credit, they eventually made restitution for the corn.) The Nauset must have gotten a chuckle, at least, when William Bradford got caught in a deer trap.

The settlers were aware there had been violent encounters with Native people in Roanoke and Jamestown, and they fully expected "mischief" from the local people in New England. Given the gruesome stories that circulated in England—that Indigenous people were cannibals who ate their captives alive—it is remarkable that they dared emigrate to North America at all.[4] They were on constant alert and never traveled without their firearms. Still, with the exception of their military commander Myles Standish, they were not trained soldiers, or even necessarily skilled outdoorsmen. They were often lost, hungry, and thirsty. If the Nauset were watching them—and there is a good chance they were as the scouting party noisily tramped through the countryside firing their muskets—they would have seen a group of men poorly equipped to survive in their surroundings. That may have given them confidence to attack.

Early one morning as an advance party of settlers was packing up their camp, they heard "a great and strange cry" and then "arrows came flying amongst us."[5] Shots were fired and more arrows flew, yet no one was hurt in what the colonists would call the First Encounter. Their fears about hostile Native people were confirmed in their minds, and they determined the area was not safe for settlement. The Nauset, for their part, were pleased that they drove away the intruders.

The English colonists eventually chose to settle at Plymouth (Patuxet) in Wampanoag territory, despite a warning in Thomas Dermer's letter that Indigenous people in that area were hostile toward the English.[6] It was now December and they needed to start building their settlement. Plymouth had many advantages: the soil was rich, there was a decent harbor and a potable water supply, much of the land had been cleared for farming by the Patuxet, and it appeared to be abandoned. So, Plymouth it would be. On December 23, 1620, they went ashore and started cutting trees for their houses.

From the very beginning the colonists heard cries and noises around them which caused great alarm, but no one approached them that winter. This was the first time the Wampanoag had seen serious settlement activity on their land, and they watched the goings-on from a distance. They were being cautious because their position had become precarious. The epidemic had hit them hard. When Samoset arrived there, he found a community that had lost up to 75 percent of its people.[7] What was worse, disease had not touched their nearest adversary, the Narragansett. Like Samoset and the Wawenock, they were now weighing their options: should they chase off the English, or invite them to become allies? What gave them the best chance of survival? In their deliberate way, they undoubtedly discussed the problem throughout the winter while they kept an eye on the foreigners. Tisquantum and Samoset would have been important sources of information about the English.

Meanwhile the colonists struggled to survive their first winter in Plymouth. Bradford sadly revealed, "In two or three months' time half of their company died, partly owing to the severity of the winter...partly to scurvy and other diseases."[8] Of the original 102 settlers, only 52 were still living after that first brutal winter.[9] Few families were left intact. As they tried to build their

The English village at Plimoth Patuxet Museum, a replica of the original settlement built by the colonists.

homes in foul winter weather, there were often only six or seven people well enough to work. It also fell to them to care for the sick. If the Wampanoag had decided to attack then, they would have met little resistance from the weakened settlers.

On the 17th of February 1621, the colonists saw two Native men at the top of a hill less than a quarter of a mile from their plantation; they made signs for the English to come to them. The English did likewise, gesturing for the two men to come to them; then they armed themselves and stood ready. Seeing no more movement from the Natives, they sent Captain Standish and Stephen Hopkins, one of the "strangers" or non-Separatists, to investigate. They could hear a large group of people in the woods, though they never saw them. They suspected they were being drawn into a trap. Shortly afterward, they brought their cannons ashore from the *Mayflower* for extra protection.

We can imagine the discussions that led to Samoset walking into Plymouth Pantation alone a month later. *How shall we make contact?* We tried to get them to come to us and that did not work, so we must go to them. *How many should we send?* One is the least threatening; they cannot feel threatened by one man. But they have weapons and it will be dangerous. *Who should it be?* Someone who can speak their language. It should be Tisquantum or Samoset.

They were the obvious choices. As an outsider to the community, Samoset may have been viewed as more expendable. Also, Tisquantum had a better grasp of English, a skill which was extremely valuable, and they would not want to risk losing him. It would be dangerous, and they knew it; they had learned about the skirmish between the settlers and the Nauset. The Englishmen carried their muskets at all times and might be quick to use them. The Wampanoag could have forced Samoset to go if he was their prisoner. Or maybe Samoset volunteered to do it.

There is one more possibility, which though unlikely is interesting to think about. Samoset walked into the plantation with "a bow and two arrows, one headed and the other unheaded."[10] This would have been common for a hunter traveling lightly. Was he out hunting one day, and decided to take it upon himself to meet the English?

Bringing a weapon into the settlement was risky—it could have been seen as a threat. With only one tipped arrow, he could not hope to defend himself against several armed Englishmen. Whatever the circumstances were that led him there, it was an important moment in his life.

That morning, Friday, March 16, 1621, was fair and warm. Samoset's appearance in the settlement was documented in *Mourt's Relation: A Journal of the Pilgrims at Plymouth,* commonly believed to be (mostly) written by one of the colony's leaders, Edward Winslow.

> And whilst we were busied hereabout, we were interrupted again, for there presented himself a savage, which caused an alarm. He very boldly came all alone and along the houses straight to the rendezvous [community building], where we intercepted him, not suffering him to go in, as undoubtedly he would out of his boldness. He saluted us in English, and bade us welcome, for he had learned some broken English among the Englishmen that came to fish at Monchiggon [Monhegan], and knew by name the most of the captains, commanders, and masters that usually come. He was a man free in speech, so far as he could express his mind, and of a seemly carriage. We questioned him of many things; he was the first savage we could meet withal. He said he was not of these parts, but of Morattiggon [Monhegan], and one of the sagamores or lords thereof...[11]

Samoset walked into the plantation with remarkable self-assurance. He showed no fear, or timidness, or hesitation. Winslow called it boldness. On the contrary he seemed completely comfortable and quickly put the colonists at ease by naming some of their countrymen who had been to Monhegan.

Winslow was impressed by the physical presence of Samoset, calling him "a tall straight man" of a "seemly carriage." He wore his hair long in the back and short in the front, and had no hair on his face—something Englishmen, who almost always wore facial hair, were inclined to note. The settlers were quick to throw a horseman's coat around him when the wind came up, as he was "stark naked, only a leather about his waist, with a fringe about a span long [nine inches]."[12] His near nakedness would have made the prim English squirm in embarrassment.

The Wampanoag had sent the right messenger. Over the past decade Samoset had met many foreigners (probably French as well as English), and had learned to read their intentions and figure out how to get what he wanted from them. This was not his homeland, so he could perhaps approach the English with more detachment than if he were negotiating for his own people. And he had the right mix of friendliness, openness, and confidence that set the tone for fruitful talks between the colonists and the Wampanoag. He treated them as his equals, not superiors, a fact that no doubt surprised them and caused them to re-evaluate the "savages" they had come to live among.

They questioned him about the local people, their sagamores, and the number and strength of their men. He answered them freely. He told them that the place where they lived was called Patuxet, and that four years earlier all the inhabitants had died during the epidemic. This is what they suspected, but they were glad for the confirmation because there would be "none to hinder our possession, or to lay claim unto it."[13] He was incredibly well informed; he knew all about the First Encounter with the Nauset, as well as Hunt's treachery and the kidnappings. He told them about the attack on Sir Ferdinando's men, and how two had survived by fleeing to Monhegan (presumably Dermer and his crewman). Sir Ferdinando Gorges was very well known in England and hearing his name could not help but impress any Englishman. Samoset also knew that the Wampanoag had taken some tools that the colonists had left in the woods and promised to return them. No one mentioned the items the English had taken from the Nauset.

They talked all that afternoon. Samoset asked for beer, having apparently acquired a taste for it from the fishermen in the north, but having none they gave him "strong water" (probably liquor). He ate a biscuit, butter, cheese, pudding, and a piece of duck, all of which he liked and was acquainted with already. By nightfall, he had overstayed his welcome. Winslow wrote "we would gladly have been rid of him" but "he was not willing to go this night."[14] The thought of sleeping with a "savage" was disconcerting to the settlers, to put it mildly.

Samoset deserves credit for asserting his will here. They thought nothing of sending him out in the night to fend for himself. Granted, he was probably accustomed to camping out, but it was March and the nights were cold. And the English had several large, warm houses to offer. So, he pushed back, politely but firmly letting them know that he—and by extension Indigenous people—would not be treated with disrespect.

Thinking to at least spare their women and children the risk of his presence, they offered to take him out to the *Mayflower* for the night, "wherewith he was well content."[15] It is worth taking a moment to think about that. Samoset may well have spent nights on board some of the fishing vessels at Pemaquid or Monhegan, and may have sailed south with Dermer; however, he was not naïve enough to think that getting on a ship with Englishmen he had just met was a safe thing to do. He knew about all the times the English had pretended to be friends with Native people, only to betray them. So why was he willing to go aboard their ship? Did he *want* to be kidnapped? The idea, crazy as it sounds, may not be that far-fetched. Most of his family and friends were likely dead, and he was starting his life over. He had heard stories about England from Tahánedo and Skicowáros, and he may have wanted to see it for himself. They had both returned safely. He had friends in England among the fishermen and sea captains who had been to Monhegan and Pemaquid. And finally, if he were a prisoner of the Wampanoag, he might have preferred to take his chances with the English. He knew the risk, and he must have felt it was worth taking.

The *Mayflower* was moored a mile and a half offshore due to the shallowness of the harbor, so getting to it required first boarding their shallop and then rowing out to the ship. That night the "wind was high and the water scant" and they could not make it to the ship, so instead they lodged Samoset at Stephen Hopkins's house and "watched him" all night.[16] It was his first night in an English house.

The next morning, they "dismissed" him with a knife, a bracelet, and a ring and he promised to return in a night or two with some beaver skins to trade. True to his word, he came back the next day (a Sunday) with "five other tall proper men." The physical description is rich; Winslow did not say whether Samoset was dressed like the others.

> [T]hey had every man a deer's skin on him, and the principal of them had a wild cat's skin, or such like on the one arm. They had most of them long hosen [leggings] up to their groins, close made; and above their groins to their waist another leather...They are of complexion like our English gypsies, no hair or very little on their faces, on their heads long hair to their shoulders, only cut before, some trussed up before with a feather, broad-wise, like a fan, another a fox tail hanging out...Some of them had their faces painted black, from the forehead to the chin, four or five fingers broad; others after other fashions, as they liked.[17]

Samoset and the five Wampanoag ate the colonists' food in great quantities, and then showed their appreciation by singing and dancing for them.

Winslow noted the nocake and tobacco they carried. They did not initiate smoking, perhaps because they were not the hosts of the meeting and it would have been improper to do so. Altogether it was a very cordial gathering.

The English refused to trade because it was Sunday, a day of no work, and they were anxious to be rid of their guests so they could get on with their religious practices. They gave the Wampanoag some "trifles" and walked them out of the settlement to the place where they had left their bows and arrows. This had been done at a direction given to Samoset—the settlers would not allow the Natives to bring any weapons into the plantation. The Wampanoag also returned the settlers' tools that had been taken in the woods, another request that Samoset fulfilled. With these two acts, he showed the English that Native people were trustworthy and reliable.

The Wampanoag departed with a promise to return in a night or two with more skins to trade. Not Samoset, however. "Samoset, our first acquaintance, either was sick, or feigned himself so, and would not go with them, and stayed with us till Wednesday morning."[18] Once again he would not leave. If it *was* an act, Winslow was not fooled. Samoset wanted to spend more time with the English, perhaps at the direction of Ousamequin to learn more about them, or simply because he was enjoying the experience. At any rate the food was probably more plentiful. Months later when Edward Winslow and Stephen Hopkins traveled to Ousamequin's home in early summer they became faint with hunger because of the Wampanoags' meager provisions. This was a difficult time of year for them, before they could forage fresh fruits and vegetables or harvest corn. They were accustomed to the lean times, but who would not prefer a full stomach to an empty one?

The next day, Thursday, March 22, Samoset returned to Plymouth accompanied by a full diplomatic company: Tisquantum, Ousamequin, Quadequina, and sixty other men. This was the famous first meeting between Ousamequin and the colonists. Samoset had laid the important groundwork for this conference to take place.

The meeting between Ousamequin and the English was a pivotal moment in the history of New England. On that day they made an agreement that both sides honored during Ousamequin's lifetime, establishing a friendly relationship that lasted until Ousamequin's death around 1661. Though they had their moments of conflict and misunderstanding, the English lived in relative peace with the Wampanoag during that time.

After some initial wariness on both sides, the English and Wampanoag traded men as insurance against any treachery, then Ousamequin and twenty of his men entered the plantation. Winslow referred to Ousamequin as "the king," and the English treated him with great deference. He was "a very lusty man, in his best years, an able body, grave of countenance, and spare of speech. In his attire little or nothing differing from the rest of his followers, only in a great chain of white bone beads about his neck [wampum]."[19]

Ousamequin was beloved by his people. In 1623 when he became sick and appeared close to death, one of his followers told Winslow that they should "never see his [Ousamequin's] like amongst the *Indians*, saying...in anger and passion he was soon reclaimed...and that he governed his men better with few strokes than others did with many."[20] Ousamequin's willingness to find common ground with his enemies was one of the most important factors in maintaining peace in the region. Samoset may well have learned some of his diplomatic skills from him.

Both parties treated the occasion with the gravity and pomp it deserved. After the colonists led the Wampanoag delegation to a building furnished with a rug and cushions on the floor for Ousamequin's comfort, the governor of Plymouth, John Carver, arrived with drum and trumpet fanfare. (The Wampanoag found the trumpets fascinating, and later asked to play them.) Then the two leaders exchanged salutations and kisses. After a drink of hard liquor, which caused Ousamequin to sweat profusely, the English offered the sachem a little fresh meat; he dutifully shared it with all of his men according to their custom. Then they got down to business.

They came to the following agreement, as written by Winslow, with Tisquantum and Samoset translating:

1. That neither he [Ousamequin] nor any of his should injure or do hurt to any of our people.

2. And if any of his did hurt to any of ours, he should send the offender, that we might punish him.

3. That if any of our tools were taken away when our people were at work, he should cause them to be restored, and if ours did any harm to any of his, we would do the like to them.

4. If any did unjustly war against him, we would aid him; if any did war against us, he should aid us.

5. He should send to his neighbor confederates, to certify them of this, that they might not wrong us, but might be likewise comprised in the conditions of peace.

6. That when their men came to us, they should leave their bows and arrows behind them, as we should do our pieces when we came to them.[21]

Though the agreement was a bit lopsided in favor of the English (who were the ones writing it down and therefore controlled what it said), Ousamequin and the Wampanoag got what they wanted out of it—military aid against any unwarranted aggression from their enemies. This was their paramount concern since they had been weakened by the epidemic. Ousamequin saw the English as a valuable ally because their guns would neutralize the Narragansett's advantage. After they had come to terms, Winslow felt the agreement was genuine; he would comment later that the settlers were often in the woods in small parties of two or three and never suffered any harm at the hands of the Wampanoag.[22]

The talks concluded after Ousamequin's brother, Quadequina, met the English. The groups parted for the night, and the Wampanoag retired to a campsite nearby with their wives and women. Only Samoset and Tisquantum were allowed to stay the night in the plantation (two others wished to, but the English would not "suffer it"). This was Tisquantum's first stay with the colonists, though he would soon come to live with them permanently.

The next day "was a very fair day; Samoset and Squanto still remained with us."[23] The date was March 23, 1621, and it was the final reference in the colonists' journals to Samoset. Though Tisquantum would become well known for his assistance to them, from his help planting corn and catching fish, to his ongoing translation and interpretation—as well as using his relationship with the English for his own ambitious ends—Samoset has never received credit for his diplomatic role in Plymouth. From the moment he met the colonists, he calmed their fears and laid the foundation for friendly relations. He showed the English how trustworthy Native people were, far from the "barbaric savages" they imagined. Most importantly, he insisted on being treated as an equal, with respect.

Samoset disappeared from the colonists'u record at this point. Ousamequin offered them another guide, Tokamahamon, when Tisquantum was not available. Tokamahamon was probably a replacement for Samoset, who had apparently returned to Pemaquid.

How he got there and if he went alone is unknown. Since there was no mention of any boats visiting Plymouth during this time he probably walked. If he was a prisoner, he either escaped or was released, perhaps because of his good service. His relationship with the colonists may not have ended when he left Plymouth. They made several trips to Maine in the colony's early years, one to Damariscove and another to Monhegan, and they eventually built a trading post on the Kennebec River.

But now it was spring and Samoset needed to get back to his village. He had been away a long time. He had missed the summer fishing season, the fall harvest season, and the fall and winter hunting seasons. His people were vulnerable to raids by the Mi'kmaq, with only a few men left alive to protect them. Even so, the risks were evidently worth it. His odyssey, though long and dangerous, may have borne just the fruit he desired. He next appears in 1623, back at home, with a wife and son.

15
SETTLERS COME TO MAINE, 1621–1624

Sir Ferdinando Gorges had not given up on his dream to build a colony in Mawooshen. The reports from John Smith, Richard Vines, Thomas Dermer, and other adventurers still painted a rosy picture of New England, in spite of the cold, and he was more anxious than ever to get there. Many others were finding their way to the Maine coast. Between the years 1607 and 1622, 109 ships logged the Pemaquid area as their destination, and Sir Ferdinando knew that if he did not send colonists soon to set down roots, someone else would beat him to it.[1] There was always the risk that the French—who were expanding into Acadia, the coastal region northeast of Mawooshen—would try to extend their territory further south.

What Sir Ferdinando needed was a fresh start, so he decided to ask for a new charter for New England. The King was happy to reward his "trusty and well-beloved servant" for his loyalty and long service.[2] King James needed loyal servants just then. His wars had been unproductive and humiliating, and when Parliament refused to give him more money he shut it down and imposed taxes directly on his overburdened subjects. The English were growing tired of his impotent leadership and their frustration was turning to anger.

Despite his incompetence there were those who believed in the monarchy and would follow the King no matter where he led. Sir Ferdinando was one. Having turned against his sovereign once during the Essex affair in 1601, Gorges would never again waver in his support for the monarchy. Others were not so faithful to the old institution, and England was beginning to split into two factions: The Royalists who supported the King and the monarchy; and the Parliamentarians who believed in Parliament's power to check the authority of the King. The rift would get much worse in the years to come, eventually leading to a brutal civil war.

Sir Ferdinando's new charter shifted the boundaries of New England slightly north of the original territory granted to the Plymouth Company. It would be governed by a new body called the Council for New England, with Sir Ferdinando conveniently serving as the Council's president. As always the colonizers were expected to "civilize" any Indigenous people they encountered, though they did not expect to find many because of what King James called that "wonderful plague" and "many horrible slaughters, and murders," which probably was a reference to the Mi'kmaq War. James issued the new charter on November 3, 1620, but not without a terrific fight in Parliament.[3]

The controversy was about fishing rights. The charter created a fishing monopoly for the members of the Council, so that now the owner of a fishing vessel would have to get a special license from the Council and pay a sizable fee for the privilege of fishing on the coast of New England, or risk the seizure of his ship and goods. Not only that, fishermen would now be prohibited from taking any wood from the land, which was a special hardship since they needed wood for their fires, fishing stages, and ship repairs. This was all too much; fishing had always been free! In an era when half of Parliament was fighting for the rights of common people, the new charter did not go over well.

The debate was still ongoing four years later when Sir Ferdinando was summoned to Parliament to answer the charge of an unfair monopoly. The renowned knight was eager to address his critics, like a school master lecturing his pupils. First, he reminded Members of Parliament that he and a few others had explored "that goodly coast" at their own cost, implying that having exclusive rights to fishing was their just reward for taking such great financial risks. He argued that settling plantations there would enlarge the King's dominions and advance the Christian religion, and if they did not seize this opportunity the French, Spanish, or Dutch certainly would, and then no Englishman would see any benefit or profit.[4]

He was just getting warmed up. His rant against English fishermen was a disturbing picture of how they treated the Native people of New England.

> [I]n their manners and behavior they are worse than the very savages, impudently and openly lying with their women, teaching their men to drink drunk, to swear and blaspheme the name of God...besides, they cozen [trick] and abuse the savages in trading and trafficking, selling them salt covered with butter instead of so much butter, and the like cozenages and deceits...they sell unto the savages muskets, fowling-pieces, powder, shot, swords, arrowheads, and other arms, wherewith the savages slew many of those fishermen, and are grown so able, & so apt, as they become most dangerous to the planters.[5]

No wonder Gorges wanted to control access to New England. These "inhumane and intolerable" mischief-makers, as he called the fishermen, were cheating and abusing the Wabanaki, who were beginning to turn hostile.[6] His testimony may have had some effect, because for the moment the Charter of New England stood as issued; the Council for New England could continue to grant patents and collect fees from any English ship sailing the coast of New England.

In 1622 the Council granted its first patents and the name "Province of Maine" was first used in connection to parts of present-day Maine and New Hampshire.[7] But the process of granting land quickly became haphazard, to put it kindly, because the Council gave grants which overlapped parcels already granted. This may have been Sir Ferdinando's fault, at least in part. He had a habit of granting land to anyone who asked him, regardless of whether it had already been granted to someone else. Then there was the problem of boundaries, which were naturally vague since there were no surveyors. It was such a mess that in 1623 they had to start over.

The Council asked the King to draw lots to reapportion the land from Cape Cod to Nova Scotia. When they met in the King's luxurious palace in the heart of London, they certainly never spared a thought for the Indigenous people already living on the land. The men who staked out their parcels on a rudimentary map of a place they knew almost nothing about congratulated each other over a glass of wine and altered the future of thousands of Indigenous people with the dash of a pen. Native peoples' rights and attachment to their homeland were of little consequence to them.

While events were playing out in London, Samoset was getting back to his life in Pemaquid. It was very different in 1621 from what it had been before the

Mi'kmaq War and the epidemic. He was now the sagamore of a small group of survivors, perhaps with a new wife. The Wawenock had to rebuild their lives based on their new circumstances, which meant accepting Europeans who were coming to their shores in greater numbers every year to fish and trade. Samoset had just come from a successful English settlement at Plymouth, and he understood that more settlers would follow. The Wawenock did not have enough people to keep them at bay, even if they wanted to.

They continued to trade with the fishermen, and European goods began to replace their handmade tools; a copper kettle was more durable than a clay pot, and a metal hatchet was much sharper than stone. They liked bells, horns, mirrors, peacock feathers, biscuits, and colored fabric, so Wawenock life began to revolve around trade. The men spent more time trapping beavers and hunting large game like moose, bear, and deer, and the women spent more time preparing the hides. As the fur business transformed into a full-time occupation for the Wawenock, they began to lose some of their traditional skills. The younger generation stopped learning how to make clay pots and arrowheads. They had less time to grow their own food and began to rely on Europeans to supply it. They were getting caught up in the cycle of a market economy.

In order to get the best trade goods and the best deal for their furs, they had to go to the fishing boats. Monhegan Island had been the favorite destination for fishermen and adventurers coming to the Pemaquid area, but increasingly the island of Damariscove was becoming popular. Situated about nine miles southwest of Pemaquid, but only about three miles from the mainland at Capemanwagan (what is now called Cape Newagen in Southport), it had a protected harbor, a sweeping view up and down the coast, and a source of fresh water. Damariscove would become known as the place that saved the settlers at Plymouth.

By 1622, things had not improved in Plymouth. The settlers found to their dismay that the seeds they had brought with them did not grow well in New England soil and their fishing nets could not hold heavy New England codfish. New colonists had arrived without adequate food supplies, and they all faced starvation. William Bradford, who became governor of the colony after the death of John Carver, got word that 30 English ships were fishing at Damariscove, so he sent Edward Winslow to get food, hoping they could count on the generosity of their fellow Englishmen. Luckily it turned out they could, and the colony was saved.[8]

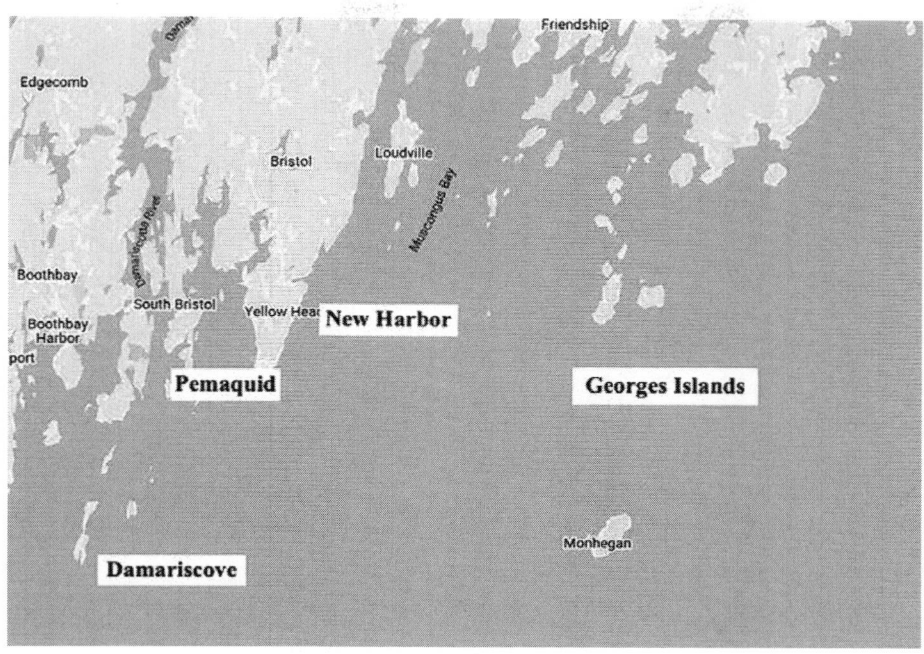

By 1623, Samoset was traveling far up and down the coast to trade. Chances are good that Damariscove was one of his stops. With thirty ships fishing there in season, it would have been an irresistible destination. He was definitely in Capemanwagan that year, because that is where he met Captain Christopher Levett, who had just been granted 6,000 acres by the Council for New England to settle a plantation.[9]

Levett, a naval officer, was in the prime of life and enthusiastic about building his own estate. At 37 years old, he was only four years older than Samoset, and a family man with several children. He was born in York, England, and he intended to build a city in Maine and name it York—a name that lives on today, though not where Levett intended. He arrived at Odiorne Point at the mouth of the Piscataqua River near present-day Portsmouth, New Hampshire in the fall of 1623. There he met Captain Robert Gorges, Sir Ferdinando's son, who was there as the newly appointed Governor-General of New England. With him were Captain Francis West, the new Admiral of New England commissioned to "restrain interlopers and such fishing ships as came to fish and trade without a license from the Council of New England"; and Reverend William Morrell, whose task was ostensibly to oversee religious affairs.[10]

Robert Gorges stayed in New England less than a year and made an unremarkable impression upon the historical record, "as he did not find the state of things here correspond to his station and way of life."[11] Captain West also quit his assignment within a year, finding the fishermen to be "stubborn fellows" who were "too strong for him."[12] Morrell stayed on an extra year, though he never made use of his authority and seemed to think it was useless to try. These3rather uncharitable characterizations of their failings were all made by William Bradford, who seemed rather annoyed that the Council for New England had sent such incompetent men to rule over him.

Apparently thirteen fishermen were wintering over on Damariscove by 1622, funded by Sir Ferdinando Gorges. To prevent the French and the Wabanaki from invading their little settlement, they built a 10-foot tall palisade, installed a cannon, and brought with them around "ten good dogs."[10]

Christopher Levett stayed about a month at Odiorne Point, and by then it was November and time to head north. The weather was raw with rain and snow, and he still needed to choose a site for his colony and build a house for himself and his men. He stopped at "Aquamenticus" (present-day York), and found that the land had been cleared, "having heretofore been planted by the savages who are all dead."[14] The same was true at Saco, which had been well populated before the Mi'kmaq War and the epidemic. Disease had hit the communities of southern Maine particularly hard because of their denser populations, and they had not yet recovered. Levett continued on to what he called "Quack," in the present-day Portland area in Casco Bay, where he found several English ships fishing in the harbor. The Wabanaki he met along the way were friendly and hospitable.

His reception at Quack was especially welcoming. He met several sagamores, including the "great sagamore of the east country" who was acknowledged to be the leader among them, as Bashabes had been. This hierarchy suggests that the Mawooshen alliance was still intact in some form. Continuing up the coast, Levett passed by Sagadahoc, or the mouth of the Kennebec River, where two ships were fishing. Referring to the Popham

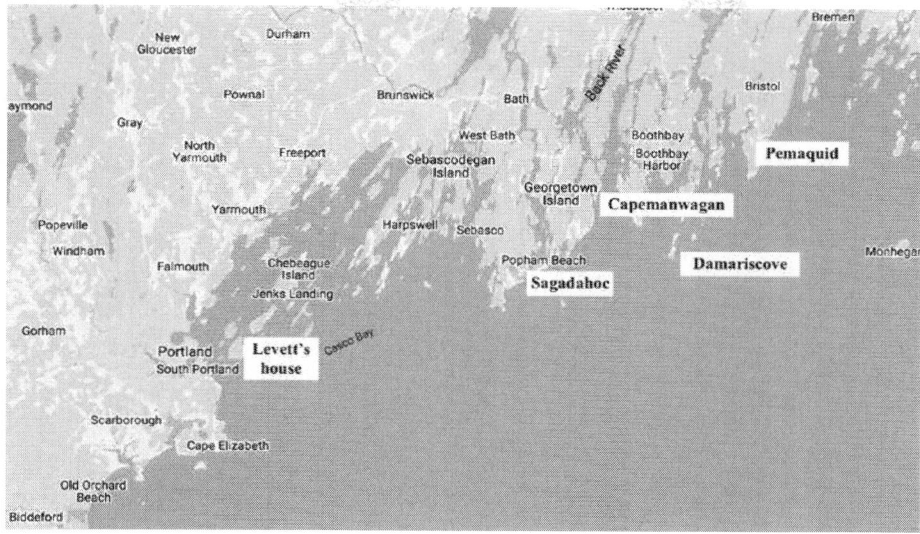

Colony, Levett noted, "For Sagadahoc I need say nothing of it, there hath been heretofore enough said by others, and I fear me too much." From Sagadahoc he proceeded to Capemanwagan, where nine ships were fishing for the season. He stayed there four nights and met many "savages," including one of special note: "a sagamore, one that hath been found very faithful to the English, and hath saved the lives of many of our nation, some from starving, others from killing."[15] It was Samoset.

It is not surprising that Levett would single him out with such distinction because of his association with Plymouth, but the comment is still a bit baffling. What did Samoset do that saved so many Englishmen's lives? How did he keep them from starving? Maybe he helped Tisquantum teach the colonists at Plymouth about farming and fishing techniques, or he told them about Damariscove which they remembered during their starving time. And whom did he save from killing? There are so many possible answers to that question. Maybe the Wampanoag were going to kill the Plymouth settlers (like they wanted to kill Dermer) and he talked them out of it. Or he was with Dermer on Martha's Vineyard and helped save him. Or there were skirmishes between the Wawenock and English fishermen and he intervened. It is all speculation, of course. If only we knew.

Levett's account is invaluable to Samoset's story, not only because he met Samoset personally, but also because he met him in his own environment. As with all accounts written by a foreigner, however, we must remember that we are looking through a European lens.

While Levett was at Capemanwagan, "there came many savages with their wives and children, and some of good account amongst them." Besides Samoset, whom he called Somerset, he mentioned by name two other sagamores: Menawormet (or Manawormet), who was probably the Wawenock sagamore of Nequasset, or present-day Woolwich; and Cogawesco, the sagamore of Casco and Quack, or the Portland area.[16] They had come many miles in the frigid temperatures of November, no easy journey especially with small children in a canoe, but it might not have been out of the ordinary; as we know the Wawenock took women and children to visit the Popham Colony in October of 1607.

When the sagamores met Levett, they showed him respect as they did to all men of authority. They paid him many compliments, calling him their "cousin" which made him not a little proud "to be adopted cousin to so many great kings at one instant."[17] Levett would soon learn that compliments were part of the Wabanaki's process of getting to know a man's character. "I find them generally to be marvelous quick of apprehension [comprehension], and full of subtlety, they will quickly find any man's disposition, and flatter and humor him strangely, if they hope to get anything of him. And yet will they count him a fool if he do[es] not show a dislike of it, and will say one to another, that such a man is a *mechecome* [fool]."[18]

After the pleasantries, Levett casually mentioned that he understood they had some coats and skins and made light of it when they did not want to trade. Then Samoset took charge. "But at last *Somerset* swore that there should be none carried out of the harbor, but his cousin *Levett* should have all." Apparently, he had judged Levett's character and found him trustworthy. The other sagamores quickly agreed and began to offer Levett some skins as gifts. But Levett told them that it was "not the fashion of English Captains always to be taking, but sometimes to take and give," and in the end they were all satisfied. Levett got the skins he wanted, and the Wabanaki found a peer they could respect.[19]

The Sagamores asked Levett where he would build his plantation and when he told them he had not yet decided, Cogawesco, the sagamore of the Portland area, invited him to settle his plantation there, saying he would be very welcome. Levett was "glad of this opportunity, that I had obtained the consent of them who as I conceive hath a natural right of inheritance."[20] Not many Europeans held the view that Indigenous people had a natural right to the land, so Samoset may have judged Levett correctly.

At this point the company parted ways, and Samoset headed north with his family while Levett sailed south with "the King, Queen, and Prince, bow and arrows, dog and kettle in my boat, his noble attendants rowing by us in their canoe."[21] It is a marvelous image. Cogawesco, with his wife and son, rode home in style in Levett's boat, escorted by his loyal men. They traveled with the things they held most dear: family, weapon, dog, and kettle. When they arrived in Portland Harbor, they were met by the masters of the ships working there. Levett made the introductions and the English were surprised when the "Queen" welcomed them to *her* country, for she had inherited it upon her father's death.

Levett had found a place to settle where the local people were friendly and welcoming. Yet he could not let go of his innate suspicions. "And thus after many dangers, much labour and great charge, I have obtained a place of habitation in *New England*, where I have built a house, and fortified it in a reasonable good fashion, strong enough against such enemies as are those savage people."[22]

There is more than a touch of irony in that statement. He feared a Wabanaki attack, which was not unjustified. Just the year before, the Jamestown settlement had been attacked by the local people and hundreds of English settlers had been murdered. (This came after years of hostile relations with the English.) The massacre would have been well known throughout England. However, as we will see, his greatest "enemy" turned out to be a fellow Englishman, an unnamed trader who defied the Council's ban on free fishing and trading. This "evil member," as Levett called him, accused the Council of sending men over with commissions "to make a prey of others" and swore he would do what he liked, backing up his threats with seventeen pieces of ordnance and fifty men.[23] He was a very well-provisioned rebel.

Levett roundly defended himself against the accusation, saying he never took advantage of anyone and even allowed others to cut timber on his land without asking for compensation. But men who had been fishing and trading in New England for years felt it was their right to do so for free and Levett's protests sounded feeble. He did not have the manpower to fend off renegades, and, apparently, he got no help from either Governor Gorges or Captain West. His only recourse was to appeal to the Council for New England to punish the rogue and set an example to all others who were likely to follow in his lawbreaking footsteps. He highlighted one instance among many of the "evil member's" misdeeds in a book titled *A Voyage into New England Begun in 1623 and ended in 1624*. It just so happened that Samoset was one of the man's victims.

It was this man's practice to travel upriver once a week, usually on Sunday (compounding the sin), so he could intercept any Wabanaki who were coming downriver to trade. Then, he would force them to deal only with him. One day, in the spring of 1624, Samoset and another sagamore named Conway were visiting Levett at his house in Casco Bay. Two men under the command of either Samoset or Conway had left some coats and beaver skins with the rogue trader, not realizing what a scoundrel he was. Samoset and Conway paddled across the harbor to retrieve their goods, but the trader refused, insisting they do business with him. They said no, they preferred to trade with Captain Levett. Levett, he said, was no captain but a jackanape and a poor fellow; they responded by calling the trader a rogue, and the situation escalated. Levett wrote how the trader and his company "fell upon them and beat them both, in so much that they came to me in a great rage against him, and said they would be revenged on his fishermen at sea, and much ado I had to dissuade one of them for going into England to tell King James of it."[24]

Samoset's passion was fully aroused. He was outraged, he wanted revenge, and he would go to England and speak to the King until he got justice! In his culture, retaliation would have been swift and severe. No sagamore could let such abuse go unanswered; if he did, he would be considered weak and his people would suffer future abuse. He needed to act.

But in 1624, Samoset faced a better equipped adversary. He also risked alienating the good along with the bad—the good Englishmen, like Levett. After Samoset and Conway calmed down, they began to worry that they had offended their friend by their talk of attacking English fishermen, so they sent an intermediary to ask Levett if he was angry with them. Demonstrating some skill with their language, Levett wrote: "I told them no, I was not angry with them for any such matter as lousy coats and skins, but if they were *matchett*, that is, naughty men, and rebellious, then I would be *mouchick hoggery*, that is, very angry, and would *cram*, that is, kill them all."[25]

What a jarring statement. The implication is that Levett was in charge and could punish them at will. At Plymouth, Samoset and the Wampanoag were on equal footing with the English; now it appeared that he and his people must bow to English authority. This was a fundamental shift in the Wabanaki-European relationship.

The reason must have been their need for protection. As emasculating as it was to submit to Levett, they had little choice—*they weren't fully armed with guns yet*. That would come later. The Europeans had an arsenal of weapons they couldn't hope to match. Levett counted only two fowling pieces, one pistol, four half-pikes, and three cutlasses among them, which were no match for seventeen cannons and fifty English muskets. For now, they had to hope that good Englishmen like Levett would administer justice for them.

Unfortunately, Levett was just as impotent as they were. He later said of the rogue trader, "[I]f such a man, condemning authority, and abusing one of the Council, and *drawing his knife upon him at his own house*, which he did, should go unpunished, then would not they care what they did hereafter" (author's emphasis).[26] The man had threatened Levett at knifepoint, and Levett did not have the authority or the manpower to handle the situation. And now, he told the Wabanaki, he was going to return to England.

Levett's warning turned out to be prophetic, and the English would have done well to pay attention to it. As the number of settlers in New England increased, so did friction with the Native people. Robert Gorges and Francis West had come to New England to set up a government and a court of law, but they both left within the year without establishing either one. Mistreatment at the hands of the English, like what Samoset and Conway suffered and with no justice on their behalf, created a simmering anger in the Indigenous community. They felt these injustices deeply; after all, they had welcomed these strangers to their homeland. Their frustration would explode in violence at the end of the century, leaving Pemaquid in ruins.

Shortly before Levett was to depart, a delegation of sagamores visited him, including Sadamoyt (the great sagamore of the east country), Menawormet, Opparunwit, Skedraguscett, Cogawesco, Conway, Samoset, and others unnamed. It was an impressive show of power. They hoped to change Levett's mind, but he had left his wife and children in England and was determined to bring them to New England personally. Satisfied that he would return, "[T]hey told me that I and my wife and children, with all my friends, should be heartily welcome into that country at any time, yea a hundred thousand times, yea *mouchicke, mouchicke*, which is a word of weight."[27]

Samoset in particular was sorry to see Levett go. Sometime that year, Samoset's wife had given birth to a son. This gift of life, after he had experienced so much death, was a true blessing. Samoset told Levett that his son and

Levett's should be brothers, and that there should be "*muchicke legamatch*, (that is friendship) betwixt them, until *Tanto* carried them to his wigwam (that is until that they died)."[28] Samoset embraced a friendship with the English that he hoped would live on in future generations.

Perhaps it was a shame that Levett never returned to Maine. No doubt the sagamores watched for his ship at the appointed time, but he never came back to his little house in Casco Bay. Levett really was poor, or at least too poor to fund the return voyage. He published his book in 1628 with the hope of raising interest and funding for his colony, but England was now at war with France and Spain and the people were overtaxed and barely getting by. Colonization was not a priority.

His book was filled with descriptions of Wabanaki people and advice for the would-be colonist. It was Levett who told of infants being bound on a cradleboard until they were three months old. He described Wabanaki society as hierarchical; sagamores scarcely spoke to sanops, or ordinary people. "*Sanops* must speak to *sanops,* and *sagamores* to *sagamores*."[29] As for women, they could inherit territory like we saw with the "Queen of Casco."

Levett's account highlighted the Wabanaki's passionate nature, but at other times he noted that their speech was slow and thoughtful, and any man who spoke too much was called a *mechecum*, or fool. Wisdom and authority were greatly respected. Levett saw no formal government or court of law, only leadership by sagamores who could rule only if they had the respect of their people.

For religion, he documented two deities: one called Squanto, who brought all their good fortune; and one they feared called Tanto, who brought all their misfortune. If one of their people became sick, it was because Tanto was angry. When they died, Tanto carried them to his wigwam in the west. (The Wawenock's Creator and Gluskabe were absent in Levett's account.) No one had seen these gods except their medicine men, who saw them only in their dreams. Because of the medicine man's supernatural powers, every sagamore kept one in his company for counsel. The medicine man was also their physician and surgeon.

Levett described the countryside he had visited with real admiration. The soil was good, there was a large variety of trees and plants, and plenty of fowl, deer, and fish to eat "if men be diligent." Still, he wanted to set the record straight. Contrary to fanciful rumors that were circulating in England, deer did not come when called, fish did not leap into the kettle, and fowl did not present themselves with spits through them.[30] He warned that colonists would have to work for their living, and illustrated the point with a cautionary tale of one man from London who, due to his own indolence and debauchery, consumed eighteen months' worth of provisions before his ship left England. The man ultimately starved to death because he refused to work.

Levett went on to say that any man who was willing to work, and who started with 18 months of provisions, could be successful. He also suggested that if wealthy citizens would voluntarily contribute money to purchase plantations for the poor, or even if every parish would invest what they spent weekly on relief for the poor, they could send those unfortunate people over to the new colonies and thus end poverty at home. There was an abundance of space and natural resources for all in America, while in England they were running out of both. It was not a completely new idea, but it was beginning to hit the mark as living conditions in England were becoming more and more intolerable.

Though Levett never made it back to Maine, his efforts to encourage colonization of New England eventually bore fruit. Meanwhile, a small number of colonists were already arriving in Maine, and Samoset was getting to know his new neighbors.

16
THE SAMOSET DEED, 1625

John Brown of Bristol, England, most likely came to Maine on one of the fishing boats making regular trips to the area. He was a blacksmith and a mason and would put those skills to good use in his new home. He brought with him his wife, Margaret, and ambition to carve out a life in a place where no Europeans had tried before.

John and Margaret, probably both in their early 20s and in the first years of their marriage, settled in New Harbor on the eastern side of the peninsula. They set to work clearing land, finding a source of water, planting a garden, and gathering a supply of firewood before winter set in. If they had foresight and resources, they brought extra provisions to see them through their first eighteen months. They built a small house at the head of the harbor using materials on hand, most likely a timber frame construction and wattle and daub interior walls, or interwoven sticks covered in a mixture of mud or clay and straw. If thatch was available John used it on the roof, and if not he had to make wooden shingles. Their home probably sat directly on the ground which, though quicker to build than using pilings or a stone foundation, would not last as long due to rot. It would have consisted of a single room, maybe 16' x 20' with a chimney at one end, and perhaps a sleeping loft in anticipation of future offspring. Despite their best efforts, it would have been a drafty place in the winter since their windows were probably simple wood frames covered with oiled paper.[1]

When Samoset heard that English settlers had arrived on the peninsula, he would have rushed to meet them. Hopefully they were as honorable as his

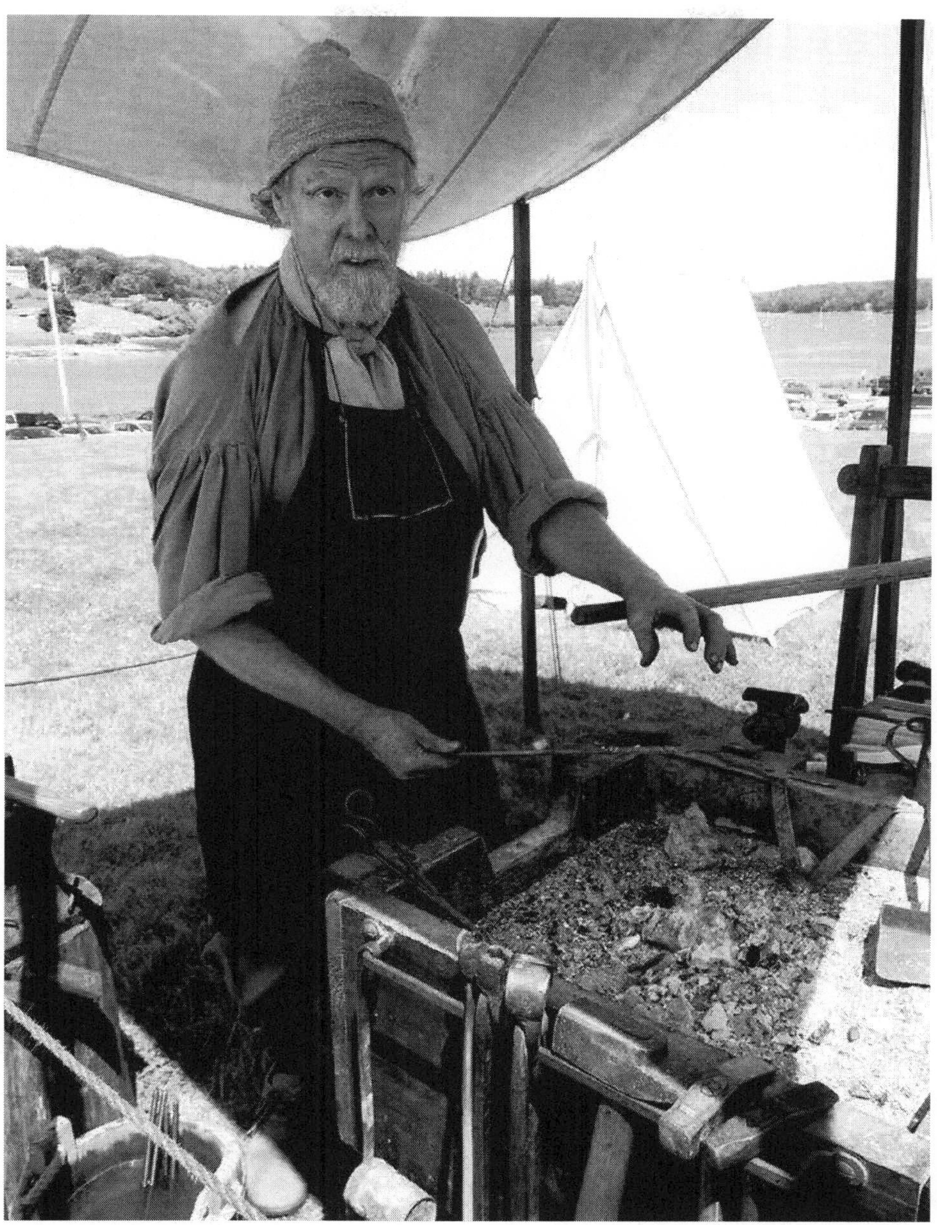

Jeff Miller demonstrates the tools and techniques of a 17th century blacksmith at a Colonial Pemaquid reenactment in 2019.

cousin, Christopher Levett. His curiosity surely would have paled in comparison to that of his wife and the other women of the village. At last, they could meet a European woman! Margaret was probably swarmed by an excited throng of women and children, eager to see what she looked like and learn everything about her. Was her skin as pale as the men's? What did she wear? How did she cook? If she brought gifts, she undoubtedly secured their friendship.

A pioneer woman like Margaret had to be hard-working, resourceful, and full of pluck. In the first years she could not count on ships arriving regularly to supply goods she needed, so she had to get by with what she brought or made herself. She and John may have been parents by this time, with one or two daughters already, so childcare would have kept her busy. Food production, though, was a top concern. She worked in the garden and did all the cooking, put up supplies for the winter and saved seeds for the spring garden. On top of this she would have helped John in any way she could.

Recreation of a 17th century house at Colonial Pemaquid State Historic Site.

Nothing in the historical account suggests there was any animosity between the Wawenock and these early English settlers. As long as the settlers treated the Wawenock fairly, they were welcomed with open arms, as we saw with Levett. Legend has it that Samoset considered John Brown a brother, which is easy to believe given how quickly he adopted Levett as his "cousin."[2] On the other hand, the legend of their friendship may have been embellished by John Brown's descendants as a way to bolster their claim that Samoset sold over 120,000 acres, almost the entire Pemaquid peninsula and land north of it, to Brown.

The Samoset deed of 1625 is infamous. It has been widely debunked as a forgery. The original deed, if there ever was one, no longer exists, which is not surprising given that in 1625 there was no place to record a deed in Maine. Original deeds from the colonial period are rare because the original went home with the purchaser and only a copy was recorded.[3] That means the original Samoset deed would have been subjected to almost 400 years of changing ownership, possible mildew and rodent damage, and the most dangerous threat: fire. We do, however, know what the deed said because the descendants of John Brown miraculously produced it about 100 years after it was created (original spelling retained in all deeds).

> To all People whome it may concern Know ye that I Capt. John Somerset & Unnongoit Indian Sagamores—they being the Propper Heirs to all the Lands on both Sides of Muscongus River Have bargained & Sold to John Brown of New Harbour this certain tract or Parcel of Land as followeth that is to Say beginnig at Pemaquid Falls and so Running a Direct Course to its Head of New Harbour from thence to the South End of Musconcus Island taking in the Island and So Running Five & Twenty miles to the country North & by East and thence Eight miles Northwest & by west and then turning and Running South & by west to Pemq- where first begun To all which Lands above bounded the Said Capt John Somerset & Unnongoit Inden Sagamores have Granted and made over to the said John Brown of New Harbour in & for Consideration of Fifty Skins to us in hand Paid to our full Satisfaction for the above mentioned Lands and we the above Said Inden Sagamors Do bind our Selves & our Heirs forever to Defend the above Said John Brown and his Heirs in the Quiet & Peaceable Possession of the above Said Lands In witness where unto I the Said

Capt John Somerset & Unongoit have Set our Hands & Seales this fifteenth Day of July in the year of our Lord God one thousand six Hundred & Twenty five

Signed Sealed In	Captain John Somerset his mark & a Seal
Presents of us	Unnongoit his mark & a Seal
William Cox	
Matthew Newman	July 24: 1626 Capt John Somerset
	and Unnogoit Indian Sagamores
	Personally appeared & acknowledged this
	Instrument to be their act and Deed at Pemaquid
	befor Abraham Short

Charlestown December 26 1720 Recd and at the Request & [illegible] of James Stilton [Stilson] and his Sister Margarit Hilton formerly Stilton [Stilson] they being the Claimers & Heirs of Said Lands accordingly Entred by Samuel Phipps one of Clarks to the Committee for Eastern Claims

PER SAMUEL PHIPPS,
One of the Clerks of the Committee for Eastern Lands[4]

If the deed is authentic, then Samoset and Unnongoit were the first Indigenous people in North America to sell land to Europeans. The earliest European settlers—mainly Spanish, French, English, and Dutch—did not purchase land from Native people because they felt it was theirs by "right of discovery" and the patents granted by their kings. Why purchase land when you did not need to? At best, some asked permission to live on Native peoples' land or accepted an invitation to live there, like Christopher Levett.

There was a sort of gentlemen's agreement between European Christian nations that whoever reached "undiscovered" territory first could claim it under the doctrine of first discovery. The English upped the ante a bit in 1580 when they added the stipulation that nations must also "possess" that territory if they were to keep it. Technically that meant they must have some of their own subjects living there, but the territories were vast and they could not possibly put a settler on every corner to secure their claims. Then the Dutch did the English one better when they purchased Manhattan from the Lenni Lenape for 60 guilders worth of goods in 1626.[5] (The Netherlands claimed the territory based on Henry Hudson's voyage of 1609.) They did this because they were flanked by English settlements to the north and south which left them vulnerable to encroachment. Knowing what a litigious people the English were, they recognized that if they purchased land legally from the locals it would be helpful in fending off English incursions into their territory.[6]

What is important to our story is that the Dutch purchased Manhattan *after* 1625 and John Brown's supposed purchase of Pemaquid. Was Brown simply ahead of his time by buying land before anyone else? As we look closer at the deed and the circumstances surrounding it, that seems more than doubtful. And what did Indigenous people think these transactions meant?

The Wabanaki did not "own" land the way Europeans did, with legal documents and fences around their property. Humans did not own the land they walked on any more than they owned the air they breathed or the ocean they paddled. But they did have territories and boundaries that they fiercely guarded. They had traditional hunting grounds and fishing places and seasonal encampments that they returned to year after year. These boundaries were well known, which is why the five captives from Pemaquid could delineate territories in Mawooshen so precisely.

A great deal has been written about whether Indigenous people understood that they were giving up the rights to their land when they "sold" it to Europeans. The answer is no, certainly not at first, since they usually continued to inhabit and use the land after the "sale." The most logical interpretation of the earliest transactions is that Indigenous people thought they were entering into a partnership with their European counterparts. *We'll share our land with you, in return for your alliance and protection from our enemies.* After the devastating loss of life from war and the epidemic, there was plenty of land and resources to share with a few foreigners.

Even better, Indigenous people may have looked at it as a windfall. In their culture, visitors were treated with great hospitality. Every time they visited their new allies, they could expect to receive gifts and food. This happened in Plymouth, where the colonists were quickly overwhelmed by a large number of Wampanoag guests and had to ask Ousamequin to put an end to the visits. In the territory of New Netherland, the Dutch had troubles of their own. The Van Rensselaers bought vast tracts of land from Mohawk and Mahican people, and their agent "had to host as many as fifty Indians at a time, feeding them and providing a steady supply of beer and brandy for the sachems." Years after the sale, he "would be out surveying the property and come across an encamped party of Indians. Rather than be indignant at the 'trespassers,' he was obliged, in accordance with their custom, to give them further presents and hospitality."[7]

The Wawenock were no different. They loved the food and gifts that George Waymouth gave them, coming back frequently for more. Forty Wawenock visited the Popham Colony, where Captain Popham fed them. Samoset made himself right at home with the Plymouth settlers and Christopher Levett, enjoying their food, gifts, and hospitality. And it was reciprocal. The Wawenock shared their bounty, even when it was meager, with their new friends. So if Samoset and the Wawenock entered into an agreement with John Brown—a deed by English reckoning, an alliance by the Wawenock's—we should not be too surprised. They never expected to leave their homeland. As far as we know, Samoset lived the rest of his life in the Pemaquid area.

In the early years the English were happy to let Native people remain on land they had purchased from them. After all, Native men were better hunters and trappers and they could provide the English with furs and meat. The situation began to change when more and more Europeans arrived and made increased demands on the land. Settlers began to assert their rights under the terms of the deeds, especially in more densely populated areas. They built fences around their properties and denied the local people the right to hunt and fish and gather nuts and berries where they had always done so. They pointed to their deeds and said *this is what you agreed to.* The Wabanaki learned quickly; deeds dating from the middle of the century often included a provision allowing the seller to continue to hunt or fish or gather nuts on the land after the sale. Sometimes they negotiated an annual payment as well, like a bushel of corn, which helped them get by in lean times.[8]

Several people were involved in the 1625 transaction. Samoset was identified as "Captain John Somerset," a name he would have borne proudly. The title "Captain" signified that he was a leader, and his English name demonstrated to both Europeans and the Wabanaki that he was an important ally of the English. Giving Native people English names became fairly common in the 17th century; they were easier to pronounce, and it was a not-so-subtle way of stripping them of their culture and identity.

Unnongoit (or Unongoit) does not appear again outside of this deed.

Wabanaki deeds were usually signed not only by the sagamore of the region but also by a second person of stature, which became a necessary precaution after a few sagamores deeded lands outside their territory.

The two men who witnessed the deed, Matthew Newman and William Cox, may have been settlers who came over with the Browns. William Cox and his descendants remained in the area (though some dispute he was in Maine at such an early date); Matthew Newman was lost to time.[9] The deed was supposedly verified to be Samoset and Unnongoit's true act the following year by Abraham Shurt (or Shurte, Short). We will learn more about Shurt, who played a significant role in the early days of the Pemaquid colony. James Stilson and Margaret Hilton were great-grandchildren of John and Margaret Brown.[10]

The Samoset deed is unique in several ways, raising red flags from beginning to end. For one, the language and format were very sophisticated for such an early deed. To create such a complicated legal document, one of the settlers had to be a lawyer or a notary with expertise in land deeds, yet there is no record that any of the early settlers had those skills. In fact, most of the settlers could not sign their own names, John Brown included. The alternative is that the settlers brought a template for the document with them. Why not then use the same template for later deeds?

The purchase price of fifty skins is also odd—not because the price was so low (it compares to the purchase price of Manhattan), but because it was a commodity that the Wawenock already had. Wabanaki people usually sold land for European goods like cloth, blankets, kettles, or food items that they had stopped growing for themselves, like corn. If no amount was specified in the deed, they probably sold the land in exchange for guns, ammunition, or liquor, items that quickly became illegal for them to purchase and therefore no Englishman would want to admit in writing that he had paid. It is of course possible that Samoset sold land for skins because they were valuable, but it stands out as being highly unusual.

The act of acknowledgment, as done by Samoset and Unnongoit in front of Abraham Shurt a year after the original deed was executed, was also out of the ordinary. Wilbur D. Spencer, who wrote a book about Maine's early settlers, reported that "No such formula of acknowledgement was required in England by the leasehold system, nor prevailed in this country until 1641, when an order of Plymouth Colony first made it a prerequisite for registration."[11] Even then, Pemaquid was not under the jurisdiction of the Plymouth Colony, or even

Massachusetts, at that early date. It was a formality that was out of place for the time and location. Moreover, Samoset would go on to sign three more deeds, none of which were thus acknowledged.

Realistically, we have to question whether Samoset knew what he was promising in this deed, or in any of the others. Not all Englishmen had the best intentions when dealing with Indigenous people; greed sometimes got in the way of virtue. Samoset probably never learned to read, so any document he put his mark on he did in good faith, trusting that it accurately reflected the verbal agreement he had made. There were, unfortunately, lots of instances when English settlers swindled Native people out of their land. Sometimes they misrepresented what was in the document, knowing the Native seller could not read it. Other times they got them drunk, charged bogus fines or let them run up debt so they were forced to sell, made a deal with someone who had no right to sell, or threatened violence.[12]

Perhaps John Brown was an honest man, but we may be giving him too much credit in this whole affair. Practically speaking, it would take a pretty high level of sophistication to pull off a monumental land purchase of more than 120,000 acres. If he had the business savvy to survey the land, draw up a deed, and get Samoset and Unnongoit to sign it, he would have also realized that without any form of English government in the area, "there could be no property where there was no jurisdiction to sanction it."[13] He lived in a legal no-man's land, which meant that his purchase could not be validated.

The red flags continue when we look at the circumstances surrounding the deed. The Wabanaki, English, and French fought two wars in Maine late in the century, causing settlers to flee for their lives. Very few thought to grab their land deeds in their haste to escape. As a result, when settlers began to trickle back into the state without their deeds, there was a great deal of confusion about property ownership and boundaries. So, the Province of Massachusetts Bay, which governed the territory of Maine in 1700, allowed settlers to register a claim for their land, provided they could produce some evidence of ownership. All claims were then recorded in *The Book of the Eastern Claims,* which was only meant to document the claims, not validate them.[14]

The Samoset deed was presented for registration in December 1720 by John Brown's great-grandchildren, James Stilson and Margaret Hilton. They simultaneously presented a second deed, from Brown to Alexander Gould (their grandfather), for a tract of land eight miles square north of New Harbor. A few things are notable and, frankly, suspicious. For one, the Brown family had never registered the Samoset deed before, even though it was supposedly in their possession for almost a century. It seems like an incredibly careless oversight for something so valuable. Secondly, Stilson and Hilton missed the filing deadline in July, but were allowed to record their claim anyway (some believe a bribe may have been involved). Next, it has been said that when compared side by side, the two deeds were remarkably similar, as if "they were drawn at the same time and by the same person," meaning that the handwriting on the two documents matched even though they were written 35 years apart.[15] An interesting point—and perhaps too coincidental —was that the second deed was witnessed by Matthew Newman and William Cox, the same two men who supposedly witnessed the Samoset deed. And lastly, soon after they presented the Samoset deed, it disappeared. A copy was filed in York County, Maine, in 1739, and supposedly another copy was on display in the Courthouse in Boston when it burned in 1747. The original has never been found, and therefore cannot be analyzed for irregularities—which is perhaps just what Stilson and Hilton intended.

Possibly the most confounding question is why Abraham Shurt, who acknowledged John Brown's purchase of 120,000 acres in 1626, would then take possession of 12,000 acres for his employers seven years later that were *within the limits of Brown's property*. Shurt came to Pemaquid as the agent of two merchants from Bristol, England—Robert Aldworth (or Aldsworth, Alsworth) and Gyles (or Giles) Elbridge—to purchase Monhegan Island, then stayed at Pemaquid to manage their affairs for decades afterward. In 1631 Aldworth and Elbridge were granted a patent from Sir Ferdinando Gorges and the Council for New England for "twelve thousand acres of land at Pemaquid, with all islands, islets adjacent, within three leagues."[16] Shurt received the patent in Pemaquid in 1633 and should have seen that there was a conflict.[17] John Brown already owned the land. Either he chose to overlook the problem, or he had never acknowledged John Brown's deed in the first place. Abraham Shurt was widely respected, and if James Stilson and Margaret Hilton wanted to make a false deed look more legitimate, adding his acknowledgment was a good way to do it. Given all the evidence, it appears that the Samoset deed presented in 1720 was written in 1720 and is most likely a forgery.

Still, there may have been a deed, or some kind of agreement, that simply did not survive. Stilson and Hilton could have created a new one in 1720 when they needed a deed to prove their claim, using language that suited their purpose. A relative of John Brown's swore in a deposition that he had seen "an Indian deed to old John Brown, of an ancient date."[18] On the contrary, John Brown's son swore that his father "had a lease of his plantation at New-Harbour, under Mr. Elbridge, and Aldsworth," which meant he did not own it.[19] Who was right? We will never know for sure. But in practical terms, John Brown *behaved* as if he owned the land, and none of the early settlers on the peninsula disputed his claim. Over his lifetime, he gave away large pieces of it to his children. Perhaps what really happened is that John Brown and his family lived there for many years with the approval of Samoset and the Wawenock, and possession was as good as ownership in early 17th century Maine.

Samoset ultimately put his mark on three other deeds, none of which were contested. The first in 1641 granted land to Richard Pearce (or Pierce), who married the Browns' oldest daughter Elizabeth. Samoset's continued closeness to the Brown family is evident—John Brown was one of the witnesses to the transaction.

> Know all men by these Pres[ts], That I Capt John Summerset a Sagamore Indian of several lands near Joyning unto Round Ponds falls by the name of Remoboose [sic], trenched [sic] away five miles Eastward four miles N. West So back to Pemeyquid River uplands & meadow and Islands & Iletts containing to about twelve miles for and in Consideration I do own myself my Heirs, Execu[rs] adm[rs] & assigns be fully paid and sattisfied before the signing hereof; Have Given, Granted, Bargained & Sold, by these Pres[ts] do absolutly Give Grant and Bargaine and sell unto Richard Pearce, Carpenter of Remobcose which is called by the English Muscongus his Heirs and assigns for Ever these Parcels of Land and medows Joyning to the Round Pond falls medows, Swamp, falls Upland Timber and Trees woods & und[r] woods, mines, & all other Priviledges belonging unto his Bounds, for the fores[d] Richard Pearce his Heirs, Execu[rs] Adm[rs] and assigns do peaceably Enjoy forever free and Clear of and from all former or later bargens Or sailes or Mortgages or Incombrances whatsoever with quiate and peaceable Possession as witness my Hand & seal, this ninth Day of January In 1641

Sign'd, Sealed & Delivered	John Summerset Sagem[r]. [Seal]
with a Turf & Twigg given	his X mark†
in behalf of Possesion of ye	Easey Gale Sagmore
whole before us witness	his X mark
Our Hands.	Dick Swalks Sage[r]
John Browne. Rich[d] Shoote	his X mark

Recorded October 24, 1729, p[r] Nathan Bowen, N. Pub.

The mark of John Summerset seems to be a sash with a tassel; that of Easey Gale resembles a written capital C upside down; and that of Dick Swalks is a semicircular scroll.[20]

This generous piece of land, containing about twelve miles of the land John Brown claimed to own according to the vague description, seemed to encompass the central part of the Pemaquid peninsula, north of New Harbor and the Pemaquid colony. The language is more typical of deeds in the 17th century. The English by then included all the geographic features of the property—meadows, islands, islets, swamps, trees, woods, and mines—so there would be no misinterpretation about who owned them going forward. Using the terms "Given, Granted, Bargained & Sold" made it clear that this transaction was final.

Mention of the turf and twig ceremony, which was the ancient practice required by English law to convey property by passing a literal piece of it from the seller to the buyer (or their agent) was not usually included in a deed and is a quaint reminder of the period. Two new sagamores were part of the transaction; the second, Dick Swalks, may very well be Dick Swash, who signed other deeds in central Maine. The deed is dated January 9, when the Wawenock would normally be living at their winter camps inland, so perhaps by 1641 they had given up their winter migration. There is no mention of what "consideration" Richard Pearce gave to the Wawenock for the land, so it may have been something illegal like firearms or alcohol. This transaction took place during a recession when tensions between Wabanaki and English people were running high. Perhaps Samoset and the Wawenock decided to sell the land because they were feeling the financial pinch or wanted to arm themselves in preparation for any trouble with the English.

The fact that Samoset rather than John Brown sold the land is significant.

If Brown had truly purchased the land described in the 1625 deed, he would have been the only person legally able to sell off a piece of it, which again calls into question the 1625 deed.

The last two deeds attributed to Samoset were both executed in 1653, presumably at the end of his life. Each mentions a place unknown to us today—Heggomeito and Soggohannago—so we do not know for certain if they were in the Pemaquid region. In the first deed Samoset conveyed land to Richard Fulford (or Fulfort, Fulfert), who married Richard Pearce's daughter Elizabeth:[21]

> The Condition of This Obligation is such that The within named Richard Fulfert may well and peaceably, have, hold Enjoy and possess from the date hereof to him & his Heirs and Assigns forever All and singular those Lands begining at the place called the passage Point and from thence alongst the shoar to the place called Heggomeito and so Two miles into the Country in Length which late were the Lands of Cap[t] Summersetts and the said Cap[t] Summersett hath granted by this Deed of Gift to the aforesaid Richard Fulfort made under his hand & Seal to possess it without any Molestation either of English or Indians.—— Sealed & Delivered in the presence of us in the Year of our Lord 1653 This first day of June.

The mark of
CAP[T] SOMERSETT

Witness
PHILLIP SWADDAN
THOMAS COLE
The mark of JOHN BROWN
The mark of John HAYMAN
RICHARD PEARSE.

The most interesting thing about this deed is that Samoset conveyed land without the participation of anyone else. Was he acting on his own without the knowledge, or consent, of his people? This deed was categorized as a gift to Fulford, which it may have been, or again something illegal was exchanged. Like with the previous two deeds, Samoset kept the land in John Brown's family, and Brown and Richard Pearce were there to act as witnesses.

Samoset's last conveyance exists only as a fragment compiled here from two accounts, but includes something extraordinary: his signature.[22]

> These present Obellygcaion (or Obbelly-gacion)…mee Captaine Sommarset of M..sc.n..s [Muscongus?] have sold unto William Parnall and Thomas Way and William England one thousand hakkurs [acres] of land in Soggohannago being quiet Possed by William Parnell and Thomas Way and William England The...day of July, 1653. The mark of Captaine Sommarset.

Samoset's signature, a bow and arrow.[23]

The old hunter and warrior signed his name with a bow and arrow. His mark on a piece of paper is all that remains of the man, his personal touch reaching out to us across the centuries. We will never know if selling Wawenock land was an act of desperation, or generosity, or simple resignation as he neared the end of his life. By this time, however, he should have understood the finality of the transactions.

The land shuffle continued after Samoset's death, when John Brown began to give away land as if he owned it himself. No one challenged him. His real estate legacy would not last, however. Over the next century and a half, property ownership in the Wawenock's homeland became a muddled mess. Wealthy English proprietors scooped up large tracts of land, but boundaries and titles were often in dispute. Tensions rose to the point that by 1811 the Commonwealth of Massachusetts had to step in to settle the cases.

In the end, only land proprietors who held a title that originated from an English patent were judged to be rightful owners.[24] "Indian deeds" were declared invalid, and the Brown family's descendants found themselves owners of nothing but worthless pieces of paper. The Wawenock's connection to the land had essentially been erased.

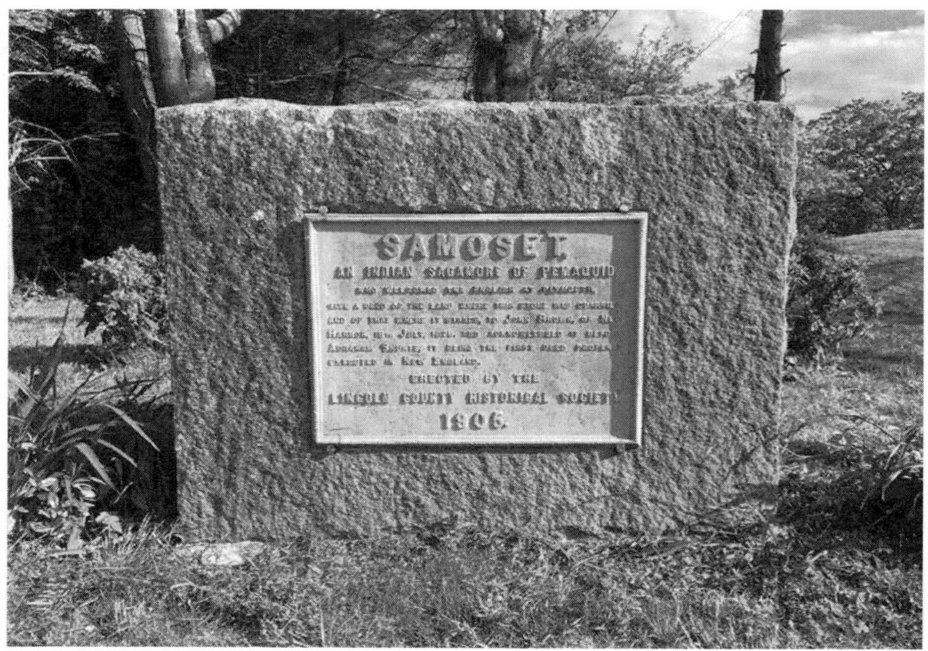

The Samoset monument that sits near the site of John Brown's house in New Harbor. The inscription reads:

SAMOSET
AN INDIAN SAGAMORE OF PEMAQUID
Who welcomed the English at Plymouth, gave a deed of the land where this stone was quarried, and of that where it stands, to John Brown, of New Harbor, 15th July, 1625, and acknowledged it before Abraham Shurte, it being the first deed properly executed in New England.
ERECTED BY THE
LINCOLN COUNTY HISTORICAL SOCIETY
1905.

PART III

Keeping the Peace, 1626–1653

17
PURITANS, PIRATES, AND THE POX, 1626-1634

Samoset's son was now a toddler. He spent most of the time with his mother and the other women of the village, running naked in the summer and listening to their songs and conversations while they prepared hides and worked at other chores. Samoset would spend more time with his son when he was big enough to learn "manly arts." Samoset's family may have grown by this time too. He may have taken another wife, which was not unheard of for sagamores who had to care for widows, orphans, and the elderly. Another wife would help with the extra work and bear more children which would add to his prestige and protect his lineage. Now that war and disease were behind them, the Wawenock population was starting to recover.

Life in the meantime followed its regular seasonal rhythm. In the spring they returned to their camp at Pemaquid, planted crops, and gathered for the alewife run and games; in the summer they fished and worked in the garden; in the fall they harvested their crops and hunted; and in the winter they dispersed to their hunting territories inland to find bigger game. The arrival of a few permanent settlers on the Pemaquid peninsula had not yet altered the traditional pattern of their lives.

Samoset lived in Pemaquid, but where exactly we do not know. The Wawenock may have lived in more than one place, moving when they let their fields lie fallow or they needed a new supply of wood or a fresh latrine. Samoset told the colonists in Plymouth that he was from Monhegan, but that was just a reference point he knew would be familiar to Europeans—the Wawenock did not actually live on Monhegan Island. Fortunately we do have a few clues that narrow down the location of his village.

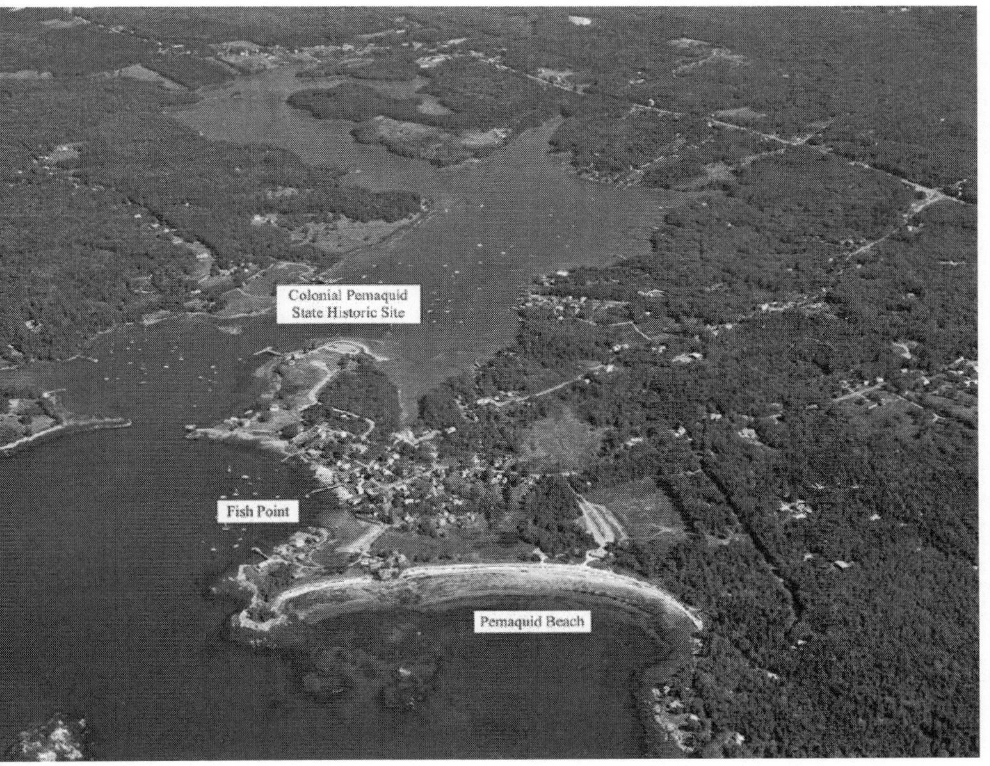

Beaches at Pemaquid. The Colonial Pemaquid State Historic Site is the most likely site of Samoset's home. Sheet film negative from the Jack Lane Photography Collection, Old Bristol Historical Society, Bristol, ME[1]

When George Popham and Raleigh Gilbert visited Tahánedo and the Wawenock in 1607, Robert Davies noted in his journal that they sailed up the Pemaquid River right to the Wawenock's "houses" and that the houses were near "the sands," suggesting a beach.[2] There are three sandy beaches near the Pemaquid River: Pemaquid Beach, Fish Point, and the Colonial Pemaquid State Historic Site, all within a half mile of each other. Davies's description best fits the Colonial Pemaquid State Historic Site. Archaeological digs at that location have uncovered a trove of Indigenous artifacts dating back around 7,500 years and up to the 17th century. This proves that Native people lived there continuously for thousands of years, including during Samoset's lifetime.[3] We can appreciate their choice to live on this idyllic, scenic point of land. Besides the appeal of its natural beauty, there is a sandy beach for easy access to the water, two rivers close by, and a natural breakwater that protects the inner harbor from wind and surf.

Robert Aldworth was one of the leading merchants of Bristol, England and established the first sugar refining house there.[5] Gyles Elbridge was a successful merchant as well with five ships to his credit, which were used to carry goods back and forth from Bristol to Pemaquid. Their financial stability was crucial to getting the settlement off to a strong start. The town of Bristol, Maine was incorporated in 1765 and named in honor of the proprietors' home port.

Fish Point has not been excavated, but digs done at Pemaquid Beach Park have uncovered Native artifacts as well, just fewer of them and none from Samoset's lifetime.[4] The evidence might be there, but modern factors have altered the 17th century landscape. Fields have been plowed, roads and houses have been built, and the sea has risen by as much as fifty feet, wiping out traces of the people who lived near the water's edge. Given the evidence that we have, it is safe to say generally that the southern tip of the peninsula was Samoset's home. When Samoset supposedly "sold" 120,000 acres to John Brown, he excluded that area from the deed—thus retaining the land that the Wawenock lived on.

When Abraham Shurt arrived in 1626, he chose the Colonial Pemaquid site as the location for the English settlement. He did so either because of, or in spite of, the Wawenock's presence there. From the Wawenock's point of view, it made sense to invite the English to live near their village. That would give them a ready market so they would not have to travel up and down the coast to trade their furs. As long as Shurt treated them fairly and stocked items they wanted, they had no need to go elsewhere. They could not have forseen how much the settlement would change their lives.

We know very little about the man who became such an important figure in Pemaquid's early history. Abraham Shurt was unmarried and in his 40s when he arrived in Pemaquid, with almost twenty years of experience working for Robert Aldworth and Gyles Elbridge in the international trade business. They set up a trade network by sending ships from Bristol filled with goods to sell to the fishermen, colonists, and Wabanaki, then Shurt loaded the ships in return with furs, fish, timber, and other goods to sell in Europe. Shurt ran the entire business from the American side. We can infer from his two decades as the manager of the settlement, during which Pemaquid grew from a fledgling fishing spot into an international trading center, that he was good at his job.

It is not clear when the physical transformation of Pemaquid began, but it was probably soon after Shurt's arrival in 1626, perhaps as early as 1627. As Samoset walked around the settlement, he would have seen carpenters, blacksmiths, coopers, and other laborers busy at work. He was already familiar with English craftsmanship, having seen it at the Popham Colony and Plymouth, but now he could watch the work up-close. Strange sounds filled the air—men sawing wood, hammering nails, pounding iron—and the harbor became a construction zone. Shurt's workers built a substantial dock where goods could be unloaded from incoming ships, as well as a large truckhouse which was probably a combination warehouse, trading post, tavern, and barracks for the workers.[6] Fishermen worked out of the harbor, hauling their boatloads of cod onto the shore to begin the messy job of processing their catch. The stench of dead fish hung in the air, while racks of fish lay drying in the sun and barrels of cod livers sat stewing on the shore.

Then there were the animals. Shurt had cattle, pigs, sheep, and chickens brought over to feed his crews and to sell to new settlers. Before long he had a thriving cattle business. It must have been a revelation to the Wawenock to see domesticated animals like these because the only animals they had tamed were dogs. They could see how easy it was for the colonists to gather eggs from their hens or slaughter cattle they did not have to hunt. Imagine their surprise the first time they saw an Englishman milk a cow. The Wawenock could probably visit the settlement whenever they wanted, free to drop in like they did at the Popham Colony. As guests they probably hoped to get a taste of exotic English food like prunes or biscuits, or receive a gift from Shurt or one of the workers.

The landscape began to change as Shurt's men cleared fields for gardens and cut down trees to build and heat their structures. They put up fences to keep their animals contained, or in the case of the pigs, let them forage their own food. Before long the Wawenock may have been competing with the English for fish, shellfish, wild nuts and berries, and small game. On the other hand, they could now easily trade furs for food.

It is possible that Samoset had already seen some of these animals at the Popham Colony, Plymouth, or on Monhegan Island. The Council for New England had ordered "every ship of sixty tons or more sailing for New England to carry two pigs, two calves, four rabbits, four hens, and one rooster" and "leave them at Monhegan for the benefit of the island fishermen."[7] If every ship complied with the order, there would have been a large stock of animals on the island.

Samoset would have closely monitored the goings-on and perhaps enjoyed sharing a smoke and a drink with Abraham Shurt, swapping stories and getting to know him. As for Shurt, he needed to foster a good relationship with his Wawenock "hosts" to keep the English safe from attack and to acquire their furs. For the settlement to succeed, Samoset and Abraham Shurt had to work together or Pemaquid would go the way of the failed Roanoke or Popham colonies.

Trading at a truckhouse would soon replace the old method of bartering with fishermen or traders wherever they found them, and it became a more stable and permanent means of exchange. Thanks to Shurt's business acumen and the robust support of proprietors Aldworth and Elbridge, Pemaquid quickly became one of the premier trading centers in New England, but other truckhouses soon followed. One of the first was built on the Kennebec River by the settlers from Plymouth.

When Edward Winslow sailed to Damariscove in 1622 to get lifesaving food supplies for the colony, he may have learned that the Wabanaki on the Kennebec River had a large supply of furs. The colonists in Plymouth were still mired in debt to the adventurers who had financed their voyage and were making very little progress paying it off. Their attempts at fishing were never very successful, but they had improved at farming—thanks in part to the seed corn they had gotten and techniques learned from the Wampanoag. By 1625 they had a bumper corn crop, which proved to be a renewable and valuable trading commodity. Maine was the logical place to do business because there were more fur-bearing animals in the colder northern climate, plus the demand for corn was greater in Maine because it did not grow well north of the Kennebec River. Even now the Wabanaki were growing less of it as they switched from food production to fur production.

Winslow sailed up the Kennebec River with a boatload of corn in 1625 and traded it for 700 pounds of beaver and other furs, and the idea of building a trading post was born. The Plymouth settlers petitioned the Crown for a patent of land along the river, and in 1628 built a truckhouse near the present capital of Augusta. It was an ideal location since they could intercept any Wabanaki who were coming downriver to trade (just like the rogue trader was doing in Casco Bay). Hopeful of more profit, they invested in another trading post in Penobscot Bay around 1631.

While the colonists from Plymouth were laying a commercial foundation in the Kennebec region, Pemaquid was starting to take shape as an English colonial village. New settlers built simple houses close to the trading post. New Harbor, too, attracted a few more families. By 1630, there may have been as many as fifteen "planters," or farmers, in Pemaquid and ten in New Harbor, along with their families.[8] But the flow of English settlers to the Pemaquid region was more of a trickle than a gush, and families tended to spread far apart rather than congregate in towns to take advantage of more farmland. Competition for settlers was about to intensify as plans for the first city in New England took shape. A powerful new force was on the way: the Puritans of the Massachusetts Bay Colony.

King James I, pitifully debilitated by arthritis, gout, and kidney stones, died on March 27, 1625. His son Charles, a patron of fine arts and music, was perhaps more sensitive than his father yet he too was hopelessly out of touch with his people. He repeated many of his father's mistakes, while making several of his own. He immediately married a French Catholic princess, which angered his subjects who hated both the French and the Catholics. Soon after, he led his country into war with both France and Spain simultaneously. Like his father, when Parliament refused to give him money to fight his wars, he dissolved it and imposed burdensome taxes directly on his subjects. He caused such widespread discontent and instability that many English citizens, especially Puritans seeking religious autonomy, chose to leave the country rather than live under his repressive regime. This decade of exodus, approximately 1630–1642, became known as the Great Migration, and was in essence a Puritan "invasion" of New England. More than twenty thousand people migrated to the Massachusetts Bay Colony—originally located around the northern part of Massachusetts Bay including Boston and Salem—in the 1630s alone, and their presence had a direct impact on Samoset and the Wawenock.[9]

King Charles I.[10]

Several things led to the Massachusetts Bay Colony's unique success. The Puritans came in large numbers, and they were generally middle-class people with solid financial resources. Many were literate, skilled craftsmen. They came in family units with the intention of building a community, and the number of women was nearly equal to the number of men. This was in contrast to the Virginia colony, where men still substantially outnumbered women and 75 percent of the population were servants working for a few wealthy landowners.[11]

Perhaps most importantly, the Puritans came with a common purpose to pursue their religious ideals, which created a strong bond among them. The Separatists in Plymouth had the same objective, but half of their company had been non-believers. Because of their small numbers and ongoing financial difficulties, they never attracted many new followers or achieved the momentum and stability that the Puritans did. Eventually their colony was absorbed by Massachusetts Bay, and the Puritans built Boston into the largest trading center in the northeast. Many of these new arrivals became very wealthy, especially in land holdings.

Tiny settlements in Maine could not compete with Boston's size and resources, especially without the "civilizing" influence of strong government and, equally important at the time, religious guidance. Without government, law and order, or clergymen to minister to the people, Maine was seen as an untamed wilderness.

The blame for this can be dropped squarely at Sir Ferdinando Gorges's feet. In 1622 he was granted the territory between the Piscataqua and Kennebec Rivers—or about half of the modern state of Maine—but he left his province to flounder without any stable leadership, making it unattractive to permanent settlers. In 1631 a small group of men arrived with a patent to settle at Sagadahoc, but "not liking the place" went to Boston instead.[12] They were not the only ones. It became common for ships carrying new settlers to stop in Maine first, and then continue to their final destination somewhere in Massachusetts.[13] Very few of those settlers stayed in Maine. Therefore, the English population in Maine in the 1630s consisted mostly of seasonal fishermen and a few independent families who could withstand life in the "wilderness," while their neighbors to the south were flourishing in a rapidly expanding economy.

The settlers of Plymouth who were seeking religious freedom were also Puritans, though technically they were Separatists because they wanted to completely "separate" from the Church of England rather than reform and "purify" it. In many instances they were more tolerant of religious differences than the Puritans, who had a very narrow and rigid definition of appropriate behavior and religious practices. The Puritans' efforts to reform the Church of England were adding to the divisiveness between Parliamentarians eager for change and Royalists loyal to the monarchy and the church.

This certainly worked in the Wawenock's favor. The large influx of settlers to Boston and the bay area caused tension with the Indigenous populations there as the English encroached on their land and tried to force them

Governor John Winthrop of the Massachusetts Bay Colony. Reprinted with permission from the National Portrait Gallery, Smithsonian Institution, gift of Dr. and Mrs. R. Ted Steinbock.[14]

to conform to the Puritan way of life. Wabanaki people did not suffer the same problem in the early years, because there was a smaller Native population and plenty of land for the relatively few colonists who lived there. Also, the Wawenock were not subjected to religious conversion like many Natives in southern New England were forced to undergo. With no clergy around, they were left to themselves. Generally, the Wawenock and other Wabanaki lived in harmony with the newcomers. In a way, they could thank the Puritans for drawing the vast majority of immigrants away from their shores.

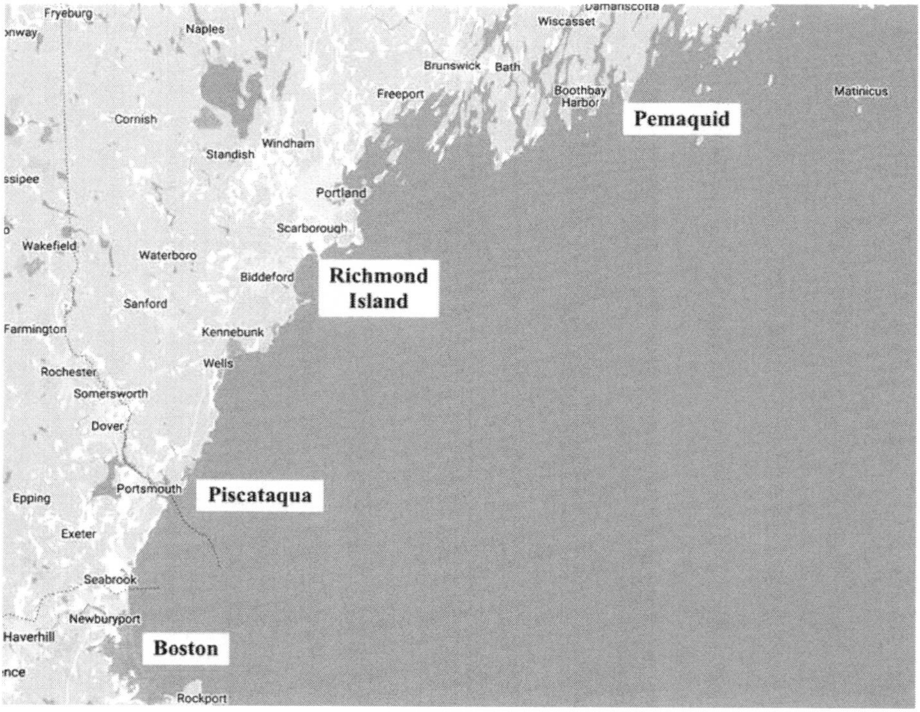

On May 11, 1855, a farmer and his son were plowing a field on Richmond Island and discovered a treasure: a broken pot filled with a ring and English coins dating from the reigns of Queen Elizabeth I to Charles I. It is believed that Walter Bagnall buried this ill-gotten loot near his trading post. COLLECTIONS OF MAINE HISTORICAL SOCIETY, ACCESSION # 819*—SOURCE FILE[15]

Of course, conflict happened as it always does when people live together, whether they are from different backgrounds or not. In one famous case a greedy trader named Walter Bagnall and his associate were murdered in the fall of 1631—by a friend of Samoset's. Bagnall had set up a trading post on Richmond Island, south of Pemaquid off the coast of present-day Cape Elizabeth, and in the words of John Winthrop, Sr., the first governor of the Massachusetts Bay Colony, he was "a wicked fellow, and had much wronged the Indians."[16] This was quite an admission coming from an Englishman, who were not inclined to side with a Native person over one of their own. Bagnall had been swindling the Wabanaki for years, and they finally had enough of it. The murderer, according to Winthrop, was "an Indian sagamore, called Squidrayset, and his company"; this was Scitterygussett, or Skedraguscett in Christopher Levett's account.[17] He was one of the sagamores who had tried to convince Levett to remain in the country. Now, he was carrying out Wabanaki justice. Bagnall was guilty, so he was punished.

Scitterygussett was taking a big risk by killing an Englishman because there was no precedent for it. Maybe he thought there would be no retaliation since no one was in charge—there was no constable, no judge, and no court at that time in Maine to hold him accountable. The Piscataqua colony in present-day Portsmouth, being the closest law enforcement body to Richmond Island (though still over fifty miles away), had to send men to deal with the problem. As it turned out, Scitterygussett was not punished and another paid the price for Bagnall's murder, albeit a year later when there was another manhunt—this time for pirates.

The fact that Pemaquid was sacked by pirates is evidence that it was flourishing. By 1632 Abraham Shurt's trading post was ripe for plunder, though he never expected to be robbed by another Englishman. Dixie Bull came to New England initially as a fur trader; he had, in fact, just been awarded a patent of land in Maine by Sir Ferdinando Gorges, so he may have planned to settle in the area.[18] His plans were dashed however when he ran afoul of some Frenchmen in Penobscot Bay who seized his boat and trade goods, leaving him destitute. Apparently, the honest route back to prosperity took too long, so he turned to piracy instead. Alcohol may have boosted his confidence. Piracy—or more euphemistically "privateering"—was common and not particularly offensive when practiced on an enemy, but Dixie Bull broke the rules when he and his crew of fifteen men, some of them detained against their will, began attacking English boats. Then they set their sights on Pemaquid.

The trading post at Pemaquid was protected by a stockade locally referred to as Shurt's Fort.[19] Shurt would have been most concerned about protecting the settlement from the French and raiding Mi'kmaq—not from one of his own countrymen. In fact Shurt may have known Dixie Bull and his men from their trading expeditions up and down the coast, making it possible that he welcomed the pirates into the fort, unaware of their new vocation. Bull and his men seized more than £500 of goods (approximately $118,000 in today's American dollars), but just as they were pulling anchor and preparing to get away a shot rang out from the fort.[20] One of Bull's men was

Pirate Dixie Bull, reenacted by James L. Nelson at Colonial Pemaquid State Historic Site.

killed, creating panic among the pirates. They managed to get away, but the bloodshed caused them to rethink things. After the looting at Pemaquid they politely paid for everything they took, and even banned excessive drinking. Dixie Bull was never captured, and no one knows for sure what happened to him; some think he went over to the French, while others think he made it safely back to England. It seems fitting that the fate of this misguided man, the first official English pirate in New England waters, is shrouded in mystery. His mystique has barely diminished over the centuries.

There is no evidence that Samoset was present during the pirate attack, but he would have certainly seen its after-effects. The English were unsettled. Law enforcement had to come all the way from the colonies in Piscataqua or Massachusetts Bay, which took months—when it came at all—leaving them terribly vulnerable. Not only might the pirates return, but they also feared a French attack. The French had recently plundered the Plymouth colony's trading post at Penobscot, and Pemaquid could be next. And now there was growing animosity among the Wabanaki because the English executed the wrong man for Walter Bagnall's murder.

A posse had been put together to hunt for Dixie Bull, and the men stopped at Richmond Island where Bagnall was killed. Though they did not find the pirates they did find a Native man nicknamed Black Will. Without evidence or a trial, they hanged him as punishment for Bagnall's murder, simply because they found him on the island.[21] Black Will was innocent, and word of the injustice spread throughout Indigenous communities in New England, stoking anger and retaliation. Anglo-Wabanaki relations began to fray, and the settlers in Maine now had four threats in their midst: pirates, the French, Mi'kmaq raiders, and their Wabanaki neighbors.[22]

The residents of Pemaquid were lucky to have the calm and steady leadership of Abraham Shurt to help them through these anxious times. He skillfully handled disagreements that arose not only among the English but among the Wabanaki as well.[23] In 1631 he was asked to negotiate the release of a sagamore's wife who had been captured in a Mi'kmaq raid in Massachusetts Bay.[24] Shurt arranged for her safe return for a ransom of wampum and furs. By dealing fairly and honestly with all parties, he cemented his reputation among Native people as a decent Englishman. This may account for why there were no Native uprisings at Pemaquid while he was the agent there. No doubt he recognized that the English situation at Pemaquid was rather precarious, with the French breathing down their necks on the eastern border, Natives all around them, and help from Piscataqua and Boston far away. He realized that the colony's chances of survival—not to mention financial success—were greater if he maintained friendly relations on all fronts.

While the English worried about pirates, the French, and possible Wabanaki attacks, the Wabanaki were about to face a new challenge of their own: the smallpox epidemic of 1633–1634. This time the disease was positively identified by Europeans who knew the symptoms. Smallpox was a virgin soil pathogen with a high mortality rate, and it quickly devastated Indigenous communities that had no immunity to it. William Bradford documented that one community on the Connecticut River lost 950 of its 1,000 members. He described their suffering:

> For want of bedding and linen and other comforts, they fall into a lamentable condition. As they lie on their hard mats, the pox breaks and matters and runs, their skin sticking to the mats they lie on, so that when they turn a whole side will flay off at once, and they will be all one gore of blood, dreadful to behold...They were swept so generally by the disease that in the end they were unable to help one another, or to make a fire or fetch a little water to drink, or to bury their dead.[25]

We can infer that the Wawenock were also affected based on a comment in 1634 by the trader on Richmond Island who replaced Walter Bagnall: "There is a great many of the Indians dead this year, both east and west from us, & a great many dies to the eastward from us."[26] Having already been the victims of one deadly epidemic, they must have been unnerved by this new one. Why were they being punished again? Once more the English—who were probably exposed to smallpox as children—were barely affected by the outbreak. While some Englishmen were glad that the epidemic cleared the land of the "savages," more charitable colonists helped those who were sick. Bradford praised his countrymen for their kindness to the suffering Natives: "But the people of the English trading-house, though they were at first afraid of the infection, seeing their woeful condition and hearing their pitiful cries, had compassion on them, and daily fetched them wood and water and made them fires, and got them food whilst they lived, and buried them when they died."[27] The survivors would not forget these acts of charity.

Smallpox would become a great killer of Indigenous people in America, resurfacing with alarming regularity for the next 200 years, even being used as a weapon of war against them.[28] Samoset survived this second wave of death, but how many others did not? His wife, his son? Nor could the Wawenock easily forget the trauma since smallpox left behind disfiguring scars. In some cases, it caused blindness. As their leader and someone who had been down this road before, Samoset had to find a way to help his weakened people once again regain their strength.

18

ALCOHOL, GUNS, A REBELLION, AND A HURRICANE, 1635

As the English expanded their trading and fishing operations, the Wawenock did their best to recover from the smallpox epidemic. There was nothing else to do but carry on. They may have been so diminished in number that Abraham Shurt had to cast his net wider for fur suppliers, because it was around this time that he expanded his trading partners to include the Kennebec and Penobscot.[1] Perhaps the business had simply outgrown the Wawenock's ability to meet the demand. Shurt was selling furs both to the European market and a burgeoning market in Boston; the Puritans were quickly becoming his best customers.[2] Now the Wawenock shared their home with Kennebec and Penobscot traders—who probably brought their families with them as well. This would have been unthinkable three decades earlier when they fought the Kennebec during the Mi'kmaq War, but in the wake of so much death it appears they were able to put aside old grievances.

Shurt stocked his trading post with goods that would entice the Kennebec and Penobscot away from the trading posts in their own territories. The Wabanaki had moved on from trinkets, feathers, mirrors, and bells that first fascinated them to practical things like "cloth, foodstuffs, clay smoking pipes and tobacco, shot, powder, kettles, axes, liquor, and beads."[3] This says a great deal about how life had changed for the Wabanaki. Now they used blankets for warmth and linen to "clean their infants."[4] They bought cloth to make clothing rather than use animal skins, either because they preferred it or because they were selling all the skins they trapped, hunted, and processed. The same could be said of food and tobacco; either they preferred what the English were selling, or they grew less of it to concentrate on fur production. We know that the trader on Richmond Island was selling coats, shirts, stockings, and shoes to the Wabanaki, and Shurt may have sold those items too.[5] European goods, clothing—and nicknames—were status symbols to the Wabanaki. Samoset, or "Captain John Somerset" as the English called him, probably took to smoking tobacco from a European pipe and wearing some articles of English clothing.

Glass beads were the English substitute for wampum, which had become hugely popular among the Wabanaki. Wampum (or wampumpeag) was a white or purple bead made primarily from quahog, periwinkle, and whelk shells found in Long Island Sound and Narragansett Bay. Natives used wampum to make decorative items like bracelets, necklaces, or belts.[6] Before 1630, wampum was quite rare in Maine and considered nearly sacred. Wampum artifacts were used to commemorate a treaty or were "worn by religious and political leaders on special occasions."[7] We saw this in 1605 when the men sent by Bashabes to meet George Waymouth were wearing "bracelets of little white round bone, fastened together upon a leather string."[8]

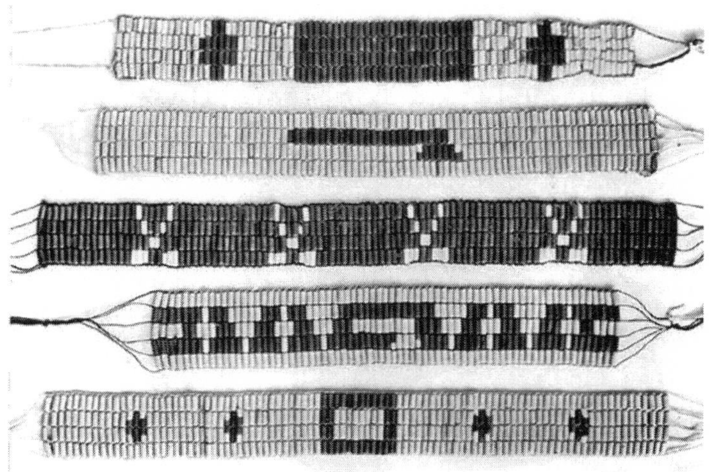

Reproductions of Penobscot ceremonial wampum belts. The mostly white belts signify peace, and the mostly blue belt denotes conflict. [9]

The colonists from Plymouth introduced large quantities of wampum at their trading post on the Kennebec River, hoping that it would become the fashion for everyone to wear, not just political and religious leaders. It took a couple of years to catch on, but once it did Bradford likened it to a drug.[10] The English imported glass beads hoping to sell them as an alternative to wampum, but wampum itself remained popular for decades.[11]

The English lost their military advantage when they taught Indigenous men how to use firearms, who quickly surpassed them in accuracy and skill. This was not difficult, because most Englishmen had very little experience with guns. Hunting was a rich man's pastime, and even the nobleman left the killing to his birds of prey and hunting dogs.[14] Though all Englishmen were required to train to be battle ready in case they were called up for war, they learned to shoot as part of a volley into a crowd of opposing soldiers, not at an individual.[15] Aim was less important than being able to reload quickly. Indigenous men, on the other hand, had to shoot accurately when they were hunting or they would go hungry, and the skill transferred well to warfare. They also knew better than to cluster together and present a large target to their enemy, thereby taking the advantage in the field.

Bradford's use of the word "drug" also applied to another staple of the trade business, which was alcohol. This was probably rum or brandy, strong stuff meant for hard drinking. The Wawenock were first exposed to it by Waymouth's crew in 1605, which they tasted "but would by no means drink."[12] But by 1624 Sir Ferdinando Gorges was complaining to Parliament that fishermen were teaching Native men "to drink drunk...and in their drunken humor to fall together by the ears, thereby giving them occasion to seek revenge."[13]

Alcohol was the Achilles heel of the Wabanaki and many other Indigenous communities. Why it became such a problem, one that has persisted for centuries, is open to question, but the reference to fishermen "teaching" them to drink until they were drunk is perhaps revealing. The Wabanaki were introduced to liquor by fishermen who drank heavily, and by unscrupulous traders who got them drunk so they could cheat them. The ones pushing alcohol were "self-selected communities of men, away from their families and from the reach of alcohol policies and other forms of social control"—in other words, men behaving badly with no moderating influences.[16] It was a rough way for the Wabanaki to start. There were few good role models to teach them to go easy, and they had no idea about alcohol's long-term effects.

The English quickly regretted introducing alcohol to Indigenous people. It made their behavior unpredictable, and at times violent. One colonist voiced disgust with his countrymen for "infecting" them with strong drink: "[S]ome of our English who to unclothe them of their beaver coat clad them with the infection of swearing and drinking, which was never in fashion with them before, it being contrary to their nature to guzzle down strong drink...until our bestial example and dishonest incitation hath too much brought them to it."[17] Colonies began to outlaw the sale of it to Native people, but the laws were difficult to enforce. Too many people were profiting from the trade to stop it.

Guns fell into the same category. The Mi'kmaq first used them in the war against the Mawooshen alliance in 1607, which opened Pandora's box. Though used primarily for hunting, every Wabanaki man needed a firearm to be on equal footing with his enemy. The English blamed the French for introducing guns to the Wabanaki, claiming a Frenchman would sell "his eyes" for beaver, but Englishmen were also guilty of supplying them with weapons.[18] This was in spite of royal proclamations in 1622 and 1630 making it illegal to sell or trade weapons of any kind to Indigenous people, or teach them how to use or repair them.[19] But proclamations from far across the ocean did little to stop illegal trafficking. The colonists wanted furs and Native people wanted guns, no matter what it took to get them.

This all leads back to Abraham Shurt and the trade going on at Pemaquid. There is no record that Shurt was selling guns and alcohol to the Wabanaki, but of course there would not be because it was illegal. However, there is evidence that Shurt was engaged in other illicit practices, namely colluding with the French.

In 1671 the French used John Brown's house in New Harbor to mark what they realistically considered to be the western boundary of Acadia.[20]

The English and French were nearly always at war, but for the moment a delicate peace existed between them. The most recent treaty of 1632 left the

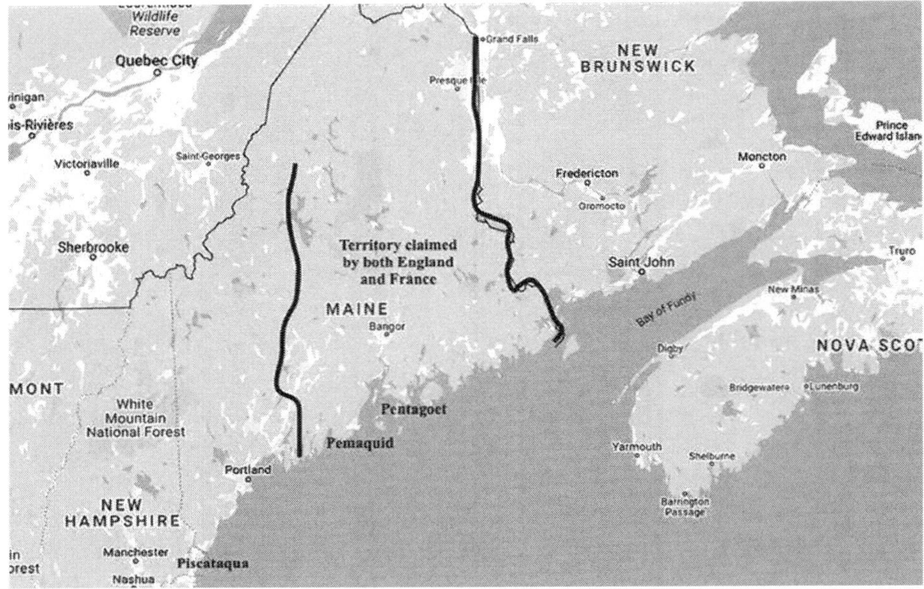

boundary between the English territory of New England and the French territory of Acadia in dispute; the English claimed the boundary was the St. Croix River, while the French claimed it was the Kennebec River, putting Pemaquid in the territory claimed by both.[21] It was an uncomfortable situation for the settlers in Pemaquid, given they were located closer to the French fort at Pentagoet (present-day Castine) than the closest English colony at Piscataqua (Portsmouth, New Hampshire).

Shurt handled the situation by making friends with his enemy. It made perfect sense as a matter of survival. The French wanted trade goods they could not get from home because the mother country was bogged down in another war, and Shurt wanted more furs than the Wabanaki in his area could provide. The French had access to a good supply of furs in the north, so the partnership would benefit them both. By trading with the French, Shurt was protecting Pemaquid better than a stockade fort and a few cannons could ever do—it took away the risk of plunder. He was also making a good profit for his employers.

Shurt was not the only Englishman trading with the French; Massachusetts Bay merchants were too. William Bradford condemned his fellow Englishmen for selling out to their longtime enemy, who had just seized their trading post in Penobscot Bay. (The French claimed it was their right to take it because the post was in French territory, and the Plymouth colonists did not have the power to contest it.) In the case of Pemaquid, Bradford's denunciation was even more harsh: "[T]he colony at Pemaquid...not only supplies them [the French], but constantly gives them intelligence of what is passing among the English."[22] Shurt did not just trade goods with the French, *he passed valuable information to them*. He was walking a fine line by giving intelligence to a former adversary, and if the two countries had been at war he never would have gotten away with it. Shurt gave the French commander of Fort Pentagoet "royal entertainment," which was reported to both Governor Bradford and Governor Winthrop.[23] They were keeping an eye on him.

As for Samoset and the Wawenock, they now shared their home not only with the English, the Kennebec, and the Penobscot, but also with the French. It must have been a busy place.

Intrigue and back channels were the order of the day, not only in New England but in old England as well, where Sir Ferdinando Gorges and other Royalists were trying to suppress the influence of the Puritans. At issue was the Puritans' increasing power and independence; if they could move to New England, set up their own government, and practice religion however they wanted, what was to stop others from doing the same? Or spreading the idea back to England? The King and the Church of England were at risk of losing control. The Great Migration proved that even the dangerous Atlantic crossing would not deter other Englishmen from following in the Puritans' footsteps. And these were hardly society's outcasts; many of the best and the brightest were leaving the country and taking their talents and resources with them.[24]

Sir Ferdinando and other Royalists sought to discredit the Puritans by accusing them of preaching sedition.[25] Though this strategy did not work, it was not in Sir Ferdinando's nature to give up easily. There was soon another plan in the works, one so bold that it nearly sparked a revolt in Boston.

Sir Ferdinando joined forces with a powerful new ally in England, the Archbishop of Canterbury William Laud, who had the ear of King Charles and a single-minded zeal to protect the Church of England's authority. Laud was finally able to convince the King to crush the Puritans' growing supremacy, and nothing less than a complete shake-up would be sufficient to knock them back on their heels.

With Laud's encouragement, the King appointed a new commission and gave its members the power to completely disassemble all colonial governments in New England. They would reset everything, beginning with the Council for New England itself, which would be dissolved and re-formed. Noblemen would once again own the land, and serfs would work it for them—no more allowing the common man to become a landowner and participate in representative government.[26] The territory of New England would be reapportioned—again—to eight of the King's loyal supporters who would receive new patents to the land.[27] Sir Ferdinando was instrumental in designing the new government and, as he fully expected, was appointed its first royal governor. He was finally going to New England, and the Puritan "experiment" would be over.

When Governor Winthrop of the Massachusetts Bay Colony learned late in 1634 about the King's commission and its plan to strip the colonies of their autonomy, he called together the ministers of all the congregations in the bay area to discuss what to do. Their decision would have been considered treasonous. They agreed that if a royal governor—in this case Sir Ferdinando Gorges—were sent to rule over them they would repulse him, and they would defend themselves against the intrusion if necessary.[28] To this end they quickly built fortifications in Dorchester, Charlestown, Fort Hill, and on Castle Island in Boston Harbor, and set up a commission to oversee all military affairs. They were preparing for Boston's first rebellion.[29]

Samoset would have been unaware of the intrigues and political maneuverings going on in England and Boston. Things were going relatively well in Pemaquid, where Abraham Shurt was simply trying to run a business, not overthrow the government. By 1635, the Wawenock were one year past the smallpox epidemic and were just regaining their footing, so the hurricane that bore down on them that summer was another devastating blow.

The Great Colonial Hurricane of 1635, a storm like no one had ever seen, has special significance in Pemaquid because of the destruction it caused. We will never know the full extent of the damage, especially to the Wawenock, but the storm is famous for sinking the 240-ton galleon *Angel Gabriel,* which had arrived in Pemaquid just ahead of the storm. She was smashed to pieces while anchored in the harbor with one seaman and three or four passengers still on board, who all perished.

The *Angel Gabriel* had a distinguished history. Sir Walter Raleigh sailed her on his second voyage to Guiana, South America in 1617 on an ill-fated search for El

Dorado; she was also famous for defeating three Spanish warships in battle in 1627.[30] The ship was now owned by Gyles Elbridge. Armed with fourteen or sixteen cannons, she could defend herself against attack but was a little slow due to the extra weight. On this voyage to Pemaquid she carried cattle and goods to re-stock Shurt's trading post and passengers destined for Massachusetts. The *Angel Gabriel* left the port of Bristol, England on June 4 along with four other ships headed to America. But not before they received a very distinguished visitor.

On May 27, while the *Angel Gabriel* sat in port waiting for favorable winds, Sir Ferdinando Gorges came aboard to see the passengers off and wish them well. He had moved from Plymouth to Bristol around 1629 when he married his fourth wife, who had an estate there. His visit was more political than social. He asked if there were any passengers going to Massachusetts Bay—the seat of sedition, he had been claiming for years—not to admonish or threaten them as they might have expected, but to "profess his good will to the people there in the bay, and promised that if he ever came there he would be a true friend unto them."[31] They were probably astounded, given how hard he had campaigned against them. They may not have known that Sir Ferdinando had been appointed their new governor, because it had only been announced the previous day.[32] In fact it is doubtful they knew about the imminent takeover of New England by the Royalists, for why would they risk the journey only to be subject to the same oppressive laws they were hoping to leave behind in England?

Warren C. Riess, marine archaeologist and Associate Research Professor Emeritus at the University of Maine, tried for years to locate the remains of the *Angel Gabriel*. He and a crew of volunteers extensively searched and mapped the inner and outer harbors at Pemaquid and the nearby coastline over the course of fifteen years starting in the 1970s, yet they found no trace of the wreck. Riess wrote a book about his efforts entitled *Angel Gabriel, The Elusive English Galleon*. Another group of researchers took up the hunt in 2018, but as of now the wreck of the *Angel Gabriel* remains lost.[33]

Sir Ferdinando was making an effort to smooth the transition to his leadership. He was not a tyrant; he sincerely thought the feudal model was better, and he wanted to change regimes peacefully—though it was rumored he was bringing 1,000 soldiers with him.[34]

The Atlantic crossing for the *Angel Gabriel* was long but mostly uneventful, and she arrived in Pemaquid by August 14. Most of the passengers disembarked and found temporary accommodations on shore. Early on the morning of the 15th, just as day was breaking, the hurricane hit. William Bradford described it as "a fearful storm of wind and rain as none living hereabouts either English or Indians ever saw."[35] It came on suddenly with amazing violence, creating waves up to 20 feet so that "many of the Indians had to climb trees for safety." Eight Narragansett in southern New England drowned trying to flee their wigwams. The winds ripped roofs off houses or blew them down altogether, pulled trees out by their roots and snapped others in half. Physical scars from the storm, especially in tree damage, would last for many years to come.[36] The legendary *Angel Gabriel*, pounded by ferocious waves, broke apart, pouring her contents of cattle, goods, and remaining passengers into the sea.

The loss of the *Angel Gabriel* and its cargo was a heavy financial blow to Gyles Elbridge, who was now the sole owner of the Pemaquid patent. (Robert Aldworth had died the year before and left his share of the enterprise to Elbridge.) While he tried to recoup his loss, the people of Pemaquid began the long process of recovering from the storm.

Because it was August, the Wawenock would have been living in Pemaquid in their wigwams by the shore. A hurricane like that would have created torrents of rain, 100 mph winds that knocked them off their feet, trees falling all around them, and a possible storm surge of 20 feet. The Wawenock had to flee for their lives. Given the severity of the storm, they may have lost their homes, their possessions, and their crops. Yet again, Samoset and the Wawenock set about rebuilding their lives.

In an interesting twist of fate, Sir Ferdinando Gorges never made it to New England. The great ship that was built to transport him and his troops fell to pieces in launching.[37] Then England plunged headlong into the chaos of civil war and the country's attention turned away from the colonies in North America, and Sir Ferdinando's plan faltered. The rebellion of 1635 was averted and the Puritans credited God with delivering them from their "adversaries."[38] How differently things might have turned out if the hand of fate had tipped the scale in Sir Ferdinando's favor instead.

19

CHANGES IN THE LAND, CIVIL WAR, RECESSION, AND THE JESUITS, 1636-1653

Sir Ferdinando Gorges, sure enough in his faith that God was not against him, saw the breaking apart of his ship only as a setback and not the end of his dreams for New England. While he regrouped, he sent his thirty-year old nephew William Gorges to act as governor of New Somersetshire—Sir Ferdinando's new but short-lived name for the province of Maine. This was far from his ultimate goal of bringing the Puritans into line, but it was a step on the path to a royal colony. William set up the first government of Maine in Saco in 1636, which must have come as a welcome relief to the colonists who would no longer have to rely on distant Piscataqua and Boston for support. He brought craftsmen "for the building of houses, and erecting of sawmills" to launch Maine's lumber industry.[1] His other contribution was to open Maine's first court. One of the first laws passed at the Saco court gave the settlers "power & authority to execute any Indians that are proved to have killed any swine of the English."[2] Like his cousin Robert, William stayed in New England only one year.

Meanwhile migration to Maine continued at a slow but steady pace, and by the middle of the decade there were a few new settlements—Saco, Pejepscot (Brunswick), Agamenticus (York), Cape Porpoise, Kittery, Scarborough, Falmouth, Sheepscot—but the population was still small and scattered, with

Maine salt marsh. REPRINTED WITH PERMISSION FROM TOM GROENING, *THE WORKING WATERFRONT*[3]

only around 700 colonists in 1640 compared to 14,000 in Massachusetts.[4] The animal population, in contrast, was growing much faster.

Domesticated animals were extremely important to every settler's life and economic prosperity. Settlers used the wool from their sheep to make clothing, horses for transportation, oxen to pull their plows, pigs for meat, chickens for eggs and meat, goats for meat and dairy, and cattle for meat, dairy, and hides. There was no need for an Englishman to hunt, except to round up his hogs when it was time to butcher them. Maine was a terrific place to breed animals because there was so much space for them to forage. And with thousands of miles of coastline and tidal rivers, Maine had an abundance of salt marsh grass that could be cut for hay.

For early settlers who had been breeding animals for a few years, it was a prosperous time because they could sell their spare livestock to new immigrants. William Bradford happily reported in 1638 that the influx of new people enriched his colony as cows were selling at £20, and sometimes as high as £28.[5]

In Pemaquid, Abraham Shurt got into the livestock business on behalf of proprietor Gyles Elbridge, and he employed men, women, and children to care for the animals and tend crops to feed the whole settlement.[6]

Great change came with the livestock, and it came quickly. Grazing animals require up to ten times more land than that used for farming, so settlers had to spread out.[7] Within four years of their arrival in Boston, some Puritans began to request permission to move to Connecticut, complaining they did not have enough land for their cattle.[8] Inevitably planters and livestock owners began to put more and more pressure on Indigenous people to sell their land.

An unintended consequence of bringing livestock to North America, one that we battle today, was the proliferation of nonnative weeds. They came in the animals' feed and were distributed through their manure. "Dandelions, chickweeds, bloodworts, mulleins, mallows, nightshades, and stinging nettles" all found fertile ground. European grasses that had adapted to livestock's heavy grazing habits quickly replaced native species. Indigenous people called plaintain 'Englishman's Foot' because it seemed to spring up wherever an Englishman walked. Ragweed, native but less common 400 years ago, exploded under the new conditions. Thorny, woody plants that could only be dug up with a plow thrived in the newly trampled and compacted soil.[9]

The weed plaintain, nicknamed "Englishman's foot" or "white man's foot" by Indigenous people.[10]

Animals were not responsible for all of the changes to the land; farmers also made an impact by overworking the soil. They tilled and planted several acres thanks to efficient oxen and plows, and their favorite crop was corn which had a high yield but quickly exhausted the soil. Indigenous planters grew beans and squash with their corn which put nutrients back into the earth, and they could move to a new field when the exhausted one stopped producing. English planters practiced monoculture and were limited to the fields they owned, so they tended to overwork them.[11] Thus their fields became less and less productive over time.

By far the most dramatic change to the land resulted from cutting down thousands of acres of forests. Europeans used wood in a myriad of ways: to build their houses, ships, furniture, and barrels; to make fences to contain their animals and mark their property boundaries; to build fires to heat their homes and cook their food. Back in England they were using coal to heat their homes because they had wiped out their forests, and here was a supply that seemed limitless. Rather than learning from their mistakes, however, they used wood as if it would never run out. Colonists built large houses because they had large families—the average number of children was 5.4 for the first generation of colonists and grew to 7.1 in following generations.[12] Their large houses not only took more wood to build but more firewood to heat. Environmental historian William Cronon estimated that a typical New England colonial family burned as much as thirty to forty cords of firewood per year, which would be "a stack of wood four feet wide, four feet high, and three hundred feet long." Each household had to cut down an entire acre of trees to heat its home every year.[13]

The colonists should have realized that with such extensive cutting they would over harvest the trees. In the more populated areas it only took ten to fifteen years before the trees were gone. Boston was running short by 1638, only eight years after the Puritans arrived. Town officials tried to regulate private cutting but it did not stop the practice, and eventually settlers had to purchase lumber and firewood far from home.[14] Certain species of trees were essentially wiped out along the coast because of their desirability: white and black oak for shipbuilding, general carpentry, and barrel staves; cedar for shingles, clapboards, and fences; pitch pine for pitch, turpentine, and resin; and majestic, tall white pines, some up to 200 feet in height, for Royal Navy masts.[15]

Massachusetts Bay towns turned to their northern neighbors for their wood supply. The provinces of New Hampshire and Maine, with their vast forests and access to rivers and the ocean for easy transportation, became lumber exporters as early as the 1630s.[16] Sawmills began to spring up on most rivers, and Pemaquid may have gotten its first grist and sawmills by the middle of the century.[17] A canal measuring about 10 feet wide, 4–5 feet deep, and 250–330 feet long was dug around the falls about three miles north of Pemaquid Beach, presumably to route water to the mills.[18]

Because of the lower population density in Maine, people there were somewhat less affected than their southern neighbors by the changes that were happening to the environment, but they experienced them all the same. Samoset and the Wawenock would have felt the differences intimately because of their familiarity with the land. Slowly, their summers began to get hotter and their winters colder.

Mass deforestation had a profound effect—it changed the way the land's inhabitants experienced the climate. This happened over time and Samoset may not have seen all of these changes, but the ecological disturbance began during his lifetime. By cutting down so many trees, the colonists laid the land bare to the sun and wind. This caused the earth to become warmer through more exposure to the sun and drier because moisture evaporated more quickly. In the winter the temperature felt colder due to increased windchill, since there were no trees to block the wind. Winter also seemed shorter because snow melted more quickly without shade from trees. With no protective blanket of fallen leaves and snow, the soil froze more deeply and could not absorb as much snow melt and spring rain. The result was increased flooding that drained off quickly; springs and streams began to dry up.[19]

Some animals had difficulty adapting to the changing habitats. Deer, for example, could not compete with English livestock for forage, and their numbers began to decline. The Wabanaki made the situation worse when they began to put pressure on animal populations by over hunting them. In pre-contact times, they only killed what they needed for their own food and clothing. Now they wanted "prestige goods"—wampum, kettles, blankets, European foodstuffs, cloth, guns, ammunition, and alcohol—that they could only get through trade, and the desire for them caused Native people to 'waste their animals' in the words of one Indigenous man.[20] Guns made their hunting more efficient, so that within a few decades they had nearly decimated the populations of deer, wild turkeys, elk, lynx, and bears.[22]

Colonists founds wolves to be a nuisance when they developed a taste for English livestock. In 1640 the court at York offered a bounty of 12 pence for any wolf killed, a practice that continued at different times in Maine's history. This wiped out the wolf population in the state.[21]

Beavers remained the Wabanaki's number one prey, but with low reproductive rates they could not withstand the onslaught of increased trapping.[23] As beavers disappeared, so did the dams and ponds they built. Pond habitats that supported ducks, geese, turkeys, mink, otter, turtles, and other wildlife began to dry up.[24] The rich soil left behind made terrific hay fields and farmland, making it more desirable to English farmers who put pressure on the local people to sell it.[25]

It became a circle of destruction Native people could not escape. Miantonomo, a Narragansett sagamore of Rhode Island, summed it up best in 1642: "[O]ur fathers had plenty of deer, & skins, our plains were full of deer as also our woods and of turkeys, and our coves full of fish and fowl, but these English having gotten our land, they with scythes cut down the grass, and their hogs spoil our clambanks, and we shall all be starved."[26]

The Wawenock had little choice but to adapt to the changes. In addition to skills they already possessed, they acquired new ones. Early journalists wrote that Indigenous people learned trades like making shingles and clapboards or repairing weapons and raising livestock.[27] The Wawenock may have hired themselves out as laborers. Perhaps Wawenock men worked at the Pemaquid sawmill or helped dig the canal; maybe women took on sewing jobs or tended the settlement's gardens. To survive in a market economy, they had to find new ways to fit into and contribute to the marketplace.

Sir Ferdinando Gorges received good news in 1639 when King Charles I upgraded his charter to the province of New Somersetshire (the name would revert permanently to Maine). The King granted him such sweeping privileges over his province that he essentially became 'an uncrowned monarch in a little kingdom of his own,' but it would come to nothing.[28] The English monarchy was teetering on the edge of a cliff and was just about to go over, and it would take Sir Ferdinando's authority with it.

The spirited knight still had every intention of going to Maine in spite of the fact that he was now more than 70 years old. Still needed in England, however, he sent his 22-year-old cousin, Thomas Gorges, as deputy governor of the province in 1640. It was an interesting choice, because Thomas was sympathetic to the Parliamentarians. This would be the third Gorges to try to establish civil government in Maine, this time based in York. It was a tall order for the young, newly minted attorney who had no experience governing. Sir Ferdinando decided to make York his grand city, the capital of all New England, yet when Thomas arrived he found nothing at all grand about it. The house that had been built to be Sir Ferdinando's residence was more like a barn, with no glass windows and furnished with only "one crock, two bedsteads & a table board." The garden was already in ruins, the field had no fence, and the grist and sawmills had fallen into disrepair.[29] It was a far cry from the glorious "City upon a hill" that the Puritans were building in Boston.[30]

To his credit, Thomas worked hard to put things right. By September, the sawmill was cutting 250 feet of lumber per tide.[31] As the resident lawyer and deputy governor he presided over the court at York, where he faced the likes of Reverend George Burdett, a charismatic but morally suspect minister who was accused of having improper relations with several married women.[32] Gorges held his ground against the licentious minister, and Burdett left the province. This left them without Burdett's spiritual guidance, though that may have been a good thing. Thomas tried (but ultimately failed) to entice a new clergyman to come to Maine; he also tried to convert the local Wabanaki to Christianity, but in that he failed as well. They were happy with their own religion and probably not impressed with the dubious ethics of the disgraced clergyman. After a few months in the country Gorges made this assessment of the province of Maine: "Long have these poor people groaned for want of government. Sin hath reigned uncontrolled. Justly hath it been termed the receptacle of vicious men. But now civil government is in its infancy...& I doubt not by the assistance of God but sin's head shall be cut off."[33] He may have been just the man to finally bring English law and order to Maine, but he did not stay long enough to finish the task.

The crisis that had been in the making between the Royalists and the Parliamentarians finally erupted late in 1640. An uprising in Scotland forced King Charles I to reopen Parliament after an eleven-year suspension, and the Parliamentarians seized the opportunity to bring charges against the King's top two advisors. Both were arrested, convicted of crimes against the state, and executed. One was Archbishop Laud, would-be reorganizer of New England and ally of Sir Ferdinando Gorges. The Parliamentarians—who leaned heavily toward Puritanism—had taken control and were clearing out their enemies. Sir Ferdinando was in an extremely precarious position.

The effect was felt almost immediately in New England. Now that Parliament was open and the King's power had been curbed, there was no need for those who had felt oppressed by his policies to leave the country. Migration to New England decreased dramatically and some settlers in New England began to pack up and return to England. With fewer settlers buying goods and no influx of new money, New England fell into recession. Cattle that had once sold for £20–30 now sold for £4–5, if a buyer could be found at all.[34] Ships in England "swung idly at their anchors waiting for passengers who never came" while in Boston fish lay unsold "for want of a ship to carry it to a market." Suddenly the settlers—and the Wawenock—were cut off from goods they had become dependent upon; the trader at Richmond Island lamented "The Country is very poor & out of clothes & linen & woolen & have not wherewith to buy."[35]

Adding to the misery, the winter of 1641–1642 was the coldest in Wabanaki memory, so extreme that fish and fowl froze in the sea and parts of Massachusetts Bay froze solid enough for horses and carts to drive over it.[36] The Wabanaki would have found hunting difficult that winter, and their troubles led to desperation, then anger. In 1642 the Wabanaki in Maine—and Indigenous people all around New England—were threatening to rise up against the English.

Thomas Gorges wrote to Sir Ferdinando in September that "the country is in great fear of the Indians. They have all combined themselves together from Penobscot to the [South?] to cut off the English. These meetings are often, dangerous words have they vented." John Winthrop likewise wrote of a rumor that the Indigenous people of southern New England were planning a great attack on the English.[37] Wabanaki men ransacked the house of merchant Thomas Purchase in Pejepscot (Brunswick) and took £15 worth of goods, then plundered two other houses. They may have had good reason to attack Purchase; he was an unscrupulous trader who was convicted of several offenses in the court at York including slander, doctoring the scales he used to weigh furs, and unpaid debts to his fellow Englishmen, including Gyles Elbridge of Pemaquid.[38] After the raid on Purchase the trouble seemed to pass and tensions eased. But it was obvious that the stress of the recession, the hard winter, and years of being mistreated by dishonest traders had stirred up resentment against the English in the old Mawooshen alliance.

The English Civil War officially began with the first armed conflict in 1642. As with most civil wars, neighbors and family members fought against one another, and the Gorges family was no exception. Thomas Gorges left Maine in 1643 to fight for the Parliamentarian cause. Sir Ferdinando, though no longer able to wield a sword, used a pen to help his monarch. He drew up elaborate battle plans that were used by the King's army to assault and conquer his home city of Bristol, which was an important victory for the Royalists.[39] The war teetered back and forth, but by 1645 the Parliamentarians had effectively triumphed and King Charles I was taken captive. He would never rule again.

It was during this time that Sir Ferdinando wrote another account of his efforts to colonize New England. It was his final chance to silence his critics and set the record straight, as he saw it at least. Even though his dream of creating a feudal colony in New England was never realized, there was no self-pity or bitterness in his words, just acceptance of the times and the circumstances of his life.

His vision for the Indigenous people who lived in New England was never realized either. After teaching them the Christian faith, he promised "to build them houses, and to provide them tutors for their breeding, and bringing up of their children, of both sexes" as well as to defend them against their enemies and not take more than what they "are willing we should be seized of."[40] The Wabanaki would have been surprised to hear this because none of these promises was fulfilled.

Fort Gorges in Casco Bay, Maine was completed in 1865 but was obsolete before it was put to use. It is now a park open to the public.[41]

In May 1647, Sir Ferdinando Gorges, loyal servant to the English crown and would-be royal governor of all New England, died at the estate of his wife at Long Ashton, near Bristol.[42] Surprisingly few memorials exist in Maine to the man who was so important to its early colonial history. His legacy has mostly been forgotten, overshadowed by the Puritans of Massachusetts Bay who would eventually take over his entire province. It may have been a blessing that he was not alive to witness that, or the death of his King and the end of the monarchy two years later. King Charles I, charged with treason against his own people, was beheaded on January 30, 1649, the only king in British history to be executed. Parliament took over the rule of the country.

In Pemaquid the more immediate concern was the death of their proprietor Gyles Elbridge in February 1644.[43] The Elbridges were Royalists, and as the royal star fell so did their fortunes. Gyles Elbridge died £3,000 in debt, a huge sum at that time.[44] He bequeathed the Pemaquid Patent to his eldest son John, who lived only two years longer than his father. (The plague was raging again in England, which may explain John's early death.[45]) John's younger brother Thomas, not yet 21 years old, inherited the patent and his father's debt. He would be the first proprietor to make Pemaquid his home, arriving around 1648, but his troubles followed him. In 1650 he was forced to spend five months in a Boston jail for non-payment of debts dating back to the wreck of the *Angel Gabriel* in 1635.

As a result of his financial problems, Thomas Elbridge had to divest himself of the Pemaquid Patent. Wealthy Massachusetts Bay merchants bought it, and other speculators followed, buying large tracts of Maine land as the Puritans' wealth grew. They were the victors in the Civil War, and to them came the spoils.[46] In the meantime homesteaders continued to add to their large families, so that by 1650 Maine had an English population of around 1,000 people.[47] (The Wabanaki population is unknown.) It was still far from the number of settlers in Massachusetts, but enough to encroach upon what was left of the Wabanaki's homeland. English farmers were now less inclined to share usage with them, and more and more the Wabanaki were dispossessed of their land. This was not what they imagined when they signed deeds and made agreements with the settlers.

Samoset and the Wawenock of Pemaquid were most likely struggling too.

By 1653 Samoset had sold three more large parcels of land and they had now lost control of most of their homeland. Samoset was around 63 years old though his age is only a guess, probably based on the estimate that he was 30 years old when he walked into Plymouth Plantation. They had been hard years, but he had guided his people through unprecedented difficulties, and they had survived when so many others had not.[48]

Samoset must have believed that making an alliance with the English was the right choice for the protection and preservation of his people. In the beginning that may have been true when the Wawenock needed European weapons to fight off the Mi'kmaq, but the balance of power shifted uncomfortably to the English when the Wawenock's numbers dwindled and they came to rely heavily on English goods. When fur-bearing animals became increasingly scarce, they realized that soon they would no longer be able to provide the two things the English wanted from them: land and furs. That left few options.

To add to their troubles, they were faced with a new enemy, more fierce and frightening than their old foes, the Mi'kmaq. An enemy that would, in fact, unite them in solidarity with the Mi'kmaq. These were the Mohawk, one of the five Haudenosaunee (Iroquois) peoples, who were aggressively pushing their way into Wabanaki territory to exploit the dwindling beaver market. The Wabanaki lived in fear of them because their warriors had a reputation—deserved or not—for cannibalism and horrible cruelty to their captives. Their raids caused widespread panic and displacement and, consequently, food insecurity when the Wabanaki had to abandon their camps and crops. Here again they could trace their troubles to the Europeans, for the beaver trade had brought this new terror down upon them.

By mid-century the pressure was building on the Wabanaki, and their relationship with the English was becoming more and more dysfunctional. English greed, falseness, and injustice angered them, but what hurt most was the Englishman's racist attitude. Their Wabanaki pride would not bear it. Most Europeans in the 17th century saw the world through a lens of white, Christian supremacy. Even though they often commented about how smart and ingenious Indigenous people were, they could not—or would not—see them as their equals. After all, treating them as inferior was profitable. The Wabanaki felt their contempt keenly—when traders cheated them, or land buyers tricked them, or the English criminal justice system failed to protect them—and they had long memories of injustices suffered. They finally realized that the English were not interested in forming a lasting relationship. They took what they wanted from Native people, then hoped they would just go away.

This was a low moment for the Wabanaki. They had been robbed of their heritage and made to feel inconsequential, and some turned to alcohol to ease their pain. Exploitative traders encouraged their drinking and let them run up debts to pay for it, continuing the cycle of dependency and oppression. They desperately needed a way out of the maelstrom that threatened to engulf them, and it was French Catholics who extended a lifeline.

The Jesuits went to Quebec to convert Indigenous people to the Catholic faith, but they were fighting a losing battle against alcoholism among the Montagnais people of the St. Lawrence River valley. The Montagnais, lamented one priest, loved brandy and wine "with an utterly unrestrained passion, not for the relish they experience in drinking them, but for the pleasure they find in becoming drunk. They imagine in their drunkenness that they are listened to, with attention, that they are great orators, that they are valiant and formidable, that they are looked up to as Chiefs, hence this folly suits them; there is scarcely a Savage, small or great, even among the girls and women, who does not enjoy this intoxication."[49]

The Kennebec people of Maine frequently traveled to Canada to trade wampum for furs with the Montagnais, and it was there they heard about the Jesuits and their efforts to eradicate alcoholism among Native people. They asked the Jesuits to send a "black gown" to their main village of Nanrantsouak (Norridgewock), located north of Augusta on the Kennebec River. Norridgewock had become a gathering place for Wabanaki who were being squeezed off their lands, and may have included some of the Wawenock. The Jesuits saw it as an opportunity to gain more converts, so they sent Father Gabriel Druillettes to Maine in 1646. He found the Wabanaki in crisis. They were dying from a new sickness, one that caused "vomiting of blood," and none of their medicine men's ministrations could stop it.[50] This may have been tuberculosis, another disease that proved deadly to Indigenous people, or possibly cirrhosis of the liver. Apparently with no concern for his own health, Father Druillettes tended to their physical and spiritual needs, caring for the afflicted with such compassion that he quickly won their affection.

Druillettes won many Wabanaki over to the Catholic faith. For those who would follow him, he asked three things. First, that they give up alcohol, which they promised to do and "fairly well kept their word." Second, since disputes arose among the various groups who were living together, he asked that they live peacefully with one another and "stop the jealousies and the quarrels which occur among those little nations." They resolved to do better and "when their lips had been too widely opened...and when their tongues had not walked straight, they came to ask pardon of one another in the Chapel." And third, he asked them to throw away their manitous, or charms. These were small items like a stone or a feather that they believed held spiritual power and gave them good fortune in the hunt or in battle. Their love and respect for him was so strong that they agreed to give them up.[51]

Christianity provided a path forward for many Wabanaki who had begun to lose their way in the new world order. Not all would convert, and Samoset may have been one of those who did not. To be sure the ones who did become Christians were not fans of certain aspects of the faith, like monogamy or the idea of burning in hell, or the fact that they could not divorce their spouse whenever they wanted.[52] But in the missions they found much-needed solace in the ritual of prayer and the joy of singing hymns together, and mission life offered them a sense of security and stability.[53] The contrast between the way Father Druillettes and the English treated them led them to hope they could find a better life with the French.

Father Druillettes was recalled to Quebec in 1647 and around thirty Wabanaki went with him to live at the mission there. Though the mission priests required them to give up many of their traditional practices and beliefs, they did not ask them to completely abandon their old way of life. The priests realized how important hunting, trapping, and fishing were to the Wabanaki's well-being. Perhaps most importantly, the Jesuits tried to shelter them from the temptation of alcohol. Converting to Catholicism was a compromise many found worth making.

Father Druillettes made a diplomatic trip to Boston and Plymouth in 1650 to seek English aid against the Haudenosaunee. The English declined to help, which served to draw the Wabanaki and French closer together. The English would later engage the Mohawk to fight on their side against the Wabanaki in the Anglo-Wabanaki wars.[54]

As relations with the English deteriorated over the next quarter of a century and the Mohawk raids continued, the Wabanaki sought out the Jesuit missions from time to time as a place of sanctuary. Some remained there permanently. The French tried to use their influence to turn the Wabanaki against the English, especially when the two countries were at war, but the Wabanaki remained their own masters. Eventually the English would live to regret such careless disposal of their Wabanaki allies. The old Mawooshen communities, along with their new allies, began to unite with determination to protect themselves and reclaim their homeland. They were regaining their strength.

EPILOGUE

Death, War, and the Destruction of Pemaquid, 1653–1696

Samoset's wigwam was hot and crowded; the smell of sweat and smoke and sickness permeated the air. Food was brought in and taken out, untouched. Day and night Samoset's family hovered, keeping the fire burning while the medicine man chanted and danced and tried various remedies to stop the inevitable: their beloved sagamore—protector, diplomat, and leader among men—was dying.

By any measure, his had been an extraordinary life. Long before his walk into Plymouth Plantation, Samoset began to navigate the alien English world which would eventually dominate his own. By learning the Englishman's language and customs he successfully bridged the cultural divide. Though he seemed to enjoy his interactions with Europeans, the needs of his own people came first. Samoset held the Wawenock together even when trauma, death, and tremendous changes to their way of life threatened to tear them apart. When the threat was a military one, he sought alliances whenever possible—like his mentors Bashabes and Ousamequin had done—believing this provided the best protection for his people. Though he traveled far and wide, he always came home to Pemaquid.

The Wawenock were subdued as they tried to carry on with their regular work while keeping one eye on Samoset's wigwam, listening and waiting. They sent messengers to alert other villages so their sagamores could come and pay their last respects. Samoset's English friends would also want to say goodbye. Then they began to make preparations to send their leader on his journey to Tanto's wigwam.

Death for the Wabanaki was not something to fear because they believed they would be reunited with those who had passed into the spirit world.

Samoset would once again see his kinsmen Tahánedo, Skicowáros, Amóret, Maneddo, and Sassacomoit, as well as the men who had fallen in the Mi'kmaq War. He would see his parents and all those who had perished in the Great Dying and the smallpox epidemic. Perhaps he had a wife or children who were waiting for him. He would be rewarded for living a virtuous life on earth with endless feasts and celebrations in the afterlife.

When at last Samoset took his final breath, the women of the village began to wail and howl. Their grief poured out in a river of sorrow. They lovingly prepared his body for the next life by dressing him in his finest clothes, arranging his hair as he liked it best, adorning his body with wampum and other finery, and painting his face one last time. They drew his knees to his chest so he would leave the world as he entered it, or to make the passage to the next world easier.

Local legend says that Samoset was buried on Louds Island in Muscongus Bay (once known as Somerset Island) where Wawenock remains have been found.[1] Given his close association with John Brown and Brown's descendants who lived on the island that is possible, but without evidence Samoset's final resting place will forever remain unknown.

After a few days, when friends had a chance to gather and they had properly celebrated his life with a feast and formal eulogies, it was time to take Samoset to his final resting place. The mourners blackened their faces with ashes to show the depth of their respect and sadness, then placed his body in a hole that had been carefully lined with sheets of bark or woven mats; his head would rest on a mound of dirt for a pillow. They howled and wailed and sang the death song as they placed items into the grave that Samoset would need in the next life: his gun and his bow and arrows, his hatchet and knife, his pipe and tobacco, food for the journey, and any other treasured items that he might need or want in the next world. His wife or wives, if any survived him, placed a lock of their hair on his chest. Then they covered him with thin sheets of brass or copper, a fitting decoration for their greatest sagamore.[2] After a final wrapping of bark or mats or perhaps a blanket to keep the dirt from his body, they filled the hole and sent him on his way.

Samoset would be revered and immortalized by his people, who would mark his passing every year by blackening their skin, along with a ritual of wailing and howling.[3] They would not, however, speak his name. It was a sacred tradition not to say the name of a sagamore after his death and considered a great insult to his memory if one did—it would be 'raising the tree too soon.'[4] Instead he would be referred to using a general term like the "great sagamore" or "our great leader" until his relatives decided an appropriate amount of time had passed. The greater the sagamore, the longer the taboo would be in place.

His death, which took place sometime after he made his mark on the last deed in July 1653, marked the end of an era. Samoset would have been the last sagamore of Pemaquid to remember what life was like before Europeans came to their shores. He had been born into a Wabanaki world, a world free from deadly epidemics, land-grabbing foreigners, and the scourge of alcohol. He could remember how self-sufficient the Wawenock had been, and the old skills, like how to make an arrowhead or polish a bowl with a beaver's tooth.

Not all the old ways had been abandoned, of course. The Wabanaki only adopted European goods and techniques that served them better than their own. They still carried their babies on cradleboards, but now they used linen cloth rather than moss to clean them. They still speared sturgeon by torchlight, but their spears were now tipped with metal prongs. They wore moccasins and snowshoes and dressed their long hair with feathers, but they added European glass beads and peacock feathers as decorations. They told Gluskabe stories by the fireside, but may have added a story or two from the Bible. English culture did not replace the things they valued, or the things that made them unique. Their attachment to each other, their land, and their traditions was as strong as ever. But now, for the Wawenock of Pemaquid at least, they would have to find their way forward without their esteemed sagamore.

After Samoset's death, life in Pemaquid went on as before, but the Wawenock lived an increasingly marginalized existence there. They continued to trade at the trading post and live wherever they could find food and feel safe from Mohawk raids. The Brown family may have allowed them to live on their land, but we cannot even be sure they remained in the Pemaquid area. Wabanaki people living in English territory west of the Penobscot River, who are known collectively as the Abenaki, generally lived the same way, on the edges of their homeland. All was certainly not well in Indigenous communities. As in 1642, when Thomas Gorges and John Winthrop reported fears of an uprising, Native people all over New England were seething with dangerous resentment against the English.

It was the same old story. They were frustrated by encroachments on their land, dishonest dealings and the ruinous pressure to buy alcohol, the imposition of English laws without English justice, and the indignity of being treated as inferiors. They were experiencing death by a thousand cuts, and the time had come to end it.

The Wabanaki who lived in French territory did not experience the same pressure and displacement as their brethren in the English colonies, not only because they were treated better by the missionaries and some of the French colonists — who were more likely to marry and live with the Wabanaki — but also because there were so few French in the territory. By 1650, there were only about 400 French people living in the vast area known as Acadia.[5]

Conflict began in Massachusetts in June 1675 with the outbreak of King Philip's War. King Philip was the English name for Pometacom (or Metacom, Metacomet), the younger son of the Wampanoag sachem Ousamequin with whom Samoset lived in 1620–'21. Hostilities erupted in Maine soon after, starting with Thomas Purchase's property in Brunswick. He was the trader whose house was ransacked in 1642 because he was cheating the Wabanaki; evidently, he was still up to his old tricks. Wabanaki raiders looted his house and killed some of his cattle in September 1675.[6] The Wabanaki killed the livestock not for food, but because they were angry that the animals ranged freely and damaged their crops with no acknowledgement or compensation from the English.

The violence escalated rapidly from there, on both sides. Fear, prejudice, and a lack of cultural understanding led some colonists to retaliate against *any* Wabanaki, even those innocent of any wrongdoing, and the Wabanaki's long-held anger exploded. Their first fatal attack was at a farmhouse in what is now Falmouth, Maine. Those who saw the smoke and went to investigate found "an old man and old woman were half in and half out of the house, near half burnt; their own son was shot through the body, and also his head dashed in pieces;

this young man's wife was dead, her head skinned, she was big with child. Two children having their heads dashed in pieces, and laid by one another with their bellys to the ground, and an oak plank laid upon their backs."[7] Such a brutal assault that included women and children seemed all out of proportion and inspired terror among the colonists.

The Wabanaki continued to unleash their pent-up frustration and fury on the settlers. They plundered and burned houses, slaughtered livestock, and killed many settlers—not sparing women or children. They took captives to use as bargaining chips or to keep as slaves; some they sold to the French. Settlers lived in fear of being caught in a surprise attack, and those living on widely dispersed farms were particularly vulnerable because they had nowhere to shelter. Forts and garrison houses were rare in those days. Fearing for their safety, the residents of Pemaquid and New Harbor fled to Damariscove and Monhegan Island in the fall of 1675.

Initially the Kennebec and Penobscot remained neutral in the conflict, and the evidence suggests the Wawenock did as well. It helped that they had a friend in Pemaquid who defended them, even at his own risk. Thomas Gardiner (or Gardner) had taken over the operation of the Pemaquid trading post and was one of the few English voices of reason in the face of mounting tensions with the Wabanaki.[8] When English officials forced the Kennebec and Penobscot to surrender their guns late that fall, afraid they would join the other Wabanaki in the fighting (again, we should include the Wawenock), Gardiner recognized the harm this would cause. He wrote to the governor of Massachusetts with his concerns: "[S]eeing that these Indians in these parts did never appear dissatisfied until their arms were taken away I doubt [the wisdom] of such actions whether they may not be forced to go to the French for relief or fight against us."[9]

Gardiner's prediction came true. Over the course of that winter many innocent Wabanaki were forced by scared, hostile colonists to abandon their homes and crops; some starved to death because their men had no guns with which to hunt. Others escaped to the Jesuit missions for safety. They emerged in the spring bitter and ready to join the war, their firearms most likely supplied by the French. By their own actions, the English had pushed those who tried to remain neutral into the war. The Wabanaki became united in the common goal of driving the English off their lands, and attacks began again with renewed force.

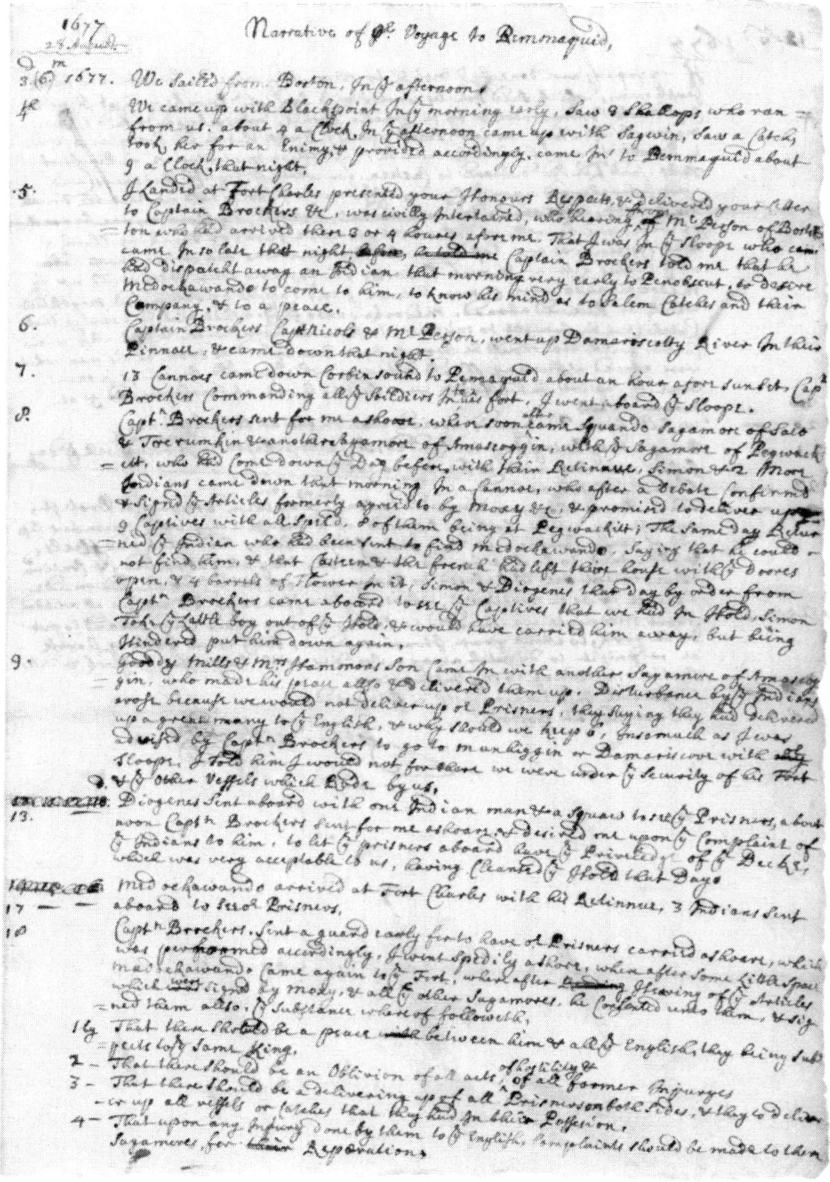
1677
28 August

Narrative of ye Voyage to Pemmaquid,

3(6) 1677. We Sailed from Boston in ye afternoon.

4th We came up with Blackpoint in ye morning early, Saw 8 Shallops who ran from us. about 4 a Clock in ye afternoon came up with Sagwin, Saw a Catch, took her for an Enimy, & provided accordingly. came in to Pemmaquid about 9 a Clock that night,

5. I Landed at Fort Charles presented your Honours Respects, & delivered your Letter to Captain Brockers &c, was civilly entertained, who haveing of Mr Pesson of Boston who had arrived there 3 or 4 houres afore me. That I was in ye Sloope who came in so late that night before, Captain Brockers told me that he had dispatcht away an Indian that morning very early to Penobscut, to desire Medockawando to come to him, to know his mind as to Salem Catches and their Company, & to a peace.

6. Captain Brockers Capt Nicols & Mr Pesson, went up Damariscotty River in their Pinnace, & came down that night.

7. 13 Cannoes came down Corbin sound to Pemaquid about an hour afore sunset, Capt Brockers Commanding all ye Soldiers into ye fort, I went aboard ye Sloope.

8. Captn Brockers sent for me ashoare, where soon after came Squando Sagamore of Saco & Tecrumkin ... Sagamore of Amascoggin, with ye Sagamore of Pegwackett, who had Come down ye Day before, with their Retinnue, Simon & 2 More Indians came down that morning in a Cannoe, who after a Debate Confirmed & Signed ye Articles formerly agreed to by Mozy &c. & promised to deliver up 9 Captives with all Speed, 8 of them being at Pegwackitt; The Same day Returned ye Indian who had been sent to find Medockawando. Saying that he could not find him, & that Casteen & the french had left their house with ye doores open, & 4 barrels of Flower in it, Simon & Diogenes that day by order from Captn Brockers came aboard to see ye Captives that we had in Hold. Simon took ye Little boy out of ye Hold, & would have carried him away, but being Hindered put him down again,

9. Goody Mills & Mrs Hammonds Son Came in with another Sagamore of Amascoggin, who made his peace also & delivered them up. Disturbance by ye Indians arose because we would not deliver up ol Prisners, they saying they had delivered up a great many to ye English, & why should we keep o', Insomuch as I was advised by Captn Brockers to go to Munhiggin or Damariscove with ye Sloope. I told him I would not for there we were under ye Security of ye Fort & ye other Vessels which Rode by us,

Diogenes sent aboard with one Indian man & a Squaw to see ye Prisners, about

13. noon Captn Brockers sent for me ashoare & desired me upon ye Complaint of ye Indians to him, to let ye prisners aboard have ye Priviledge of ye Decks, which was very acceptable to us, having Cleansed ye Hold that Day.

Medockawando arrived at Fort Charles with his Retinnue, 3 Indians sent

17 — aboard to see ol Prisners,

18 Captn Brockers sent a guard early first to have ol Prisners carried ashoare, which was performed accordingly, I went speedily ashore, when after some Little Space Medockawando Came again to ye Fort, where after hearing ye Articles which were signed by Mozy, & all ye other Sagamores, he Consented unto them, & signed them also, ye Substance whereof followeth,

1ly That there should be a peace between him & all ye English, they being Subjects to ye same King,

2 — That there should be an Oblivion of all acts of hostility & of all former Injuryes

3 — That there should be a delivering up of all Prisners on both sides, & they to deliver up all vessels or Catches that they had in their Possession,

4 — That upon any Injury done by them to ye English, Complaints should be made to their Sagamores, for Reparation.

First page of terms agreed to during peace talks held at Pemaquid to end King Philip's War, August 1677. COLLECTIONS OF MAINE HISTORICAL SOCIETY, 15560[10]

By the summer of 1676, the settlers of Pemaquid and New Harbor had returned to their farms. In August they were warned about attacks just west of them and they fled once again to Monhegan Island, only just in time. From the island they could see clouds of smoke rise from their homes burning on the mainland. The two villages were completely destroyed, with the exception of John Brown's house in New Harbor. It was supposedly spared in deference to his friendship with Samoset.[11] With no homes to return to and no help coming, the settlers scattered to Boston, northern Massachusetts, and the Portsmouth area for refuge.

King Philip's War changed the course of Anglo-Wabanaki relations for good. Warfare became the way of things in Maine and New England for decades to come. The Wabanaki, French, and English waged new wars in 1688, 1703, 1721, 1744, and 1754 with only enough breathing room between each conflict for settlers to trickle back into the state.[12] The same problems persisted with broken treaties added to their mutual distrust, and with each act of bloodshed the chances that they could ever live together peacefully became more and more remote.

English refugees from King William's War fled south again as they did during King Philip's War; most took shelter in Massachusetts. Some of the refugees who landed in Essex County were caught up in the famous Salem Witch Trials of 1692. Several of the accusers—and two people who were executed as witches—had lived in Maine. One historian believes that the fear generated by the Wabanaki attacks led to the hysteria of the witch hunt.[13]

Initially Pemaquid played an important role in the wars as England's most eastern garrison and a central location for peace talks with the Wabanaki. In 1677, the English built Fort Charles, named for King Charles II, for the protection of settlers who began to feel confident enough to return to their homes. But Pemaquid was destined for destruction. On August 2, 1689, one year into King William's War, a large force of Wabanaki warriors—aided by the French—attacked the settlement, killing or capturing all of the settlers and the troops stationed at the fort. Among those captured and taken to Canada were Margaret Stilson, the granddaughter of John and Margaret Brown, along with four of her children: James,

Excavation of the barracks and a replica of the bastion of Fort William Henry, originally built in 1692.

Margaret, John, and Mary. (Her children, James and Margaret, would later produce the infamous Samoset deed in 1720.) Margaret's husband and infant child were killed in the attack.[14] Samoset's close relationship to the Brown family no longer protected them.

The attack of 1689 was well planned and executed, with the intention of taking hostages and wiping out the settlement. It was a complete success. The Wabanaki burned the fort and all the houses to the ground which, in the words of one captive, "made a terrible blast, and was a melancholy sight to us poor captives, who were sad spectators."[15] Pemaquid had now been completely destroyed for a second time.

Pemaquid's final defeat came at the hands of a joint Wabanaki-French attack in 1696. The provincial government of Massachusetts, which by then had absorbed all the settlements in Maine, built a new stone fortress in Pemaquid in 1692, "the finest thing that had been seen in these parts of America." It had a 29-foot tower with a commanding view of the harbor, 14–18 mounted guns, and walls that were up to six feet thick in places.[16] The English boasted that Fort William Henry was "strong enough to resist all the Indians in America and has so much discouraged them that they have laid down their arms and sent their Sagamores to beg for an everlasting peace." But, to their everlasting embarrassment, an attack force of 400–500 French and Wabanaki fighters forced its surrender in a day.[17] Pemaquid's glory days were over.

The Wabanaki successfully chased English settlers out of Maine as far south as Wells.[18] Ironically, when there were almost no English residents left in the territory, Maine got the stable government it had always lacked when it was incorporated into the Province of Massachusetts in 1691. It would remain a part of Massachusetts until it achieved statehood in 1820.[19]

King William's War ended in 1699 with massive displacement and enormous loss of human life for both the English and the Wabanaki. Though the Wabanaki had succeeded in driving most of the settlers off their land, they were hardly prospering. Constant warfare had disrupted their food supply and famine had become a relentless concern. Sometimes they sought relief at one of the French mission villages outside Quebec, but there they faced periodic outbreaks of smallpox and other diseases, including influenza and measles.[20] The French, for their part, did not always prove to be good allies. At times they used the Wabanaki for their own ends, urging them to go to war with the English and the Haudenosaunee because it suited their own purposes. They turned out to be poor trading partners as well, charging inflated prices for limited goods. The Wabanaki were partially motivated to sue for peace with the English so they could re-establish trade with them.

Abenaki people may have suffered the most as a result of the wars, because they were not able to return to their homelands. The government of Massachusetts sent raiding parties to Maine that destroyed everything they could find: crops, canoes, wigwams, villages. With this constant harassment the Abenaki could not safely go home, and their fortunes fell further and further.

The cycle of war and displacement continued until all Wabanaki were finally subdued, along with the French, in the French and Indian War (also known as the Seven Years War) of 1754–'63.

> **Wabanaki people who lived east of the Wawenock's homeland, in French territory, fared a little better. The Penobscot, Maliseet, Passamaquoddy, and Mi'kmaq retained some of their former territories and have communities there today.**

Through all the upheavals of the Anglo-French-Wabanaki wars, it is easy to lose sight of the Wawenock. They never came back to live in Pemaquid or any other Wawenock territory after the wars, which would have grieved Samoset. Who were the Wawenock if not "the people of the bay?" The coast of Maine was part of their identity. But Samoset was also a pragmatist. If he taught his people anything, it was that they should do what it took to survive. For the Wawenock, this meant heading north to Canada, to live among the French and other Wabanaki refugees. Many

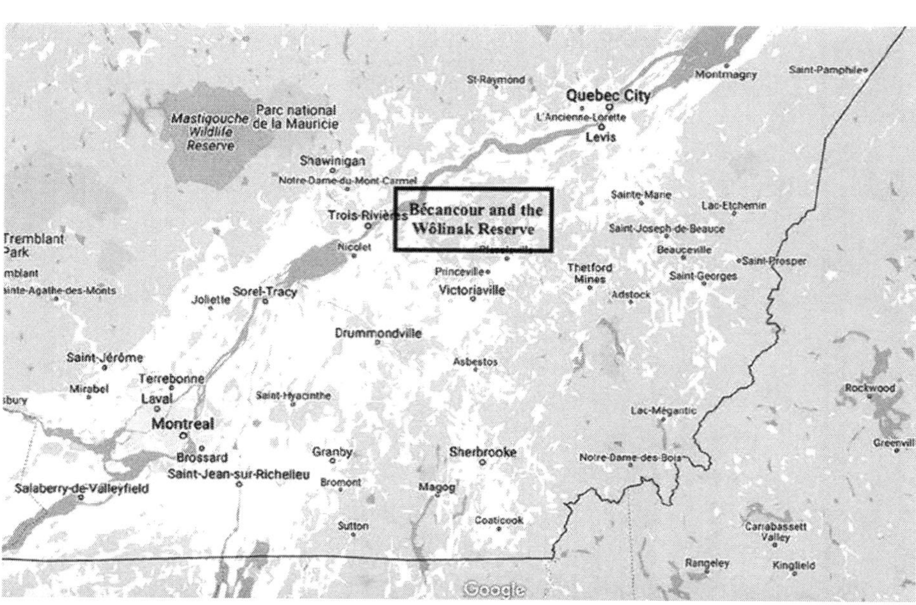

Wawenock moved to the Wôlinak reserve set aside by the French government for Wabanaki people near Bécancour, about halfway between Montreal and Quebec. It consisted of an area of around 200 square miles near the Bécancour River. And even though the Jesuits themselves readily admitted that "the country in which they lived is much better than this one with regard to food, to hunting, and to fishing," the Wabanaki could at least be safe there.[21]

Perhaps the biggest misconception about the Wawenock is that they no longer exist—that they all died of disease or war. Anthropologist Frank Speck documented twenty-three Wawenock people living in Bécancour in 1914, while other Wawenock families had moved to various towns in Canada. Some were living with the Montagnais as hunters and trappers. These were large families who would have descendants living today, but now they are more likely to identify themselves as Abenaki or another group in government censuses, so they are hard to trace. Some of their family names, such as Neptune and Nicholas, are shared with other Wabanaki, and there are undoubtedly many people with Wawenock ancestry living among the Wabanaki and First Nations. A hundred years ago Speck noted that Wawenock elder François Neptune could still speak the language and remembered the old stories, and a few elders knew the names of some of the dances, but integration had been so complete with other communities that "they know almost nothing of their own people." Without constant attention, the language and culture have been forgotten.[22]

Though Samoset's story and the history of the Wawenock of Pemaquid are unique, they mirror what other Indigenous people experienced during colonization: the culture clash with Europeans and racist treatment at their hands; the trauma of mass death by war and disease; the upheaval of their traditional way of life and loss of their homeland; and forced integration into new communities. Non-Native people have not always been willing to face the part they played in this history.

It has been over 400 years since the English built their first colony in Maine, and the Wabanaki are still fighting to regain their rights. They have made progress. In the 1970s the Penobscot Nation, the Passamaquoddy Tribe of Indians, and the Houlton Band of Maliseets received federal recognition, and in 1980 they won a landmark settlement with the federal government. As compensation for giving up their claim to 12.5 million acres of land taken in unratified treaties, they received a financial settlement to purchase land and set up a trust fund. In 1991, the Aroostook Band of Mi'kmaqs was officially recognized by the federal government, but without a settlement.[23] The Abenaki people who lived west of the Penobscot River have not been federally recognized because they were extensively displaced during the wars. Criteria for recognition include being able to prove "continued tribal existence" and "continued contact with the tribe," a difficult threshold for many communities whose people were so widely dispersed.[24] Without federal recognition the Abenaki are not eligible for federal programs specific to Indigenous people, like health care and education, or to receive reparations.

Meanwhile the federally recognized Wabanaki continue to work through legal channels to reclaim their sovereignty. As it stands now, Maine Wabanaki are subject to Maine laws but have control over local issues. In February 2020, Sherri Mitchell of the Penobscot Nation testified to the Maine Legislature's Judiciary Committee that the underlying beliefs standing in the way of sovereignty are "rooted in racially motivated paternalism that publicly calls into

Pemaquid Point Lighthouse.[25]

Remains of English settlers' houses at Colonial Pemaquid State Historic Site.

question the capacity of Wabanaki peoples to govern themselves."[26] She spoke a hard truth; our European forefathers imbued us with a sense of superiority and entitlement. White supremacy lives on, and the Wabanaki are still battling it. After 400 years, they are not about to give up the fight. It helps that, in the words of one Indigenous scholar, "Patience is a quality possessed in abundance by indigenous communities."[27]

Today anyone can visit Samoset's homeland on the beautiful Pemaquid peninsula. The landscape has not changed drastically, so it is easy to imagine what it looked like in Samoset's day. Still, it has been unmistakably marked by the colonists who came from England. Clapboard houses dot the shoreline and moss-covered stone walls are evidence of old property boundaries. Fishermen gather in New Harbor early in the morning to share a cup of coffee and a laugh before heading out for the day's catch. At the height of summer, tourists swim at Pemaquid Beach or test their balance on the rocky outcropping at Pemaquid Point, now overlooked by an iconic lighthouse.

Visitors to the Colonial Pemaquid State Historic Site can see traces of the English settlement that existed when Samoset lived there. They can walk through the ancient village and peer into the stone cellars of the early settlers' houses, a solid reminder of their time there. A small museum displays Wawenock and European artifacts that date back hundreds, even thousands, of years.

The Wawenock may no longer be there physically, but they will always have a presence on the coast of Maine. Their bones lie in the ground. Currently around 9,000 of Maine's citizens identify themselves as American Indian, or about 0.7 percent of the population, and though small the number is growing.[28] They have worked hard to make their voices heard and keep their languages

Students at Bristol Elementary School on the Pemaquid peninsula perform a Wabanaki dance that they learned during Diversity Week, March 2020.

and traditions from disappearing. Maulian Dana, Penobscot Nation Tribal Ambassador and Wabanaki Alliance President, put it eloquently: “Indigenous people stand on the shoulders of our ancestors who were silenced and oppressed in our homeland. We all honor their powerful legacy of stewardship, self-determination, diplomacy, and being connected to the land and one another. We will be ancestors someday and we are showing our descendants how we keep our values and life ways strong.”[29]

Samoset’s story puts a human face on Native peoples’ struggle during the period when our ancestors first met. If we remember the brave man who risked his life to walk into Plymouth Plantation on that day in March 1621, as well as what he and his people endured and achieved, then we will honor their memory. If we strive to treat each other like brothers, as Samoset asked of Christopher Levett, then we will be on the path toward conciliation and healing.

NOTES

Introduction - pages 13-17

1. Edward R. Belcher, "Notes on Cole's Hill," Pilgrim Hall Museum, accessed August 10, 2020, https://pilgrimhall.org/pdf/Notes_Coles_Hill.pdf.
2. Dwight B. Heath, ed., *Mourt's Relation: A Journal of the Pilgrims at Plymouth* (Bedford, MA: Applewood Books, 1963), 51.
3. Fannie Hardy Eckstorm, *Indian Place-Names of the Penobscot Valley and the Maine Coast* (Orono, ME: University Press, 1960), 102; Frank G. Speck, Wawenock *Myth Texts from Maine* (Washington: Government Printing Office, 1928), 170, http://www.gutenberg.org/files/49951/49951-h/49951-h.htm.
4. "Wawenock Homelands," Davistown Museum, accessed August 10, 2020,http://www.davistownmuseum.org/historicalmarker.html.
5. Joseph Bruchac, *The Faithful Hunter: Abenaki Stories* (Greenfield Center, NY: Greenfield Review Press, 1988), unpaged introduction.
6. "Maine Memory Network: 1500-1667 Contact & Conflict," Maine Historical Society, accessed August 10, 2020, https://www.mainememory.net/sitebuilder/site/895/page/1306/print; Dean R. Snow and Kim Lanphear, "European Contact and Indian Depopulation in the Northeast: The Timing of the First Epidemics," *Ethnohistory* 35, no. 1 (Winter 1988): 24.
7. Helen Camp, *Pemaquid Lost and Found* (Pemaquid, ME: Ancient Pemaquid Restoration, 1967), 4; Herbert Milton Sylvester, *Samoset: An Appreciation* (Boston: W. B. Clarke Company, 1910), 11, https://archive.org/details/samosetanapprecioosylviala/page/n23/mode/2up.
8. George Parker Winship, ed., *Sailors Narratives Of Voyages Along The New England Coast, 1524-1624* (Boston: Houghton, Mifflin & Company, 1905), 271.

Part I: Samoset's Early Life and Precolonial Times, approximately 1590-1605

Chapter 1: Background - pages 20-24

1. Chris Newell, Co-Founder and Director of Education, Akomawt Educational Initiative, Personal communication with the author, March 14, 2021.Helen Camp, *Pemaquid Lost and Found* (Pemaquid, ME: Ancient Pemaquid Restoration, 1967), 4.Neill DePaoli, Park Manager and Historical Archaeologist, Colonial Pemaquid State Historic Site, Personal communication with the author, January 8, 2022.
4. Arthur Spiess and Leon Cranmer, "Native American Occupations at Pemaquid: Review and Recent Results," *The Maine Archaeological Society Bulletin* 41, no. 2 (2001): 22.
5. Steven A. Walton, "Iron Beginnings in America," Building Community: Medieval Technology and American History, Penn State University, accessed August 11, 2020, http://www.engr.psu.edu/mtah/articles/iron_beginnings.htm.
6. Denise Schmandt-Besserat, "The Evolution of Writing," University of Texas, last modified January 25, 2014, https://sites.utexas.edu/dsb/tokens/the-evolution-of-writing/; "Variables: The Story of...Writing," Guns, Germs and Steel, PBS, accessed August 11, 2020, http://www.pbs.org/gunsgermssteel/variables/writing.html; Ewan

Clayton, "Where did writing begin?," British Library, accessed March 16, 2021, https://www.bl.uk/history-of-writing/articles/where-did-writing-begin#.

7. David Cressy, "Levels of Illiteracy in England, 1530-1730," *The Historical Journal* 20, no. 1 (Mar., 1977): 13, https://www.jstor.org/stable/2638587.
8. Megan Gambino, "A Salute to the Wheel," *Smithsonian Magazine*, June 17, 2009, https://www.smithsonianmag.com/science-nature/a-salute-to-the-wheel-31805121/.
9. David S. Cook, *Above the Gravel Bar: The Native Canoe Routes of Maine* (Solon, ME: Polar Bear & Company, 2007), 23.
10. "Variables: The Story of...Horses," Guns, Germs and Steel, PBS, accessed August 11, 2020, https://www.pbs.org/gunsgermssteel/variables/horses.html.
11. "'Penobscot Sense of Place,' a lecture by James Francis, Wednesday, February 26, 2020," YouTube, accessed May 3, 2021, https://www.youtube.com/watch?v=SYBmhQmp_zE.
12. James Axtell, *The European and the Indian: Essays in the Ethnohistory of Colonial North America* (New York: Oxford University Press, 1981), 161.

Chapter 2: Spring - pages 25-34

1. Reuben Gold Thwaites, ed., *The Jesuit Relations and Allied Documents: Travels and Explorations of the Jesuit Missionaries in New France 1610—1791, Vol. III Acadia 1611-1616* (Cleveland: The Burrows Brothers Company, 1898), 108, http://moses.creighton.edu/kripke/jesuitrelations/relations_03.html; Howard S. Russell, *Indian New England Before the Mayflower* (Hanover, NH: University Press of New England, 1980), 38.
2. Russell, *Indian*, 38.
3. Ruth Holmes Whitehead and Harold McGee, *The Micmac: How Their Ancestors Lived Five Hundred Years Ago* (Halifax: Nimbus Publishing, 1983), 21.
4. Russell, *Indian*, 36.
5. Helen Camp, *Pemaquid Lost and Found* (Pemaquid, ME: Ancient Pemaquid Restoration, 1967), 4.
6. Whitehead, *The Micmac*, 35.
7. Russell, *Indian*, 165.
8. Chris Newell, Co-Founder and Director of Education, Akomawt Educational Initiative, Personal communication with the author, March 14, 2021.
9. Nan Fischer, "Ancient Companion Planting: The Three Sisters," Mother Earth Gardener, Winter 2017-2018, https://www.motherearthgardener.com/organic-gardening/techniques/planting-a-three-sisters-garden-zm0z17wzcwil.
10. Russell, *Indian*, 92; Hannah Newton, "The Sick Child in Early Modern England, 1580-1720," Endeavour, June 2014, 38(2): 122–129, National Center for Biotechnology Information, https://www.ncbi.nlm.nih.gov/pmc/articles/PMC4330552/.
11. Russell, Indian, 76-77; Campwillowlake, "Indian colored corn stock, 1137420983" iStock, accessed March 2, 2021, https://www.istockphoto.com/photo/indian-colored-corn-gm1137420983-303316206.
12. Harald E. L. Prins and Bunny McBride, *Asticou's Island Domain: Wabanaki Peoples at Mount Desert Island 1500-2000, Vol. 2* (Boston: National Park Service, 2007), 435-504, https://www.nps.gov/parkhistory/online_books/acad/wabanaki_peoples_vol2.pdf.
13. Frank G. Speck, *Penobscot Man: The Life History of a Forest Tribe in Maine* (Orono, ME: The University of Maine Press, 1998), 114-115; Russell, Indian, 191.
14. Speck, *Penobscot Man*, 115.
15. Chris Newell, Personal communication with the author, March 14, 2021.
16. C. Keith Wilbur, *New England Indians, 2nd ed.* (Saybrook, CT: Globe Pequot, 1996), 63.
17. Speck, *Penobscot Man*, 59-63.

18. Nick Stasulis, Data Section Chief of the Maine Office of the New England Water Science Center, Personal communication with the author, October 31, 2016.
19. Reuben Gold Thwaites, ed., *The Jesuit Relations and Allied Documents: Travels and Explorations of the Jesuit Missionaries in New France 1610—1791, Vol. LXVII, Lower Canada, Abenakis, Louisiana 1716-1727, 214* (Cleveland: The Burrows Brothers Company, 1900), http://moses.creighton.edu/kripke/jesuitrelations/relations_67.html.
20. Hannah Laclaire, "'Fish less' to protect endangered salmon," *The Times Record*, May 16, 2019, A1.
21. George Parker Winship, ed., *Sailors Narratives Of Voyages Along The New England Coast, 1524-1624* (Boston: Houghton, Mifflin & Company, 1905), 73, 74, 78, 79, 80, 87
22. "Bowl, Waltes - HM6613.1," Mi'kmaq Waltes, c. 1850-1900, Hudson Museum, University of Maine, accessed March 23, 2021, https://hudsonmuseum.pastperfectonline.com/search.
23. Russell, *Indian*, 112.
24. Edith Favour, *Indian Games, Toys, and Pastimes of Maine And The Maritimes* (Bar Harbor, ME: The Robert Abbe Museum, 1974), 5.
25. Speck, *Penobscot Man*, 254-5.
26. Favour, *Indian Games*, 15.
27. Ibid., 12-17.

Chapter 3: Summer - pages 35-39

1. George Parker Winship, ed., *Sailors Narratives Of Voyages Along The New England Coast, 1524-1624* (Boston: Houghton, Mifflin & Company, 1905), 148-9.
2. Colin Woodard, "2018 was deadly for right whales," *Morning Sentinel*, January 21, 2018, Digital Maine Library: ProQuest; "North Atlantic Right Whale," NOAA Fisheries, accessed August 11, 2020, https://www.fisheries.noaa.gov/species/north-atlantic-right-whale; 6381380, "North Atlantic Right Whale, 1207994628" iStock, accessed March 2, 2021, https://www.istockphoto.com/photo/north-atlantic-right-whale-gm1207994 628-349000035.
3. Frank G. Speck, *Penobscot Man: The Life History of a Forest Tribe in Maine* (Orono, ME: The University of Maine Press, 1998), 270.
4. Winship, *Sailors*, 122-123.
5. Howard S. Russell, *Indian New England Before the Mayflower* (Hanover, NH: University Press of New England, 1980), 160.
6. Ibid., 100.
7. Speck, *Penobscot Man*, 236-237.
8. Henry Lorne Masta, *Abenaki Indian Legends, Grammar and Place-Names* (Toronto: Global Language Press, 2008), 32; "Penobscot Dictionary," accessed May 4, 2021, https://penobscot-dictionary.appspot.com/entry/search/; "motewolon, ptewolon," Passamaquoddy-Maliseet Language Portal, accessed May 4, 2021, https://pmportal.org/dictionary/motewolon-ptewolon.

Chapter 4: Fall - pages 40-46

1. Howard S. Russell, *Indian New England Before the Mayflower* (Hanover, NH: University Press of New England, 1980), 176.
2. David Hackett Fischer, *Champlain's Dream* (New York: Simon & Schuster, 2008), 252.
3. Colin Woodard, "Commentary: When Indians Ruled Maine's Seas," *Portland*

Press Herald, December 14, 2014, https://www.pressherald.com/2014/12/14/commentary-when-indians-%E2%80%A8ruled-maines-seas/.

4. George Parker Winship, ed., *Sailors Narratives Of Voyages Along The New England Coast, 1524-1624* (Boston: Houghton, Mifflin & Company, 1905), 72; 76.
5. Frank G. Speck, *Penobscot Man: The Life History of a Forest Tribe in Maine* (Orono, ME: The University of Maine Press, 1998), 206.
6. Ibid., 206.
7. SC1/series 45X. Massachusetts Archives Collection, v. 31 pp. 103-105. Massachusetts Archives, Boston, Massachusetts; Colin G. Calloway, ed., *Dawnland Encounters: Indians and Europeans in Northern New England* (Hanover, NH: University Press of New England, 1991), 92.
8. Speck, *Penobscot Man*, 79-81.
9. "The Passenger Pigeon," *Smithsonian*, Smithsonian Institution Archives, accessed August 12, 2020, https://www.si.edu/spotlight/passenger-pigeon.
10. Russell, *Indian*, 179.

Chapter 5: Winter - pages 47-51

1. Eva L. Butler and Wendell S. Hadlock, *Dogs of the Northeastern Woodland Indians* (Bar Harbor, ME: The Robert Abbe Museum, 1994), 7, 27, 35.
2. Frank G. Speck, *Wawenock Myth Texts from Maine*, (Washington: Government Printing Office, 1928), 169, Project Gutenberg, http://www.gutenberg.org/ ebooks/49951.
3. Ibid., 181-182.
4. Howard S. Russell, *Indian New England Before the Mayflower* (Hanover, NH: University Press of New England, 1980), 45.
5. Neal Salisbury, *Manitou and Providence: Indians, Europeans, and the Making of New England, 1500-1643* (New York: Oxford University Press, 1982), 39; Mary Ellen Lepionka, "Manitou in Context," Historic Ipswich, accessed August 12, 2020, https://historicipswich.org/2018/02/07/manitou-in-context/.
6. Russell, *Indian*, 44.
7. Ibid.
8. Lisa Therrien, "Moose in middle of forest in winter, 1128971796" iStock, accessed March 1, 2021, https://www.istockphoto.com/photomoose-in-middle-of-forest-in-winter-gm1128971796-298075458.
9. John Josselyn, *An Account of Two Voyages to New-England, Made during the years 1638, 1663* (Boston: William Veazie, 1865), 100.
10. "Snowshoe - HM7028.1," HM7028 Penobscot Children's Snowshoes c. 1900, Hudson Museum, University of Maine, accessed April 7, 2021, https://hudsonmuseum.past perfectonline.com/search.
11. Edith Favour, I*ndian Games, Toys, and Pastimes of Maine And The Maritimes* (Bar Harbor, ME: The Robert Abbe Museum, 1974), 4.
12. "2004.24.1835 Game of Su-Ha (Snake Game)," Peabody Museum of Archaeology and Ethnology at Harvard University, accessed March 23, 2021, https://pmem.unix.fas.harvard.edu:8443/peabody/.
13. Russell, *Indian*, 69.

Chapter 6: The European Invasion, 1492-1604 - pages 52-62

1. Claudio Valdes, "Barcelona Christopher Columbus monument, 483098754" iStock, accessed March 24, 2021, https://www.istockphoto.com/photobarcelona-christopher

-columbus-monument-gm483098754-70427591.
2. Heather Pringle, "Cabot, cod and the colonists," *Canadian Geographic*, July/August 1997, 35, http://www.academia.edu/2443638/CABOT_COD_AND_THE_COLONISTS.
3. "Journal of the First Voyage of Columbus," American Journeys Collection, accessed August 12, 2020, 111, http://www.americanjourneys.org/pdf/AJ-062.pdf.
4. Heather Murphy and Aimee Ortiz, "Columbus Day or Indigenous Peoples' Day? Depends Where You Are," *New York Times*, October 13, 2019, https://www.nytimes.com/2019/04/28/us/columbus-day-Indigenous-peoples.html.
5. Dutch Scenery, "Ancient nautical astrolabe with lenses isolated on a white back ground, 161847133" iStock, accessed March 23, 2021, https://www.istockphoto.com/photo/ancient-astrolabe-with-lenses-isolated-on-white-gm161847133-23079276.
6. Samuel Eliot Morison, *The European Discovery of America: The Northern Voyages A.D. 500-1600* (New York: Oxford University Press, 1971), 132.
7. 3D Sculptor, "Caravel In The Ocean, 537636540" iStock, accessed March 2, 2021, https://www.istockphoto.com/photo/caravel-in-the-ocean-gm537636540-95430831.
8. *What Life was Like in the Realm of Elizabeth: England AD 1533-1603* (Alexandria: Time-Life Books, 1998), 124; Morison, European Discovery, 131-133.
9. John Josselyn, *An Account of Two Voyages to New-England, Made during the years 1638, 1663* (Boston: William Veazie, 1865), 9.
10. Tim Lambert, "The Population of Ancient England," A History of English Population, accessed August 12, 2020, http://www.localhistories.org/population.html.
11. Pringle, "Cabot," 36.
12. Cecily Hilleary, "Native Groups Call on Vatican to Retract 500-Year-Old Charter," Voices of America, accessed March 17, 2021, https://www.voanews.com/usa/native-groups-call-vatican-retract-500-year-old-charter.
13. Joseph Nicolar, *The Life and Traditions of the Red Man* (Durham, NC: Duke University Press, 2007), 115.
14. Charlton Ogburn, "The Longest Walk: David Ingram's Amazing Journey," *American Heritage*, April/May 1979, Vol. 30 Issue 3, https://www.americanheritage.com/longest-walk-david-ingrams-amazing-journey.
15. Plowden Charles Jennett Weston, ed., *The Land Travels of Davyd Ingram and others in the years 1568-9: From the Rio de Minas in the Gulph of Mexico to Cape Breton in Acadia* (London: 1856), Documents Connected with the History of South Carolina, 8-10, https://archive.org/stream/documentsconnec00wetogoog#page/n12/mode/2up.
16. "Sir Humphrey Gilbert Compton Castle," Wikimedia Commons, last modified November 5, 2017, https://commons.wikimedia.org/wiki/File:Sir_Humphrey_Gilbert_Compton_Castle.jpg.
17. Morison, *European Discovery*, 464; 467.
18. Ibid., 566.
19. Ibid., 572.
20. Ibid., 574.
21. Ibid., 576.
22. Ibid., 577.

Part II: Meeting Europeans, 1605-1625

Chapter 7: The Kidnapping, 1605 - pages 64-78

1. Ann Marie Plane, *Colonial Intimacies: Indian Marriage in Early New England* (Ithaca: Cornell University Press, 2002), 50; William Wood, New England's Prospect (Amherst, MA: University of Massachusetts Press, 1977), 83.
2. "A reading edition of William Morrell's 'New England', 1625," Early Modern Whale, accessed August 12, 2020, http://roy25booth.blogspot.com/2011/06/reading-edition-of-william-morrells-new.html.
3. David B. Quinn and Alison M. Quinn, eds., *The English New England Voyages 1602-1608* (London: The Hakluyt Society, 1983), 266.
4. Ibid., 267.
5. Ibid., 268.
6. Ibid., 268-269.
7. Frank G. Speck, *Penobscot Man: The Life History of a Forest Tribe in Maine* (Orono, ME: The University of Maine Press, 1998), 150.
8. Quinn and Quinn, English New England, 270.
9. David C. Morey, ed., *The Voyage of Archangell: James Rosier's Account of the Waymouth Voyage of 1605, A True Relation* (Gardiner, ME: Tilbury House Publishers, 2005), 49.
10. William Bradford, *Of Plymouth Plantation* (Mineola, NY: Dover Publications, 2006), 14.
11. Morey, *Voyage*, 48.
12. Quinn and Quinn, *English New England*, 273.
13. Morey, *Voyage*, 54.
14. Ibid., 52.
15. Ibid., 55.
16. Ibid., 59.
17. Quinn and Quinn, *English New England*, 98.
18. Morey, *Voyage*, 63.
19. Ibid.
20. Ibid., 63-5.
21. Ibid., 64.
22. Quinn and Quinn, *English New England*, 283.
23. Ibid., 284.
24. Ibid.
25. Ibid., 287.
26. Ibid., 295.
27. George Parker Winship, ed., *Sailors Narratives Of Voyages Along The New England Coast, 1524-1624* (Boston: Houghton, Mifflin & Company, 1905), 96.
28. Quinn and Quinn, English New England, 297.
29. Ibid., 297-298.

Chapter 8: The Wawenock in England, 1605-1606 - pages 79-90

1. George Parker Winship, ed., *Sailors Narratives Of Voyages Along The New England Coast, 1524-1624* (Boston: Houghton, Mifflin & Company, 1905), 147.
2. Ibid., 151.
3. "Abnaki-Penobscot Possession," Native Languages of the Americas, accessed August 13, 2020, http://www.native-languages.org/abna_possession.htm.

4. Fannie Hardy Eckstorm, I*ndian Place-Names of the Penobscot Valley and the Maine Coast* (Orono, ME: University Press, 1960), xxiii.
5. "Algonquian languages," Wikipedia, last modified August 12, 2020, https://en.wikipedia.org/wiki/Algonquian_languages.
6. Eckstorm, *Indian Place-Names*, 5; "Penobscot Dictionary," accessed May 25, 2021, https://penobscot-dictionary.appspot.com/entry/4880775333806080/; James Francis, Sr., Penobscot Tribal Historian, Personal communication with the author, May 24, 2021.
7. Eckstorm, *Indian Place-Names*, 69.
8. Winship, *Sailors*, 74.
9. "Vocabulary in Native American Languages: Wabanaki Indian Words," Native Languages of the Americas, accessed August 13, 2020, http://www.native-languages.org/wabanaki_words.htm.
10. "Penobscot Dictionary," accessed May 6, 2021, https://penobscot-dictionary.appspot.com/entry/search/bear/1; "The Passamaquoddy-Maliseet Dictionary," Passamaquoddy-Maliseet Language Portal, accessed May 6, 2021, https://pmportal.org/browse-dictionary/m?page=92; Fannie Hardy Eckstorm, *Old John Neptune and Other Maine Indian Shamans* (Orono: Marsh Island Reprint, University of Maine at Orono, 1980), 51; David B. Quinn and Alison M. Quinn, eds., *The English New England Voyages 1602-1608* (London: The Hakluyt Society, 1983), 310.
11. Claes Janszoon Visscher II, "London panorama, 1616," Public domain via Wikimedia Commons, last modified October 26, 2020, https://commons.wikimedia.org/wiki/File:London_panorama,_1616b.jpg.
12. Quinn and Quinn, *English New England*, 340.
13. James Phinney Baxter, ed., *Sir Ferdinando Gorges and his province of Maine: Including the Brief relations, the Brief narration, his defence, the charter granted to him, his will, and his letters, Vol. I* (Boston: The Prince Society, 1890), 15.
14. "Sir John Popham Restored to His Former Glory," Harvard Law Today, accessed March 25, 2021, https://today.law.harvard.edu/sir-john-popham-restored-former-glory/.
15. Dean R. Snow, "The Ethnohistoric Baseline of the Eastern Abenaki," *Ethnohistory*, Vol. 23, No. 3 (Summer, 1976): 302.
16. Ibid., 300.
17. Pat Higgins, "Popham Colony," The Maine Story, accessed August 13, 2020, http://www.mainestory.info/maine-stories/popham-colony.html.
18. "The First Charter of Virginia; April 10, 1606," The Avalon Project of Yale Law School, accessed August 13, 2020, https://avalon.law.yale.edu/17th_century/va01.asp.
19. Christopher Lee, 1603: *The Death of Elizabeth I and the Birth of the Stuart Era* (London: Review, 2004), 192.
20. Alden T. Vaughan, *Transatlantic Encounters: American Indians in Britain, 1500-1776* (New York: Cambridge University Press, 2009), xi; 11; 42.
21. Ibid., xii.
22. John de Critz (attributed), "James I England," Public domain via Wikimedia Commons, last modified February 6, 2021, https://commons.wikimedia.org/wiki/File:JamesI England.jpg.
23. Stephen Inwood, *A History of London* (New York: Carroll & Graf, 1998), 208.
24. Peter Ackroyd, Rebellion: *The History of England from James I to the Glorious Revolution* (New York: Thomas Dunne Books, 2014), 19.
25. Ibid., 16.
26. Quinn and Quinn, *English New England*, 302.

Chapter 9: The Return to Pemaquid, 1606-1607 - pages 91-97

David B. Quinn and Alison M. Quinn, eds., *The English New England Voyages 1602-1608* (London: The Hakluyt Society, 1983), 364.
2. Ibid., 341.
3. Ibid., 367-8.
4. Henry Otis Thayer, *The Sagadahoc Colony, Comprising the Relation of a Voyage Into New England* (Forgotten Books, 2012), 164; Alexander Brown, *The First Republic in America: an Account of the Origin of this Nation, written from Records then (1624) concealed by the Council, rather than from the Histories then licensed by the Crown* (Boston: Houghton, Mifflin & Company, 1898), 52, https://archive.org/stream/firstrepublicinaoobrowuoft/firstrepublicinaoobrowuoft_djvu.txt.
5. Brown, *First Republic,* 18-19.
6. Thayer, *Sagadahoc*, 163.
7. Ibid.
8. Quinn and Quinn, *English New England*, 337, 345.
9. Ibid., 80-81.
10. Ibid., 426.
11. Thayer, *Sagadahoc*, 58.
12. Stephen Luscombe, "Meeting the Native Americans," The British Empire, accessed August 14, 2020, http://www.britishempire.co.uk/maproom/popham/meetingnatives.htm; William Cullen Bryant, Sydney Howard Gay, and Noah Brooks, Scribner's P*opular History of the United States from the Earliest Discoveries of the Western Hemisphere by the Northmen to the Present Time, Vol. I* (New York: Charles Scribner's Sons, 1898), 384, https://hdl.handle.net/2027/mdp.39015070225712.
13. Quinn and Quinn, *English New England*, 427-8.
14. Ibid., 428.
15. Ibid.
16. Ibid.

Chapter 10: The Popham Colony, 1607-1608 - pages 98-113

1. David B. Quinn and Alison M. Quinn, eds., *The English New England Voyages 1602-1608* (London: The Hakluyt Society, 1983), 428.
2. Fannie Hardy Eckstorm, I*ndian Place-Names of the Penobscot Valley and the Maine Coast* (Orono, ME: University Press, 1960), 129.
3. Quinn and Quinn, *English New England*, 429.
4. Ibid., 430.
5. Ibid., 442.
6. John Hunt, "St. Georges Fort plan, Phippsburg, 1607, 7542," Collections of Maine Historical Society, Maine Memory Network, accessed August 14, 2020, https://www.mainememory.net/artifact/7542.
7. Jeffrey P. Brain, "The John Hunt Map of the First English Colony in New England," *Northeast Historical Archaeology* 37, no. 1 (April 27, 2011): 70-71, accessed August 14, 2020, http://www.britishempire.co.uk/maproom/popham/johnhunt.pdf.
8. "Letters between King Philip III and Don Pedro de Zúñiga (1607–1608)," Encyclopedia Virginia, accessed August 14, 2020, https://www.encyclopediavirginia.org/Letters_between_King_Philip_III_and_Don_Pedro_de_Zuniga_1607-1608.
9. Eckstorm, *Indian Place-Names*, 114.
10. Quinn and Quinn, *English New England*, 433.

11. George Parker Winship, ed., *Sailors Narratives Of Voyages Along The New England Coast, 1524-1624* (Boston: Houghton, Mifflin & Company, 1905), 69-70.
12. Quinn and Quinn, *English New England*, 438.
13. Ibid., 450.
14. Ibid., 439.
15. Ibid., 473.
16. Ibid., 413.
17. Ibid.
18. Ibid., 447.
19. Ibid., 449.
20. Ibid., 450.
21. Ibid.
22. Ibid., 461.
23. Ibid., 455-6.
24. Ibid., 456.
25. Ibid., 350.
26. Ibid., 453-454.
27. James Phinney Baxter, *Sir Ferdinando Gorges and His Province of Maine Including the Brief Relation, the Brief Narration, His Defence, the Charter Granted to Him, His Will, and His Letters, Vol. I* (Boston: The Prince Society, 1890), 206.
28. Alfred A. Cave, "Why Was the Sagadahoc Colony Abandoned? An Evaluation of the Evidence," *The New England Quarterly*, 68, no. 4 (Dec., 1995), 625.
29. Henry Otis Thayer, *The Sagadahoc Colony, Comprising the Relation of a Voyage Into New England* (Forgotten Books, 2012), 107.
30. William H. Tabor, "Maine's Popham Colony," Athena Review, accessed August 15, 2020, http://www.athenapub.com/AR/10popham.htm.

Chapter 11: Fishing and War, 1607-1615 - pages 114-128

1. James Phinney Baxter, *Sir Ferdinando Gorges and His Province of Maine Including the Brief Relation, the Brief Narration, His Defence, the Charter Granted to Him, His Will, and His Letters, Vol. II* (Boston: The Prince Society, 1890), 17, https://ia802606.us.archive.org/6/items/sirferdinandogo02baxt/sirferdinandogo02baxt.pdf.
2. Ibid., 17-18.
3. Neill DePaoli, "Life on the Edge: Community and Trade on the Anglo-American Periphery, Pemaquid, Maine, 1610-1689," (PhD diss., University of New Hampshire, 2001), 27.
4. Donald S. Johnson, *Charting the Sea of Darkness: The Four Voyages of Henry Hudson* (New York: Kodansha International, 1995), 101.
5. Ibid., 102.
6. *Voyages of Samuel de Champlain, Vol. II: 1604-1610* (Boston: The Prince Society, 1878), 143, https://www.americanjourneys.org/pdf/AJ-115.pdf.
7. Johnson, Charting, 102.
8. Ibid., 103.
9. Alden T. Vaughan, *Transatlantic Encounters: American Indians in Britain, 1500-1776* (New York: Cambridge University Press, 2009), 67.
10. E. A. Churchill, "A Most Ordinary Lot of Men: The Fishermen at Richmond Island, Maine, in the Early Seventeenth Century," *The New England Quarterly*, 57, no. 2 (June 1984): 187.
11. Paul Daiute, Volunteer Interpreter at Colonial Pemaquid State Historic Site, Personal

communication with the author, July 27, 2019.

12. Churchill, "Most Ordinary," 189.
13. Patrick M. Malone, *The Skulking Way of War: Technology and Tactics among the New England Indians* (Lanham, MD: Madison Books, 2000), 26; John Warner Barber, *The History and Antiquities of New England, New Jersey, and Pennsylvania* (Hartford: H. S. Parsons & Col, 1846), 174.
14. Churchill, "Most Ordinary," 185.
15. Ibid., 194.
16. "John Smith," Historic Jamestowne, accessed August 16, 2020, https://historicjamestowne.org/history/pocahontas/john-smith/.
17. John Smith, *A Description of New England or, the Observations and Discoveries of Captain John Smith, (Admiral of That Country), in the North of America, in the Year of Our Lord 1614, with the Success of Six Ships That Went the Next Year, 1615* (Rochester: George P. Humphrey, Colonial Tracts, 1898), 1.
18. Ibid.,1.
19. Ibid.; John Smith, *A Description of New England (1616): An Online Electronic Text Edition* (Electronic Texts in American Studies, 1616), 18, https://digitalcommons.unl.edu/cgi/viewcontent.cgi?article=1003&context=etas.
20. Smith, *Description*, Colonial Tracts, 1-2.
21. Ibid., xii.
22. Ibid., 7.
23. Ibid., 11.
24. James Reeve, Simon van de Pass, and John Smith, "New England the most remarqueable parts thus named. by the high and mighty Prince Charles, nowe King of great Britaine," Osher Map Library, University of Southern Maine, accessed March 25, 2021, https://oshermaps.org/map/12548.0001.
25. Smith, *Description*, Colonial Tracts, 7.
26. Ibid., 12.
27. Ibid., 11.
28. Ibid., 29.
29. Malone, *Skulking*, 7-8.
30. Ibid., 23.
31. Ibid.; James Axtell, *The European and the Indian: Essays in the Ethnohistory of Colonial North America* (New York: Oxford University Press, 1981), 139.
32. Axtell, *European*,138.
33. Ibid., 146.
34. Malone, Skulking, 21.
35. Ibid., 19.
36. Ibid., 23.
37. Ibid., 20.
38. Axtell, *European*,182.
39. *Voyages*, 138.
40. Baxter, *Sir Ferdinando* Vol. II, 19.
41. Helen B. Camp, *Archaeological Excavations at Pemaquid, Maine 1965-1974* (Augusta, ME: The Maine State Museum, 1975), 75; Neill DePaoli, Park Manager and Historical Archaeologist, Colonial Pemaquid State Historic Site, Personal conversation with the author, July 26, 2020.
42. *Voyages*, 150.
43. David B. Quinn and Alison M. Quinn, eds., *The English New England Voyages 1602-1608* (London: The Hakluyt Society, 1983), 433.

44. *Voyages*, 150.
45. Neal Salisbury, *Manitou and Providence: Indians, Europeans, and the Making of New England, 1500-1643* (New York: Oxford University Press, 1982), 93.
46. Dean R. Snow, "The Ethnohistoric Baseline of the Eastern Abenaki," *Ethnohistory*, Vol. 23, No. 3 (Summer, 1976): 302.
47. "Facing Hatchet Mountain," Hope History, accessed August 17, 2020, http://www.hopehist.com/Himages/HD402.html.
48. William D. Williamson, *The History of the State of Maine; From Its First Discovery, A.D. 1602, to the Separation, A.D. 1820, Inclusive* (Hallowell, ME: Glazier, Masters & Smith, 1829), 215-216.

Chapter 12: The Great Dying, 1616-1619 - pages 129-133

1. Dean R. Snow and Kim M. Lanphear, "European Contact and Indian Depopulation in the Northeast: The Timing of the First Epidemics," *Ethnohistory* 35, no. 1 (Winter 1988): 16-19.
2. Neal Salisbury, *Manitou and Providence: Indians, Europeans, and the Making of New England, 1500-1643* (New York: Oxford University Press, 1982), 57.
3. Snow and Lanphear, "European Contact," 24.
4. Salisbury, *Manitou*, 106.
5. Alfred Goldsworthy Bailey, T*he Conflict of European and Eastern Algonkian Cultures 1504-1700: A Study in Canadian Civilization* (Toronto: University of Toronto Press, 1976), 21.
6. James Phinney Baxter, *Sir Ferdinando Gorges and His Province of Maine Including the Brief Relation, the Brief Narration, His Defence, the Charter Granted to Him, His Will, and His Letters, Vol. II* (Boston: The Prince Society, 1890), 18-19, https://ia802606.us.archive.org/6/items/sirferdinandog002baxt/sirferdinandog002baxt.pdf.
7. Ibid., 19.
8. James Phinney Baxter, *Sir Ferdinando Gorges and His Province of Maine Including the Brief Relation, the Brief Narration, His Defence, the Charter Granted to Him, His Will, and His Letters, Vol. I* (Boston: The Prince Society, 1890), 219-220.
9. Timothy L. Bratton, "The Identity of the New England Indian Epidemic of 1616-19," *Bulletin of the History of Medicine* 62, no. 3 (Fall 1988): 354.
10. Bratton, "Identity," 382.
11. Snow and Lanphear, "European Contact," 24.
12. William Bradford, *Of Plymouth Plantation* (Mineola, NY: Dover Publications, 2006), 56.
13. Ibid., 63.
14. Gordon Harris, "The Great Dying 1616-1619, 'By God's visitation, a wonderful plague,'" accessed August 17, 2020, https://historicipswich.org/2017/09/01/the-great-dying/.
15. Salisbury, *Manitou*, 72.

Chapter 13: Getting to Plymouth, 1619-1620 - pages 134-144

1. William Bradford, *Of Plymouth Plantation* (Mineola, NY: Dover Publications, 2006), 51-52.
2. Dwight B. Heath, ed., *Mourt's Relation: A Journal of the Pilgrims at Plymouth* (Bedford, MA: Applewood Books, 1963), 51.
3. Heath, *Mourt's*, 70; John Smith, *A Description of New England or, the Observations and Discoveries of Captain John Smith, (Admiral of That Country), in the North of America, in the Year of Our Lord 1614, with the Success of Six Ships That Went the Next Year, 1615* (Rochester: George P. Humphrey, Colonial Tracts, 1898), 30.

4. James Phinney Baxter, *Sir Ferdinando Gorges and His Province of Maine Including the Brief Relation, the Brief Narration, His Defence, the Charter Granted to Him, His Will, and His Letters, Vol. I* (Boston: The Prince Society, 1890), 209.
5. Smith, *Description*, 30.
6. Heath, *Mourt's*, 55.
7. "The Cupids Colony and John Guy," Heritage Newfoundland & Labrador, accessed August 17, 2020, http://www.heritage.nf.ca/articles/exploration/cupids.php.
8. John Smith, *The Generall Historie of Virginia, New-England, and the Summer Isles: With the Names of the Adventurers, Planters, and Governours from Their First Beginning, Ano: 1584. To This Present 1624. With the Procedings of Those Severall Colonies and the Accidents That Befell Them in All Their Journyes and Discoveries. Also the Maps and Descriptions of All Those Countryes, Their Commodities, People, Government, Customes, and Religion Yet Knowne. Divided into Sixe Bookes. By Captaine Iohn Smith, Sometymes Governour in Those Countryes & Admirall of New England* (London: I.D. and I.H. for Michael Sparkes, 1624), 229, https://docsouth.unc.edu/southlit/smith/smith.html.
9. James Phinney Baxter, *Sir Ferdinando Gorges and His Province of Maine Including the Brief Relation, the Brief Narration, His Defence, the Charter Granted to Him, His Will, and His Letters, Vol. II* (Boston: The Prince Society, 1890), 27, https://ia802606.us.archive.org/6/items/sirferdinandogo02baxt/sirferdinandogo02baxt.pdf.
10. Baxter, *Sir Ferdinando Vol. I*, 213-215.
11. Neal Salisbury, *Manitou and Providence: Indians, Europeans, and the Making of New England, 1500-1643* (New York: Oxford University Press, 1982), 103.
12. Baxter, *Sir Ferdinando Vol. I*, 220.
13. Bradford, *Of Plymouth*, 53.
14. Ibid., 54.
15. David J. Silverman, "Massasoit," *National Geographic History*, November/December 2020, 76; Chris Newell, Executive Director of the Abbe Museum and Senior Partner to Wabanaki Nations, Personal communication with the author, March 14, 2021.
16. Baxter, *Sir Ferdinando Vol. II*, 20-21.
17. Alden T. Vaughan, *Transatlantic Encounters: American Indians in Britain, 1500-1776* (New York: Cambridge University Press, 2009), 65-66.
18. "History of Henry VIII, Act V, Scene 4," OpenSource Shakespeare, accessed August 17, 2020, https://www.opensourceshakespeare.org/views/plays/play_view php?WorkID=henry8&Act=5&Scene=4&Scope=scene.
19. Baxter, *Sir Ferdinando Vol. II*, 28.
20. Fannie Hardy Eckstorm, Indian Place-Names of the Penobscot Valley and the Maine Coast (Orono, ME: University Press, 1960), 171-2; Baxter, Sir Ferdinando Vol. I, 220.
21. Baxter, Sir Ferdinando Vol. I, 214, 220.
22. Ibid., 221.
23. Carville Earle, "Environment, disease and mortality in early Virginia," *Journal of Historical Geography* 5, no. 4 (1979): 368, https://sultanaeducation.org/wp-content/uploads/2014/06/Earle-Environment-Disease-and-Mortality.pdf8; James Horn, *A Land As God Made It: Jamestown and the Birth of America* (New York: Basic Books, 2005), 56-57, 237-8.
24. Bradford, *Of Plymouth*, 53; Baxter, *Sir Ferdinando Vol. I*, 219; *Mourt's* p. 52.
25. Bradford, *Of Plymouth*, 53-54.
26. Baxter, Sir Ferdinando Vol. II, 29; Baxter, Sir Ferdinando Vol. I, 219.
27. Heath, *Mourt's*, 52.
28. Baxter, *Sir Ferdinando Vol. I*, 221.
29. Bradford, *Of Plymouth*, 54.

Chapter 14: Meeting the Colonists, 1621 - pages 145-156

1. William Bradford, *Of Plymouth Plantation* (Mineola, NY: Dover Publications, 2006), 81.
2. Ken Wiedemann, "Mayflower Asail, 614235256," iStock, accessed May 27, 2021, https://www.istockphoto.com/photo/mayflower-asail-gm614235256-106225885.
3. "Mayflower Compact," History, last modified September 20, 2019, https://www.history.com/topics/colonial-america/mayflower-compact.
4. Bradford, *Of Plymouth*, 14.
5. Dwight B. Heath, ed., *Mourt's Relation: A Journal of the Pilgrims at Plymouth* (Bedford, MA: Applewood Books, 1963), 35.
6. Bradford, *Of Plymouth*, 53.
7. "Wampanoag History," First Nations Histories, accessed August 17, 2020, https://www.tolatsga.org/wampa.html.
8. Bradford, *Of Plymouth*, 50.
9. "Who were the Pilgrims?" Plimoth Plantation, accessed August 17, 2020, https://plimoth.org/learn/just-kids/homework-help/who-were-pilgrims.
10. Heath, *Mourt's*, 51.
11. Ibid., 50-51.
12. Ibid., 51.
13. Heath, *Mourt's*, 51.
14. Ibid., 52.
15. Ibid.
16. Ibid.
17. Ibid., 53.
18. Ibid., 54.
19. Ibid., 57,
20. Edward Winslow, *Good News from New England* (Amherst: University of Massachusetts Press, 2014), 80.
21. Heath, Mourt's, 56-57.
22. Ibid., 58.
23. Ibid., 59.

Chapter 15: Settlers Come to Maine, 1621-1624 - pages 157-169

1. "Maine Historical Society," *Brunswick Telegraph*, July 19, 1872.
2. Henry S. Burrage, *The Beginnings of Colonial Maine 1602-1658* (Portland, ME: Marks Printing House, 1914), 145; "The Charter of New England: 1620," The Avalon Project of Yale Law School, accessed August 18, 2020, https://avalon.law.yale.edu/17th_century/mass01.asp.
3. Avalon Project, "Charter."
4. James Phinney Baxter, *Sir Ferdinando Gorges and His Province of Maine Including the Brief Relation, the Brief Narration, His Defence, the Charter Granted to Him, His Will, and His Letters, Vol. II* (Boston: The Prince Society, 1890), 41, https://ia802606.us.archive.org/6/items/sirferdinandogo02baxt/sirferdinandogo02baxt.pdf.
5. Ibid., 42.
6. Ibid., 42-43.
7. Burrage, *Beginnings*, 164, 167; Mary Frances Farnham, ed., *Documentary History of the State*

of Maine Vol. VII Containing The Farnham Papers 1603-1688 (Portland, ME: The Thurston Print, 1901), 64.

8. Edward Winslow, *Good News from New England* (Amherst: University of Massachusetts Press, 2014), 67.
9. John Johnston, *A History of the Towns of Bristol and Bremen in the State of Maine, Including the Pemaquid Settlement* (Albany: Joel Munsell, 1873), 46.
10. William Bradford, *Of Plymouth Plantation* (Mineola, NY: Dover Publications, 2006), 79.
11. Ibid., 86.
12. Ibid., 79.
13. Sydney V. James, Jr., ed., *Three Visitors to Early Plymouth: Letters About the Pilgrim Settlement in New England During Its First Seven Years* (Bedford, MA: Applewood Books, 1997), 15-16.
14. Christopher Levett, *A Voyage into New England Begun in 1623 and Ended in 1624. Performed by Christopher Levett, his Majesties Woodward of Somersetshire, and one of the Councell of New-England* (London: William Jones, 1628), 92.
15. Ibid., 101-102; Fannie Hardy Eckstorm, *Indian Place-Names of the Penobscot Valley and the Maine Coast* (Orono, ME: University Press, 1960), 123.
16. Levett, Voyage, 101-102.
17. Ibid, 102.
18. Ibid., 116.
19. Ibid., 103.
20. Ibid., 104.
21. Ibid.
22. Ibid., 105.
23. Ibid., 107-108.
24. Ibid., 109.
25. Ibid.
26. Ibid., 113.
27. Ibid., 112.
28. Ibid.
29. Ibid.,117.
30. Ibid., 119-120.

Chapter 16: The Samoset Deed, 1625 - pages 170-184

1. Neill DePaoli, "Life on the Edge: Community and Trade on the Anglo-American Periphery, Pemaquid, Maine, 1610-1689," (PhD diss., University of New Hampshire, 2001), 71-72.
2. Helen Camp, *Pemaquid Lost and Found* (Pemaquid, ME: Ancient Pemaquid Restoration, 1967), 4.
3. Emerson W. Baker, "'A Scratch with a Bear's Paw': Anglo-Indian Land Deeds in Early Maine," *Ethnohistory* 36, no. 3 (Summer 1989): 236.
4. John Johnston, *A History of the Towns of Bristol and Bremen in the State of Maine, Including the Pemaquid Settlement* (Albany: Joel Munsell, 1873), 54-55; *Order of Both Branches of the Legislature of Massachusetts, to Appoint Commissioners to Investigate the Causes of the Difficulties in the County of Lincoln; and the Report of the Commissioners Thereon, with the Documents in Support Thereof* (Boston: Munroe & French, 1811), 106-7.
5. Russell Shorto, *The Island at the Center of the World: The Epic Story of Dutch Manhattan and the Forgotten Colony That Shaped America* (New York: Vintage Books, 2005), 54-55.
6. Francis Jennings, *The Invasion of America: Indians, Colonialism, an The Cant*

of Conquest (Chapel Hill: Published for the Omohundro Institute of Early American History and Culture, Williamsburg, Virginia by the University of North Carolina Press, 2003), 132.

7. Shorto, *Island*, 57-58.
8. Baker, "Scratch," 244.
9. Johnston, *History*, 55; Sybil Noyes, Charles Thornton Libby, and Walter Goodwin Davis, *Genealogical Dictionary of Maine and New Hampshire* (Baltimore: Genealogical Publishing Co., Inc., 2002), 168.
10. Wilbur D. Spencer, *Pioneers on Maine Rivers* (Baltimore: Genealogical Publishing Co., Inc., 1973), 326.
11. Ibid., 328.
12. Jennings, *Invasion*, 144-145.
13. Ibid., 130.
14. *Order of Both Branches*, 21.
15. Spencer, *Pioneers*, 328.
16. Johnston, *History*, 57.
17. James Otis, *The Story of Pemaquid* (New York: Thomas Y. Crowell & Co., 1902), 30, https://archive.org/details/storyofpemaquid01otis/page/n9/mode/2up?q=patent.
18. *Order of Both Branches*, 111.
19. Ibid., 115.
20. *The New England Historical and Genealogical Register, Published Quarterly, Under the Patronage of the New England Historic Genealogical Society, for the Year 1859, Volume XIII* (Boston: Samuel G. Drake, 1859), 365, https://archive.org/details/newengland histo35unkngoog/page/n376/mode/2up.
21. *Publications of the Colonial Society of Massachusetts, Volume VI: Transactions 1899, 1900* (Boston: The Colonial Society of Massachusetts, 1904), 21, https://babel.hathitrust.org/cgi/pt?id=hvd.32044013641758&view=1up&seq=57.
22. J. Wingate Thornton, *Ancient Pemaquid: An Historical Review* (Portland: Brown Thurston, 1857), 56; Rufus King Sewall, *Ancient Dominions of Maine* (Bath, ME: Elisha Clark and Company, 1859), 104.
23. Thornton, *Ancient Pemaquid*, 60; Sewall, *Ancient Dominions*, 104.
24. Johnston, *History*, 495-6.

Part III: Keeping the Peace, 1626-1653

Chapter 17: Puritans, Pirates, and the Pox, 1626-1634 - pages 186-199

1. Jack Lane, *Aerial views of Pemaquid Beach, Johns Bay, & Bradley Shore*, catalog no. 2018.002. cn438-04, 1995, sheet film negative, The Jack Lane Photography Collection, Old Bristol Historical Society, Bristol, ME, accessed March 17, 2021, https://oldbristolhistoricalsociety.pastperfectonline.com/photo/A14AAD16-1221-4924-B249-275161536087. David B. Quinn and Alison M. Quinn, eds., The English New England Voyages 1602-1608 (London: The Hakluyt Society, 1983), 427-8.
2. David B. Quinn and Alison M. Quinn, eds., *The English New England Voyages 1602-1608* (London: The Hakluyt Society, 1983), 427-8.
3. Arthur Spiess and Leon Cranmer, "Native American Occupations at Pemaquid: Review and Recent Results," *The Maine Archaeological Society Bulletin* 41, no. 2 (2001): 2, 6, 24.
4. Kathleen E. Callum, "The Geoarcheology of the Nahanada Site (16-90): Pemaquid Beach, Bristol, Maine," (MS diss., The University of Maine, May 1994), 90.
5. Neill DePaoli, "Beaver, Blankets, Liquor, and Politics: Pemaquid's Fur Trade, 1614-1760," *Maine History* 33, no. 3-4 (1993-4): 176.
6. Neill DePaoli, "Life on the Edge: Community and Trade on the Anglo-American Periphery, Pemaquid, Maine, 1610-1689," (PhD diss., University of New Hampshire, 2001), 72.
7. Ibid., 41.
8. James Sullivan, *History of the District of Maine* (Augusta, ME: Maine State Museum, 1975),167, 390-1.
9. Lynn Betlock, "New England's Great Migration," New England Historic Genealogical Society, accessed August 19, 2020, https://www.americanancestors.org/new-englands-great-migration.
10. "King Charles I after original by van Dyck," Public domain via Wikimedia Commons, last modified January 19, 2021, https://commons.wikimedia.org/wiki/File:King_Charles_I_after_original_by_van_Dyck.jpg.
11. Betlock, "New England's."
12. Henry S. Burrage, *The Beginnings of Colonial Maine 1602-1658* (Portland, ME: Marks Printing House, 1914), 204.
13. James Phinney Baxter, ed., *The Documentary History of the State of Maine, Vol. III. Containing the Trelawny Papers* (Portland, ME: Hoyt, Fogg, and Donham, 1884), 46, https://books.google.com/books?id=IoEOAAAAIAAJ&pg=PA63&source=gbs_toc_r&cad=4#v=onepage&q&f=false.
14. "John Winthrop," Smithsonian's National Portrait Gallery, accessed August 19, 22020, https://npg.si.edu/object/npg_NPG.2004.1.
15. Bruce Bourque, "Richmond Island's Pot of Gold: A fascinating tale of early Maine," MaineBoats, accessed August 19, 2020, https://maineboats.com/print/issue-157/richmond-island's-pot-gold; Maine Memory Network, Accession # 819—Source File (item not searchable in catalog), https://www.mainememory.net.
16. James Kendall Hosmer, ed., *Winthrop's Journal "History of New England" 1630-1649 Volume I: Normal School* (New York: Charles Scribner's Sons, 1908), 69, http://www.noblenet.org/salem/reference/wp-content/uploads/2017/08/Original-Narratives-of-Early-American-History-Winthrops-Journal-vol.-1.pdf.
17. Ibid.
18. *Records of the Council for New England* (Cambridge: John Wilson and Son, 1867), 57-58, https://books.google.com/books?id=v7JXAAAAcAAJ&pg=RA1-PA57&g=RA1-PA57&dq=council+for+new+england+dixie+bull&source=bl&ots=zGAIA8pb1x&sig=ACfU3UowohkCJ9opSeNyAX5fiuue9ys_kg&hl=en&sa=X&ved=2ahUKEwjZoZHAjvrmAhWJiOAKHVIPByAQ6AEwB30ECAgQAQ#v=onepage&q=council%20for%20new%20

england%20dixie%20bull&f=false.

19. "Pemaquid," Maine: An Encyclopedia, accessed August 19, 2020, https://maineanencyclopedia.com/pemaquid/; John Johnston, *A History of the Towns of Bristol and Bremen in the State of Maine, Including the Pemaquid Settlement* (Albany: Joel Munsell, 1873), 64.
20. Eric Nye, "Pounds Sterling to Dollars: Historical Conversion of Currency," accessed June 6, 2021, https://www.uwyo.edu/numimage/currency.htm.
21. Hosmer, *Winthrop's Journal, Vol. I*,, 98; Johnston, History, 65.
22. William D. Williamson, *The History of the State of Maine; From Its First Discovery, A.D. 1602, to the Separation, A.D. 1820, Inclusive* (Hallowell, ME: Glazier, Masters & Smith, 1829), 251.
23. DePaoli, "Life," 46.
24. Johnston, History, 59; Hosmer, *Winthrop's Journal Vol. I*, 67-68; Mary Ellen Lepionka, "Who Were the Agawam Indians, Really?" Historic Ipswich on the Massachusetts North Shore, accessed August 19, 2020, https://historicipswich.org/2019/10/07/who-were-the-agawam-indians-really/.
25. William Bradford, *Of Plymouth Plantation* (Mineola, NY: Dover Publications, 2006), 172-3.
26. Baxter, *Documentary History Vol. III*, 47.
27. Bradford, *Of Plymouth*, 173.
28. John Duffy, "Smallpox and the Indians in the American Colonies," *Bulletin of the History of Medicine* 25, no. 4 (July-August 1951): 341.

Chapter 18: Alcohol, Guns, a Rebellion, and a Hurricane, 1635 - pages 200-208

1. Neill DePaoli, "Beaver, Blankets, Liquor, and Politics: Pemaquid's Fur Trade, 1614-1760," *Maine History* 33, no. 3-4 (1993-4): 177.
2. Ibid., 178.
3. Ibid., 177.
4. Reuben Gold Thwaites, ed., *The Jesuit Relations and Allied Documents: Travels and Explorations of the Jesuit Missionaries in New France 1610—1791, Vol. III Acadia 1611-1616* (Cleveland: The Burrows Brothers Company, 1898), 75, http://moses.creighton.edu/kripke/jesuitrelations/relations_03.html.
5. James Phinney Baxter, ed., *The Documentary History of the State of Maine, Vol. III*. Containing the Trelawny Papers (Portland, ME: Hoyt, Fogg, and Donham, 1884), 25-26, https://books.google.com/books?id=IoEOAAAAIAAJ&pg=PA63&source=gbs_toc_r&cad=4#v=onepage&q&f=false.
6. Patrick M. Malone, *The Skulking Way of War: Technology and Tactics among the New England Indians* (Lanham, MD: Madison Books, 2000), 37.
7. Neal Salisbury, Manitou and Providence: *Indians, Europeans, and the Making of New England, 1500-1643* (New York: Oxford University Press, 1982), 149.
8. David B. Quinn and Alison M. Quinn, eds., T*he English New England Voyages 1602-1608* (London: The Hakluyt Society, 1983), 287.
9. Frank Speck, "Wabanaki Wampum Belts," Public domain via Wikimedia Commons, last modified August 19, 2020, https://commons.wikimedia.org/wiki/File:Wabanaki_Wampum_Belts.png. David B.
10. William Bradford, *Of Plymouth Plantation* (Mineola, NY: Dover Publications, 2006), 128.
11. Emerson Woods Baker II, "Trouble to the Eastward: The Failure of Anglo-Indian Relations in Early Maine," (PhD diss., The College of William and Mary, 1986), 141.
12. George Parker Winship, ed., S*ailors Narratives Of Voyages Along The New England Coast,*

1524-1624 (Boston: Houghton, Mifflin & Company, 1905), 117.

13. James Phinney Baxter, *Sir Ferdinando Gorges and His Province of Maine Including the Brief Relation, the Brief Narration, His Defence, the Charter Granted to Him, His Will, and His Letters, Vol. II* (Boston: The Prince Society, 1890), 42, https://ia802606.us.archive.org/6/items/sirferdinandogo02baxt/sirferdinandogo02baxt.pdf.
14. Malone, *Skulking*, 52-53.
15. Ibid., 56-57.
16. John W. Frank, Roland S. Moore, and Genevieve M. Ames, "Public Health Then and Now: Historical and Cultural Roots of Drinking Problems Among American IIndians," *American Journal of Public Health* 90, no. 3 (March 2000): 348.
17. William Wood, *New England's Prospect* (Amherst, MA: University of Massachusetts Press, 1977), 79.
18. Ibid.
19. King James I, "Prohibiting Disorderly Trading to New England," Proclamation November 6, 1622, 33 and King Charles I, "Forbidding Disorderly Trading with the Savages," Proclamation November 24, 1630, 66, accessed August 19, 2020, https://www.gutenberg.org/files/46167/46167-h/46167-h.htm#x1630_November_24.
20. Neill DePaoli, "Life on the Edge: Community and Trade on the Anglo-American Periphery, Pemaquid, Maine, 1610-1689," (PhD diss., University of New Hampshire, 2001), 270; Alaric Faulkner and Gretchen Fearon Faulkner, *The French at Pentagoet 1635-1674: An Archaeological Portrait of the Acadian Frontier* (Augusta, ME: The Maine Historic Preservation Commission and The New Brunswick Museum, 1987), 26-27.
21. Henry S. Burrage, *The Beginnings of Colonial Maine 1602-1658* (Portland, ME: Marks Printing House, 1914), 266-7.
22. William Bradford, *Of Plymouth Plantation* (Mineola, NY: Dover Publications, 2006), 178.
23. "Edward Winslow to John Winthrop, April 16, 1637," Massachusetts Historical Society: Winthrop Family Papers, accessed August 20, 2020, https://www.masshist.org/publications/winthrop/index.php/view/PWF03d315.
24. James Phinney Baxter, *Sir Ferdinando Gorges and His Province of Maine Including the Brief Relation, the Brief Narration, His Defence, the Charter Granted to Him, His Will, and His Letters, Vol. I* (Boston: The Prince Society, 1890), 162; James Kendall Hosmer, ed., *Winthrop's Journal "History of New England" 1630-1649 Volume I: Normal School* (New York: Charles Scribner's Sons, 1908), 127, http://www.noblenet.org/salem/reference/wp-content/uploads/2017/08/Original-Narratives-of-Early-American-History-Winthrops-Journal-vol.-1.pdf. 105; Richard Mather, *Journal of Richard Mather. 1635. His Life and Death. 1670.* (Boston: David Clapp, 1850), 12, https://babel.hathitrust.org/cgi/pt?id=loc.ark:/13960/t7mp56r0f&view=1up&seq=18.
25. Hosmer, *Winthrop's Journal Vol. I*, 101; Baxter, Sir Ferdinando Vol. I, 159.
26. Burrage, *Beginnings*, 230; Hosmer, *Winthrop's Journal Vol. I*, 135.
27. Baxter, *Sir Ferdinando Vol. I*, 167.
28. Hosmer, *Winthrop's Journal Vol. I*, 145.
29. Ibid., 130; Burrage, *Beginnings*, 233.
30. Warren C. Riess, *Angel Gabriel The Elusive English Galleon: Its History and the Search for Its Remains* (Bristol, ME: 1797 House, 2001), 22.
31. Mather, Journal, 7-8.
32. Baxter, *Sir Ferdinando Vol. I*, 169-170.
33. Sam Shepherd, "Hallowell man leading state's effort to locate a centuries-old shipwreck in Bristol," *Kennebec Journal*, November 23, 2018, https://www.centralmaine.com/2018/11/23/hallowell-man-leading-states-effort-to-locate-a-centuries-old-shipwreck-in-bristol/.

34. Baxter, *Sir Ferdinando Vol. I*, 172.
35. Bradford, *Of Plymouth*,178.
36. Ibid., 179.
37. Baxter, *Sir Ferdinando Vol. I*, 172.
38. Hosmer, *Winthrop's Journal Vol.* I, 152.

Chapter 19: Changes in the Land, Civil War, Recession, and the Jesuits, 1636-1653 - pages 209-222

1. James Phinney Baxter, *Sir Ferdinando Gorges and His Province of Maine Including the Brief Relation, the Brief Narration, His Defence, the Charter Granted to Him, His Will, and His Letters, Vol. II* (Boston: The Prince Society, 1890), 58, https://ia802606.us.archive.org/6/items/sirferdinandogo02baxt/sirferdinandogo02baxt.pdf.
2. *Province and Court Records of Maine: Vol. I*, (Portland, ME: Maine Historical Society, 1991),
3. Tom Groening, personal communication with the author, March 4, 2021.
4. "1500-1667: Contact & Conflict," Maine Memory Network, accessed August 20, 2020, https://www.mainememory.net/sitebuilder/site/895/page/1306/print; "Population in the Colonial and Continental Periods," Census, 9, accessed August 20, 2020, https://www2.census.gov/prod2/decennial/documents/00165897ch01.pdf.
5. William Bradford, *Of Plymouth Plantation* (Mineola, NY: Dover Publications, 2006), 195.
6. Neill DePaoli, "Life on the Edge: Community and Trade on the Anglo-American Periphery, Pemaquid, Maine, 1610-1689," (PhD diss., University of New Hampshire, 2001), 100; John Johnston, *A History of the Towns of Bristol and Bremen in the State of Maine, Including the Pemaquid Settlement* (Albany: Joel Munsell, 1873), 84.
7. William Cronon, *Changes in the Land: Indians, Colonists, and the Ecology of New England* (New York: Hill and Wang, 2003), 139.
8. James Kendall Hosmer, ed., *Winthrop's Journal "History of New England" 1630-1649 Volume I*: Normal School (New York: Charles Scribner's Sons, 1908), 132, http://www.noblenet.org/salem/reference/wp-content/uploads/2017/08/Original-Narratives-of-Early-American-History-Winthrops-Journal-vol.-1.pdf.
9. Cronon, *Changes*,142-4.
10. "Plaintain weed," Organic Seeds, accessed August 20, 2020, https://organicseeds.top/plantain_weed.
11. Cronon, *Changes*, 150-1.
12. Richard Archer, "New England Mosaic: A Demographic Analysis for the Seventeenth Century," *The William and Mary Quarterly* 47, no. 4 (October 1990): 486.
13. Cronon, *Changes*, 119-20.
14. Ibid., 121.
15. Ibid., 110-2.
16. Ibid., 109.
17. Johnston, *History*, 67.
18. Ibid.; DePaoli, "Life," 120.
19. Cronon, *Changes*, 122-6.
20. Ibid., 98.
21. *Province and Court*, 77; "Gray Wolf," Maine Department of Inland Fisheries & Wildlife, accessed August 20, 2020, https://www.maine.gov/ifw/docs/endangered/graywolf_20_21.pdf.
22. Cronon, *Changes*, 100-1.
23. Ibid., 99.
24. "Ecology of the Beaver," Ecology.info, accessed August 20, 2020, http://www.ecology.

info/beaver-ecology.htm.

25. Cronon, *Changes*, 107.
26. W. N. Chattin Carlton, ed., *Relation of the Pequot Warres Written in 1660 by Lieutenant Lion Gardener* (Hartford: Hartford Press, 1901), 25-26, https://digitalcommons.unl.edu/cgi/viewcontent.cgi?referer=https://www.google.com/&httpsredir=1&article=1038&context=etas; Neal Salisbury, *Manitou and Providence: Indians, Europeans, and the Making of New England, 1500-1643* (New York: Oxford University Press, 1982), 13.
27. Cronon, Changes, 112, 163.
28. Emerson W. Baker, "The World of Thomas Gorges: Life in the Province of Maine in the 1640s," in *American Beginnings: Exploration, Culture, and Cartography in the Land of Norumbega*, ed. Emerson W. Baker, Edwin A. Churchill, Richard S. D'Abate, Kristine L. Jones, Victor A. Konrad, and Harald E. L. Prins (Lincoln: University of Nebraska Press, 1994), 263.
29. James Phinney Baxter, S*ir Ferdinando Gorges and His Province of Maine Including the Brief Relation, the Brief Narration, His Defence, the Charter Granted to Him, His Will, and His Letters, Vol. I* (Boston: The Prince Society, 1890), 181; Robert E. Moody, ed., The Letters of Thomas Gorges, Deputy Governor of the Province of Maine 1640-1643 (Portland, ME: Maine Historical Society, 1978), 1.
30. "City Upon a Hill," Digital History, accessed August 20, 2020, http://www.digitalhistory.uh.edu/disp_textbook.cfm?smtID=3&psid=3918.
31. Moody, *Letters*, 13.
32. *Province and Court*, 70-71, 73-75.
33. Moody, Letters, 17.
34. Johnston, *History*, 84.
35. Baxter, *Sir Ferdinando Vol. I, 188; James Phinney Baxter, ed., The Documentary History of the State of Maine, Vol. III. Containing the Trelawny Papers* (Portland, ME: Hoyt, Fogg, and Donham, 1884), 310, 321, https://books.google.com/books?.
36. Moody, *Letters*, 100; James Kendall Hosmer, ed., *Winthrop's Journal "History of New England" 1630-1649 Volume II* (New York: Charles Scribner's Sons, 1908), 54, http://www.noblenet.org/salem/reference/wp-content/uploads/2017/08/Original-Narratives-of-Early-American-History-Winthrops-Journal-vol.-2.pdf.
37. Moody, *Letters*, 120; Hosmer, *Winthrop's Journal Vol. II*, 74.
38. *Province and Court*, 56-58; 65; 67; 78; 80-81.
39. Baxter, *Sir Ferdinando Vol. I*, 192.
40. Ibid., 240.
41. Dougall Photography, "Fort Gorges in Portland Maine Harbor, 177046973" iStock, accessed March 27, 2021, https://www.istockphoto.com/photofort-gorges-in-portland-maine-harbor-gm177046973-26543684..
42. Henry S. Burrage, *The Beginnings of Colonial Maine 1602-1658* (Portland, ME: Marks Printing House, 1914), 340
43. Burrage, *Beginnings*, 306.
44. DePaoli, "Life," 93.
45. Ibid., 86.
46. Ibid., 126-8.
47. "Population," Census, 9.
48. Gordon M. Day, *Identity of the Saint Francis Indians*, Mercury Series (Ottawa: University of Ottawa Press, 1981), 30.
49. Reuben Gold Thwaites, ed., *The Jesuit Relations and Allied Documents: Travels and Explorations of the Jesuit Missionaries in New France 1610—1791, Vol. XI* (Cleveland: The Burrows Brothers Company, 1898), 194, http://moses.creighton.edu/kripke/

jesuitrelations/relations_11.html.

50. Reuben Gold Thwaites, ed., *The Jesuit Relations and Allied Documents: Travels and Explorations of the Jesuit Missionaries in New France 1610—1791, Vol. XXVIII Hurons, Iroquois, Lower Canada 1645-1646* (Cleveland: The Burrows Brothers Company, 1898), 203, 213, http://moses.creighton.edu/kripke/jesuitrelations/relations_28.html.
51. Reuben Gold Thwaites, ed., *The Jesuit Relations and Allied Documents: Travels and Explorations of the Jesuit Missionaries in New France 1610—1791, Vol. XXXI Iroquois, Lower Canada, Abenakis 1647* (Cleveland: The Burrows Brothers Company, 1898), 188-191, http://moses.creighton.edu/kripke/jesuitrelations/relations_31.html.
52. James Axtell, *The European and the Indian: Essays in the Ethnohistory of Colonial North America* (New York: Oxford University Press, 1981), 77-8.
53. Kenneth M. Morrison, "The People of the Dawn: The Abnaki and Their Relations with New England and New France, 1600-1727" (PhD diss., University of Maine, 1975), 112-116.
54. Ibid., 101-102.

Epilogue: Death, War, and the Destruction of Pemaquid, 1653-1696 - pages 223-237

1. Charles B. McLane, *Islands of Mid-Maine Coast, Volume III, Muscongus Bay and Monhegan Island* (Gardiner, ME: Tilbury House, 1992), 185.
2. Helen B. Camp, *Archaeological Excavations at Pemaquid, Maine 1965-1974* (Augusta, ME: The Maine State Museum, 1975), 75.
3. David B. Quinn and Alison M. Quinn, eds., *The English New England Voyages 1602-1608* (London: The Hakluyt Society, 1983), 350-1.
4. James Axtell, *The European and the Indian: Essays in the Ethnohistory of Colonial North America* (New York: Oxford University Press, 1981), 126.
5. John G. Reid, *Acadia, Maine, and New Scotland: Marginal Colonies in the Seventeenth Century* (Toronto: University of Toronto Press, 1981), 103.
6. John Johnston, *A History of the Towns of Bristol and Bremen in the State of Maine, Including the Pemaquid Settlement* (Albany: Joel Munsell, 1873), 117.
7. James Phinney Baxter, ed., *Documentary History of the State of Maine, Vol. VI Containing the Baxter Manuscripts*, (Portland, ME: The Thurston Print, 1900), 89, https://books.google.com/books?id=IXlQAQAAIAAJ&pg=PR15&lpg=PR15&dq=deposition+of+thomas+stevens,+september+4,+1688&source=bl&ots=BylmMI Jeq&sig=ACfU3U2 efud5LdZRuD DroufgbI4cHr9ZJg&hl=en&sa=X&ved=2ahUKEwiHnozG2v70 AhUPknIEHceBBXcQ6AEwAnoECAYQAQ#v=onepage&q=deposition%20of%20thomas%20stevens%2C%20september%204%2C%201688&f=false; "The History of Falmouth," accessed June 7, 2021, https://www.falmouthme.org/sites/g/files/vyhlif556/f/uploads/history.pdf.
8. Neill DePaoli, "Life on the Edge: Community and Trade on the Anglo-American Periphery, Pemaquid, Maine, 1610-1689," (PhD diss., University of New Hampshire, 2001), 303.
9. Baxter, *Documentary History Vol. VI*, 91-92.
10. "Narrative of voyage to Pemaquid, 1677, Item15560" Collections of Maine Historical Society, Maine Memory Network, accessed August 23, 2020, https://www.mainememory.net/sitebuilder/site/982/page/1407/display.
11. Helen Camp, *Pemaquid Lost and Found* (Pemaquid, ME: Ancient Pemaquid Restoration, 1967), 4.

12. "1668-1774 Settlement & Strife," Maine Memory Network, accessed August 23, 2020, https://www.mainememory.net/sitebuilder/site/897/page/1308/print.
13. Mary Beth Norton, *In the Devil's Snare: The Salem Witchcraft Crisis of 1692* (New York: Vintage Books, 2003), 12.
14. Sybil Noyes, Charles Thornton Libby, and Walter Goodwin Davis, *Genealogical Dictionary of Maine and New Hampshire* (Portland, ME: Genealogical Publishing Co., 2002), 662-3; The New York Genealogical and Biographical Record, Volume LI, 1920 (New York: New York Genealogical and Biographical Society, 1920), 29-32.
15. John Giles, *Memoirs of Odd Adventures, Strange Deliverances, Etc. in the Captivity of John Giles, Esq., Commander of the Garrison on Saint George River, in the District of Maine* (Cincinnati: Spiller & Gates, 1869), 11.
16. Cotton Mather, *Magnalia Christi Americana; or, the Ecclesiastical History of New England, from its First Planting, in the Year 1620, unto the Year of our Lord 1698, Vol. II, Book VII* (Hartford: Silas Andrus & Son, 1853), 619. https://books.google.com/books?id=foY5s7bsqDQC&printsec=frontcover&source=gbs_ge_summary_r&cad=0#v=onepage&q&f=false.
17. J. W. Fortescue, ed., *Calendar of State Papers, Colonial Series, America and West Indies, January, 1693-May, 1696. Preserved in the Public Record* (London: Mackie and Co., 1903), 157, https://books.google.com/books?id=kNIJAAAAIAAJ&pg=PA156&lpg=PA156&dq=william+phips+letter+to+earl+of+nottingham+september+1693&source=bl&ots=sDgN-P62sV&sig=ACfU3U3vMlBjVdzft2yfvKW-JGCr1hSezw&hl=en&sa=X&ved=2ahUKEwicoaW9t-HpAhXngXIEHaoAIgQ6AEwAXoECAsQAQ#v=onepage&q=william%20phips%20letter%20to%20earl%20of%20nottingham%20september%201693&f=false.
18. Michael Dekker, *French & Indian Wars in Maine* (Charleston: The History Press, 2015), 37; DePaoli, "Life," 259.
19. Williamson, *History*, 600.
20. Colin G. Calloway, *The Western Abenakis of Vermont, 1600-1800: War, Migration, and the Survival of an Indian People* (Norman, OK: University of Oklahoma Press, 1990), 36-37, https://books.google.com/books?id=EB2Q1un0tzkC&pg=PA37&lpg=PA37&dq=disease+outbreaks+at+french+missions+17th+century&source=bl&ots=vl5IBpNNrZ&sig=ACfU3U0xP1P5TtWMPs-en5qL7-kH7xmH3A&hl=en&sa=X&ved=2ahUKEwj8tuTpjIzqAhXxkHIEHdgrBYoQ6AEwBHoECAoQAQ#v=onepage&q=disease%20outbreaks%20at%20french%20missions%2017th%20century&f=false.
21. Reuben Gold Thwaites, ed., *The Jesuit Relations and Allied Documents: Travels and Explorations of the Jesuit Missionaries in New France 1610—1791, Vol. LXII Lower Canada, Iroquois, Ottawas 1681-1683* (Cleveland: The Burrows Brothers Company, 1900), 41, http://moses.creighton.edu/kripke/jesuitrelations/relations_62.html.
22. Frank G. Speck, Wawenock *Myth Texts from Maine*, (Washington: Government Printing Office, 1928), 176-7, http://www.gutenberg.org/files/49951/49951-h/49951-h.htm.
23. Diana Scully, "Maine Indian Claims Settlement: Concepts, Context, and Perspectives," 12, accessed August 24, 2020, http://archive.abbemuseum.org/downloads/d_scully_land claims.pdf.
24. United States Department of the Interior, Office of Federal Acknowledgement, *The Official Guidelines to the Federal Acknowledgment Regulations*, 25 CFR 83, Washington, DC: US Department of the Interior, 1997, 36-37, accessed March 22, 2021, https://www.bia.gov/sites/bia.gov/files/assets/as-ia/ofa/admindocs/OfficialGuidelines.pdf.
25. Ron and Patty Thomas, "Pemaquid Point Lighthouse Maine, 1213940804" iStock, accessed March 27, 2021, https://www.istockphoto.com/photo/pemaquid-point-lighthouse-maine-gm1213940804-353006603.

26. Sherri Mitchell, "Denial of tribal sovereignty is an 'archaic remnant of a racist past,'" Maine Beacon, accessed August 24, 2020, https://mainebeacon.com/denial-of-tribal-sovereignty-is-an-archaic-remnant-of-a-racist-past/.
27. Linda Tuhiwai Smith, *Decolonizing Methodologies: Research and Indigenous Peoples* (London: Zed Books, 2012), 160.
28. "Maine: 2010: Summary Population and Housing Characteristics 2010 Census of Population and Housing," United States Census 2010, 40, accessed August 24, 2020, https://www.census.gov/prod/cen2010/cph-1-21.pdf; "Maine: 2000: Census 2000 Profile," United States Census 2000, 2, accessed August 24, 2020, https://www.census.gov/prod/2002pubs/c2kprof00-me.pdf; "1990 Census of Population General Population Characteristics Maine," Census '90, 56, accessed August 24, 2020, https://www2.census.gov/library/publications/decennial/1990/cp-1/cp-1-21.pdf; "QuickFacts Maine," United States Census Bureau, accessed March 19, 2022, https://www.census.gov/quickfacts/ME.
29. Maulian Dana, "Wabanaki Alliance," *Facebook*, May 3, 2021, https://www.facebook.com/WabanakiAlliance.